Alexander Motyl

# NATIONAL QUESTIONS

## Theoretical Reflections on Nations and Nationalism in Eastern Europe

## Bibliografische Information der Deutschen Nationalbibliothek
Die Deutsche Nationalbibliothek verzeichnet diese Publikation in der Deutschen Nationalbibliografie; detaillierte bibliografische Daten sind im Internet über http://dnb.d-nb.de abrufbar.

## Bibliographic information published by the Deutsche Nationalbibliothek
Die Deutsche Nationalbibliothek lists this publication in the Deutsche Nationalbibliografie; detailed bibliographic data are available in the Internet at http://dnb.d-nb.de.

Cover illustration by Alexander Motyl

ISBN-13: 978-3-8382-1675-1
© *ibidem*-Verlag, Stuttgart 2022
Alle Rechte vorbehalten

Das Werk einschließlich aller seiner Teile ist urheberrechtlich geschützt. Jede Verwertung außerhalb der engen Grenzen des Urheberrechtsgesetzes ist ohne Zustimmung des Verlages unzulässig und strafbar. Dies gilt insbesondere für Vervielfältigungen, Übersetzungen, Mikroverfilmungen und elektronische Speicherformen sowie die Einspeicherung und Verarbeitung in elektronischen Systemen.

All rights reserved. No part of this publication may be reproduced, stored in or introduced into a retrieval system, or transmitted, in any form, or by any means (electronic, mechanical, photocopying, recording or otherwise) without the prior written permission of the publisher. Any person who does any unauthorized act in relation to this publication may be liable to criminal prosecution and civil claims for damages.

Printed in the EU

# Soviet and Post-Soviet Politics and Society (SPPS)
ISSN 1614-3515

**General Editor:** Andreas Umland,
*Stockholm Centre for Eastern European Studies*, andreas.umland@ui.se

**Commissioning Editor:** Max Jakob Horstmann,
London, mjh@ibidem.eu

## EDITORIAL COMMITTEE*

### DOMESTIC & COMPARATIVE POLITICS
Prof. **Ellen Bos**, *Andrássy University of Budapest*
Dr. **Gergana Dimova**, *University of Winchester*
Dr. **Andrey Kazantsev**, *MGIMO (U) MID RF, Moscow*
Prof. **Heiko Pleines**, *University of Bremen*
Prof. **Richard Sakwa**, *University of Kent at Canterbury*
Dr. **Sarah Whitmore**, *Oxford Brookes University*
Dr. **Harald Wydra**, *University of Cambridge*

### SOCIETY, CLASS & ETHNICITY
Col. **David Glantz**, *"Journal of Slavic Military Studies"*
Dr. **Marlène Laruelle**, *George Washington University*
Dr. **Stephen Shulman**, *Southern Illinois University*
Prof. **Stefan Troebst**, *University of Leipzig*

### POLITICAL ECONOMY & PUBLIC POLICY
Dr. **Andreas Goldthau**, *Central European University*
Dr. **Robert Kravchuk**, *University of North Carolina*
Dr. **David Lane**, *University of Cambridge*
Dr. **Carol Leonard**, *Higher School of Economics, Moscow*
Dr. **Maria Popova**, *McGill University, Montreal*

### FOREIGN POLICY & INTERNATIONAL AFFAIRS
Dr. **Peter Duncan**, *University College London*
Prof. **Andreas Heinemann-Grüder**, *University of Bonn*
Prof. **Gerhard Mangott**, *University of Innsbruck*
Dr. **Diana Schmidt-Pfister**, *University of Konstanz*
Dr. **Lisbeth Tarlow**, *Harvard University, Cambridge*
Dr. **Christian Wipperfürth**, *N-Ost Network, Berlin*
Dr. **William Zimmerman**, *University of Michigan*

### HISTORY, CULTURE & THOUGHT
Dr. **Catherine Andreyev**, *University of Oxford*
Prof. **Mark Bassin**, *Södertörn University*
Prof. **Karsten Brüggemann**, *Tallinn University*
Dr. **Alexander Etkind**, *University of Cambridge*
Dr. **Gasan Gusejnov**, *Moscow State University*
Prof. **Leonid Luks**, *Catholic University of Eichstaett*
Dr. **Olga Malinova**, *Russian Academy of Sciences*
Dr. **Richard Mole**, *University College London*
Prof. **Andrei Rogatchevski**, *University of Tromsø*
Dr. **Mark Tauger**, *West Virginia University*

## ADVISORY BOARD*

Prof. **Dominique Arel**, *University of Ottawa*
Prof. **Jörg Baberowski**, *Humboldt University of Berlin*
Prof. **Margarita Balmaceda**, *Seton Hall University*
Dr. **John Barber**, *University of Cambridge*
Prof. **Timm Beichelt**, *European University Viadrina*
Dr. **Katrin Boeckh**, *University of Munich*
Prof. em. **Archie Brown**, *University of Oxford*
Dr. **Vyacheslav Bryukhovetsky**, *Kyiv-Mohyla Academy*
Prof. **Timothy Colton**, *Harvard University, Cambridge*
Prof. **Paul D'Anieri**, *University of Florida*
Dr. **Heike Dörrenbächer**, *Friedrich Naumann Foundation*
Dr. **John Dunlop**, *Hoover Institution, Stanford, California*
Dr. **Sabine Fischer**, *SWP, Berlin*
Dr. **Geir Flikke**, *NUPI, Oslo*
Prof. **David Galbreath**, *University of Aberdeen*
Prof. **Alexander Galkin**, *Russian Academy of Sciences*
Prof. **Frank Golczewski**, *University of Hamburg*
Dr. **Nikolas Gvosdev**, *Naval War College, Newport, RI*
Prof. **Mark von Hagen**, *Arizona State University*
Dr. **Guido Hausmann**, *University of Munich*
Prof. **Dale Herspring**, *Kansas State University*
Dr. **Stefani Hoffman**, *Hebrew University of Jerusalem*
Prof. **Mikhail Ilyin**, *MGIMO (U) MID RF, Moscow*
Prof. **Vladimir Kantor**, *Higher School of Economics*
Dr. **Ivan Katchanovski**, *University of Ottawa*
Prof. em. **Andrzej Korbonski**, *University of California*
Dr. **Iris Kempe**, *"Caucasus Analytical Digest"*
Prof. **Herbert Küpper**, *Institut für Ostrecht Regensburg*
Dr. **Rainer Lindner**, *CEEER, Berlin*
Dr. **Vladimir Malakhov**, *Russian Academy of Sciences*

Dr. **Luke March**, *University of Edinburgh*
Prof. **Michael McFaul**, *Stanford University, Palo Alto*
Prof. **Birgit Menzel**, *University of Mainz-Germersheim*
Prof. **Valery Mikhailenko**, *The Urals State University*
Prof. **Emil Pain**, *Higher School of Economics, Moscow*
Dr. **Oleg Podvintsev**, *Russian Academy of Sciences*
Prof. **Olga Popova**, *St. Petersburg State University*
Dr. **Alex Pravda**, *University of Oxford*
Dr. **Erik van Ree**, *University of Amsterdam*
Dr. **Joachim Rogall**, *Robert Bosch Foundation Stuttgart*
Prof. **Peter Rutland**, *Wesleyan University, Middletown*
Prof. **Marat Salikov**, *The Urals State Law Academy*
Dr. **Gwendolyn Sasse**, *University of Oxford*
Prof. **Jutta Scherrer**, *EHESS, Paris*
Prof. **Robert Service**, *University of Oxford*
Mr. **James Sherr**, *RIIA Chatham House London*
Dr. **Oxana Shevel**, *Tufts University, Medford*
Prof. **Eberhard Schneider**, *University of Siegen*
Prof. **Olexander Shnyrkov**, *Shevchenko University, Kyiv*
Prof. **Hans-Henning Schröder**, *SWP, Berlin*
Prof. **Yuri Shapoval**, *Ukrainian Academy of Sciences*
Prof. **Viktor Shnirelman**, *Russian Academy of Sciences*
Dr. **Lisa Sundstrom**, *University of British Columbia*
Dr. **Philip Walters**, *"Religion, State and Society", Oxford*
Prof. **Zenon Wasyliw**, *Ithaca College, New York State*
Dr. **Lucan Way**, *University of Toronto*
Dr. **Markus Wehner**, *"Frankfurter Allgemeine Zeitung"*
Dr. **Andrew Wilson**, *University College London*
Prof. **Jan Zielonka**, *University of Oxford*
Prof. **Andrei Zorin**, *University of Oxford*

*While the Editorial Committee and Advisory Board support the General Editor in the choice and improvement of manuscripts for publication, responsibility for remaining errors and misinterpretations in the series' volumes lies with the books' authors.*

# Soviet and Post-Soviet Politics and Society (SPPS)
ISSN 1614-3515

Founded in 2004 and refereed since 2007, SPPS makes available affordable English-, German-, and Russian-language studies on the history of the countries of the former Soviet bloc from the late Tsarist period to today. It publishes between 5 and 20 volumes per year and focuses on issues in transitions to and from democracy such as economic crisis, identity formation, civil society development, and constitutional reform in CEE and the NIS. SPPS also aims to highlight so far understudied themes in East European studies such as right-wing radicalism, religious life, higher education, or human rights protection. The authors and titles of all previously published volumes are listed at the end of this book. For a full description of the series and reviews of its books, see www.ibidem-verlag.de/red/spps.

**Editorial correspondence & manuscripts** should be sent to: Dr. Andreas Umland, Department of Political Science, Kyiv-Mohyla Academy, vul. Voloska 8/5, UA-04070 Kyiv, UKRAINE; andreas.umland@cantab.net

**Business correspondence & review copy requests** should be sent to: *ibidem* Press, Leuschnerstr. 40, 30457 Hannover, Germany; tel.: +49 511 2622200; fax: +49 511 2622201; spps@ibidem.eu.

**Authors, reviewers, referees, and editors** for (as well as all other persons sympathetic to) SPPS are invited to join its networks at www.facebook.com/group.php?gid=52638198614
www.linkedin.com/groups?about=&gid=103012
www.xing.com/net/spps-ibidem-verlag/

## Recent Volumes

242 Sebastian Schäffer (Ed.)
Ukraine in Central and Eastern Europe
Kyiv's Foreign Affairs and the International Relations of the Post-Communist Region
With a foreword by Pavlo Klimkin
ISBN 978-3-8382-1615-7

243 Volodymyr Dubrovskyi, Kalman Mizsei, Mychailo Wynnyckyj (Eds.)
Eight Years after the Revolution of Dignity
What Has Changed in Ukraine during 2013–2021?
With a foreword by Yaroslav Hrytsak
ISBN 978-3-8382-1560-0

244 Rumena Filipova
Constructing the Limits of Europe
Identity and Foreign Policy in Poland, Bulgaria, and Russia since 1989
With forewords by Harald Wydra and Gergana Yankova-Dimova
ISBN 978-3-8382-1649-2

245 Oleksandra Keudel
How Patronal Networks Shape Opportunities for Local Citizen Participation in a Hybrid Regime
A Comparative Analysis of Five Cities in Ukraine
With a foreword by Sabine Kropp
ISBN 978-3-8382-1671-3

246 Jan Claas Behrends, Thomas Lindenberger, Pavel Kolar (Eds.)
Violence after Stalin
Institutions, Practices, and Everyday Life in the Soviet Bloc 1953–1989
ISBN 978-3-8382-1637-9

247 Leonid Luks
Macht und Ohnmacht der Utopien
Essays zur Geschichte Russlands im 20. und 21. Jahrhundert
ISBN 978-3-8382-1677-5

248 Iuliia Barshadska
Brüssel zwischen Kyjiw und Moskau
Das auswärtige Handeln der Europäischen Union im ukrainisch-russischen Konflikt 2014-2019
Mit einem Vorwort von Olaf Leiße
ISBN 978-3-8382-1667-6

249 Valentyna Romanova
Decentralisation and Multilevel Elections in Ukraine
Reform Dynamics and Party Politics in 2010–2021
With a foreword by Kimitaka Matsuzato
ISBN 978-3-8382-1700-0

*I dedicate this book to the Ukrainian victims of fascist Russia's genocidal war.*


*In memoriam of my friends, colleagues, and teachers at the Harriman Institute:*
Edward Allworth, Nick Arena, Serhii Berezovenko, Seweryn Bialer, Oded Eran, Henry Ergas, Neil Felshman, Dan Gutterman, John Hazard, Peter Juviler, Michael Lucas, Cathy Nepomnyashchy, Marshall Shulman, Mark von Hagen, Janet Willen.

# Contents

Preface ................................................................................. 9

1   The Modernity of Nationalism: Nations, States, and Nation-States in the Contemporary World ...................... 11

2   Liberalism, Nationalism, and National Liberation Struggles ........................................................................... 29

3   Inventing Invention: The Limits of National Identity Formation ............................. 43

4   Imagined Communities, Rational Choosers, Invented Ethnies ................................................................. 65

5   The Social Construction of Social Construction ..................... 89

6   Why Is the KGB Bar Possible? Binary Morality and Its Consequences .................................. 113

7   Building Bridges and Changing Landmarks: Theory and Concepts in the Study of Soviet Nationalities .. 141

8   Negating the Negation: Russia, Not-Russia, and the West ............................................ 163

| | | |
|---|---|---|
| 9 | Can Ukraine Have a History? | 177 |
| 10 | Should Ukraine Forget Its History? | 191 |
| 11 | The Holodomor and History: Bringing Ukrainians Back In | 203 |
| 12 | The Paradoxes of Paul Robert Magocsi: The Case for Rusyns and the Logical Necessity of Ukrainians | 217 |
| 13 | The Ukrainian Nationalist Movement and the Jews: Theoretical Reflections on Nationalism, Fascism, Rationality, Primordialism, and History | 225 |
| 14 | On Nationalism and Fascism | 257 |
| 15 | Putin's Russia as a Fascist Political System | 267 |

# Preface

*National Questions* consists of thirteen articles and two speeches. All deal with nations, national identity, and nationalism. The earliest article appeared in 1991; the latest in 2016. Remarkably or not, given that the articles span 25 years, they actually hang together, forming a coherent whole that amounts to a book, and not just a collection. There are some repetitions (and, possibly, contradictions), but they don't (I hope) upset the overall narrative arc, which begins with discussions of national identity and nationalism, moves on to the Soviet, post-Soviet, and Ukrainian contexts, and concludes with assessments of nationalism's relationship with fascism, in general and with regard to Vladimir Putin's criminal regime in particular.

Readers will notice my obsessive concern with and interest in concepts and conceptual clarity—for which I am eternally grateful to Giovanni Sartori. They will also notice my belief that theory, however frustrating and inconclusive, is as indispensable as analytic logic—especially of the kind practiced by Arthur Danto; that comparison is always useful, if not indeed imperative; and that, notwithstanding the slipperiness of concepts, empirical reality, both now and in the past, does in fact exist and can and must be known for theory to make any sense.

New York City, 2022

Alexander J. Motyl

# 1

## The Modernity of Nationalism
## Nations, States and, Nation-States in the Contemporary World*

What is nationalism? Above all, nationalism is a word—a rather obvious point, to be sure, but one that goes a long way toward resolving the confusion so evident in many interpretations of nationalism. In emphasizing that nationalism is first and foremost a word, I wish to underline the fact that it is neither a thing that can be physically grasped, such as a rock or tree—a fact that, as John Armstrong points out, makes its referent ontologically no less real than those associated with the so-called economic "base"[1] —nor a phenomenon that can be comprehended without the mediation of some concept. Determining what nationalism is, therefore, is in the first place a definitional task and not an empirical challenge. We establish what nationalism is not by examining the beliefs or behaviors of self-styled nationalists, but, as Giovanni Sartori recommends,[2] by investigating the multiple meanings that the term nationalism possesses, isolating its defining and central characteristics and then determining which meaning is most appropriate in given circumstances.

The point is that nationalism, like revolution, state, class, modernity, development and most other weighty social science terms, is what William Connolly calls an "essentially contested

---

* First printed in: *Journal of International Affairs*, 45, no. 2 (Winter 1992), pp. 307-323. Reprinted with permission of the original publisher. I thank Reneo Lukic and the Institute for World Affairs for the opportunity to present an earlier draft of this paper at their seminar on 8 August 1991.
1 John A. Armstrong, "The Autonomy of Ethnic Identity: Historic Cleavages and Nationality Relations in the USSR," in Alexander J. Motyl, ed., *Thinking Theoretically about Soviet Nationalities* (New York: Columbia University Press, 1992) pp. 23-44.
2 Giovanni Sartori, "Guidelines for Concept Analysis," in Giovanni Sartori, ed., *Social Science Concepts* (Beverly Hills, CA: Sage, 1984) pp.15-85.

concept" — that is to say, a word that resonates with a number of different meanings.³ Does nationalism therefore possess every meaning that is, or can be, ascribed to it? Of course not. Such an approach to the problem of defining is no solution: It leads only to the creation of ungainly and internally self-contradictory megaphenomena that serve merely to depict a multitude of details that may or may not be logically related.⁴ In a word, nationalism, like any other essentially contested concept, is either something — some one thing — or it is nothing, that is to say everything. And inasmuch as its being everything subverts any attempt to grasp the phenomenon, nationalism evidently must be deemed only one thing: The word must be given only one meaning and thus "attached" to only one phenomenon.

Does such an approach not distort "reality"? Does it not overly simplify, indeed caricature, that which is "in reality" enormously complex? The answer to both questions must be an emphatic "no," but — and this point is critical — only if we accept the view that we can grasp phenomena exclusively by means of the mediating influence of language, a point argued conclusively by Sartori.⁵ The alternative view, that language is just a vehicle at best, or a nuisance at worst, with no tangible relationship with the "objective reality," would appear to require epistemological assumptions that run counter to much of twentieth-century philosophy.

## What, Then, Is Nationalism?

The answer to the question "what is nationalism?" depends on the definition and, more substantively, on the definer. This is to say that the meaning of nationalism, like the meaning of every essentially contested concept, is neither value-neutral nor divorced from context — be it that of the political, social and cultural environment within which the word is used or that of the text within which the

---

3 William E. Connolly, *The Terms of Political Discourse* (Lexington, MA: D.C. Heath, 1974) pp. 9-44.
4 Alexander J, Motyl, "Concepts and Skocpol: Ambiguity and Vagueness in the Study of Revolution," *Journal of Theoretical Politics*, 4, no. 1 (January 1992).
5 Sartori, pp. 15-22.

term is nested. Defining nationalism obviously permits no definetive solution. Meanings will vary from person to person and from context to context. The task before scholars is not to impose a uniform meaning on their colleagues, which would be impossible both practically and epistemologically, but to ensure that the way nationalism is used in their own texts is uniform. Internal consistency is the goal. Where consistency is lacking, confusion usually reigns, discussions of semantics masquerade as discussions of substance, description substitutes for explanation and, ironically, despite all the effort expended on understanding nationalism, "it" remains as mysterious as it always seemed.

As we would expect, the meanings assigned to nationalism in much scholarship and most political discourse reveal more about the users of the term than about the phenomenon. A complete listing of current scholarly and nonscholarly understandings of nationalism would reveal that it is used to denote virtually everything and everyone however remotely related to nations. Thus, nationalists appear to be people who belong to nations, who love their nations and aspire to their well-being, who desire some form of political self-government for their nations, even up to independent statehood, and, last but not least, who hate everything but their nations. That is to say, nationalists are all living people, inasmuch as the self-conscious cultural communities that are nations represent the dominant form of contemporary social organization, and belonging to nations, love of nations, self-government of nations and hatred of other nations are ubiquitous. Used in so broad a manner, one that is almost equivalent to life itself, nationalism becomes meaningless.

Further complicating the definitional problem is that users of the term often ascribe to it an exclusively pejorative connotation. The adjectives that are frequently appended to the word—such as suicidal, irrational, hyper and emotional—reveal that nationalism is merely a code word for exaggerated national sentiment.[6] Indeed,

---

6   Jack Snyder, "The New Hypernationalism in Europe: Searching for Antidote," unpublished manuscript (New York: December 1990). "Suicidal nationalism" is, of course, President Bush's term.

Conor Cruise O'Brien explicitly defines nationalism as "a conglomerate of emotions."[7] (So, too, I add, are love, hate and, alas, virtually everything else!) Not surprisingly, those who speak of nationalism in this manner see it only within others and never within themselves. Thus, Alan Dershowitz's *Chutzpah* is considered bold and daring by American critics, while *The Japan That Can Say No* is denounced for its arrogance; Brooklyn youths who assault blacks are rightly called racist thugs, while Moscow youths who assault Jews are always nationalists.

The following examples are also illustrative. By any definition, American behavior during the 1991 war with Iraq, and especially during the so-called "Operation Welcome Home," must qualify as the apogee of exaggerated national sentiment. Nevertheless, few Americans would consider their own behavior nationalist. In contrast, were some Balkan nation to stage such a "conglomerate of emotions," were the Germans to wave as many flags as Americans do, were the Japanese to express themselves in forms that Americans generally do ("We're Number One!" being a typical sentiment), even fewer Americans would refrain from calling their behavior a typical manifestation of backward thinking, of emotionalism, of irrationality, of, well, nationalism.

Compare also President Bush's State of the Union message on 29 January 1991 with Saddam Hussein's interview with Cable News Network the day before. Appeals to God abound in both texts, both Americans and Iraqis are depicted as inspired by the divine and both are considered to be the bearers of world salvation.[8] To be sure, the terminology is different: Hussein's language is Middle Eastern and strikes Western ears as odd; Bush was far more in tune with the dominant discourse in the West. But beneath the surface, the substance of both texts was remarkably similar. Yet few if any Americans would consider Bush to be the functional equivalent of Hussein. None would dare extend the Hitler analogy to the American president, although the content of

---

7   Conor Cruise O'Brien, "Nationalists and Democrats," *New York Review of Books*, 15 August 1991, p. 29.
8   See *New York Times*, 30 January 1991; 31 January 1991.

his speech was in fact only marginally different from Hussein's interview.

## Defining Nationalism

How should nationalism be defined? I shall not answer this question in this article, although I do, of course, have my own preferences.[9] The most important points to keep in mind when defining nationalism are: First, the definition should not rest on the erroneous view of concepts as being descriptive of a reality that is divorced from the conceptualization of it; second, it should not conflate defining characteristics with central or associated ones; and third, it should avoid creating megaphenomena that subvert attempts at explanation.

With these cautionary words, I suggest that nationalism, if it is to be a useful concept, should be endowed with only one of the possible meanings noted above; the others may then be demoted to the rank of central characteristics that generally appear to "go with" the defined phenomenon. That is, nationalism may be a political ideology or ideal that argues that nations should have their own states (or enjoy self-rule); it may be the belief that the world is divided into nations and that this division is both proper and natural; it may be love of one's nation; and, finally, it may be the belief that one's own nation should stand above all other nations. In simple terms, these views of nationalism boll down, respectively, to the following beliefs: in the nation-state, in self-government, in national identity, in national well-being and in national superiority.[10] As these or other beliefs are not forms of behavior, individuals or groups with such beliefs may attempt to translate them into reality, but the specific actions they undertake cannot, by

---

9  See Alexander J. Motyl, *Sovietology, Rationality, Nationality: Coming to Grips with Nationalism in the USSR* (New York: Columbia University Press, 1991), where I define nationalism as a "political ideal that views statehood as the optimal form of political organization for each nation," p. 53.

10  Classic views of nationalism as a thing of the mind are Hans Kohn, *The Idea of Nationalism* (New York: Macmillan, 1944) and Elie Kedourie, *Nationalism* (London: Hutchinson, 1966).

definition, be nationalism — unless we make the absurd assumption that beliefs invariably translate automatically into behavior.[11]

If and when we employ the above definitions, it is imperative that we do so in an even-handed manner that permits the term nationalism to be maximally applicable to a variety of situations, including one's own. Thus, if nationalism is belief in the nation-state, then it can be found only amongst those nations that lack their own states, and to speak of contemporary American or French nationalism would be illogical. If nationalism is belief in self-government, then the pool of potential candidates expands to include those individuals and movements that aspire to autonomy: In this sense, even the ostensibly quiescent Turkmen would have to be considered fervid nationalists. If nationalism is belief in nations and in national identity, then we are all nationalists. If nationalism is dedication to a nation's well-being, then, again, we are all nationalists. Finally, if nationalism is some form of chauvinism or supremacism, then we would have to admit that it is manifest in East and West, North and South — indeed, as I suggested above, no less in the United States than in Iraq, no less in Great Britain than in Romania.

A dispassionate application of the concept of nationalism leads us to the conclusion that nationalism, in all of the above five designations, is not only alive and well in the West, which claims to be everything but nationalist, but that it is also quite modern. True, fewer groups may be striving for the nation-state in the West than in other parts of the world (although this claim appears questionable in light of the Quebecois, Basque, Puerto Rican, Corsican, Scottish, Welsh, Northern Irish and South Tyrolean independence movements), but only because nation-states already emerged in Europe and North America some one hundred years ago.[12] National identity, national well-being, chauvinism and the desire for self-government, however, remain fully enthroned in the United States, Canada and Western Europe. The desire of East

---

11  See Motyl, *Sovietology, Rationality, Nationality*, pp. 49-52.
12  See Edward Tiryakian and Ronald Rogowski, eds., *New Nationalisms of the Developed West* (Boston: Allen & Unwin, 1985).

European nations or of Third World nations to attain their own states or to be nationalist in the other four senses of the term are thus nothing but attempts to be like the modern world. That is to say, to be nationalist, in any or all of the senses of the term, is to be modern — naturally, if by modernity we mean that which the self-styled modern world is or claims to be.

## Nationalism and Modernity

But there are also more substantive reasons for suspecting that nationalism is not about to leave the world stage and that West Europeans and Americans will, *nolens volens*, continue to be among the world's most important promoters of the idea. As I will argue below, the central elements of what generally passes for modernity promote all "forms" of nationalism. Democracy, the market and secularism strengthen the nation and reinforce its current hegemony. Contemporary values regarding social justice and the dynamics of the international system strengthen the state and, thus, willy-nilly its current incarnation, the nation-state. Education, urbanization and industrialization create national elites, who, together with nations and states, represent the necessary conditions of the actual striving for nation-states and self-government. The discourse of human rights enormously facilitates this pursuit, while democracy acts as the sufficient condition of its emergence. Because the nation and the state are, respectively, the dominant social and political organizing principles of the contemporary world, the continued striving of national elites for their own states is inevitable in a world of democracy and human rights.

If, on the other hand, nationalism is defined as, say, a form of chauvinism, then the above division of factors into necessary, facilitating and sufficient ones would obviously be different. The existence of elites and states with national identities would only facilitate chauvinism; the ubiquity of the nation would be necessary to its emergence, while democracy and the market might suffice to produce it. Although the perception of others as "other" will be with us for a long time, national differentiation on its own does not produce chauvinism. For such attitudes to arise, nations must be brought into contact and competition, in which some lose and others win. Democracy and the market are two forces that compel individuals and groups to compete unremittingly, that produce winners and losers continually — it goes without saying that there will always be bad winners and sore losers — and that encourage groups to pursue their interests on the basis of their semiotic self-understanding, their cultural "groupness." Add to this combustible mixture the modern state, which acts as an arena within which struggles can be pursued, and another potent element contributes to conflict and competition. And if, as seems likely, the state becomes the preserve of some dominant group, we may expect ethnic animosities only to intensify.

## The Modernity of Nations

Fundamental to my argument is the proposition that the nation and the nation-state are, as I stated above, the dominant forms of organization in the modern world. Of course, the claims that modern countries make are quite different: namely, that they are modern precisely because they are on the verge of abandoning the nation-state and demoting the nation. This self-perception, which I believe is both self-serving and fundamentally wrong, seems to be part and parcel of the discourse of human rights that has been appropriated by the elites of these countries and which functions to legitimize their rule internally, to preserve their hegemony externally and to isolate "Europe" from troubling developments in neighboring states. We need not take this self-perception too seriously as a practical program, except perhaps to ask, as I do at the end of this essay, what the subtext is of so unabashedly ideological a formulation.

Despite such rhetoric, neither the nation — as a self-conscious cultural community — nor the state — as a political organization with a monopoly of violence in some territory — appears to be on the verge of extinction. Ethnic groups in the United States and Canada are very much in the process of asserting their nationhood, even as Washington and Ottawa desperately struggle to foster pan-ethnic identities. The peoples of Western Europe, both the majority nations and the minorities, are all reclaiming their history, asserting their prerogatives and establishing themselves as bona fide corporate entities. To be sure, people are learning foreign languages, traveling and developing multiple identities, but none of these characteristics contravenes the fact that the background on which all of these trends are taking place is the nation. And if the emergence of a self-confident Japan, a reunified Germany and a beleaguered America is a portent of things to come, we may expect the sense of national identity and the feeling of belongingness to a nation to continue to grow. The trend may change, of course, but there seem to be few indications of why it should anytime in the near future.

Why and how nations emerged several centuries ago are questions that John Armstrong, Benedict Anderson, Ernest Gellner, Carlton Hayes, Eric Hobsbawm and many others have attempted to answer, but these issues do not concern us here.[13] Far more important is explaining why nations, which are regularly denounced for their supposedly atavistic qualities, still exist. Although a definitive answer is probably impossible, critically important to the nation's continued hold on humanity are, as I suggested above, secularism, democracy and the market. Thus, Anthony D. Smith has argued that the crisis of the intelligentsia, a crisis that had much to do with the emergence of secularism in a religious world, was directly responsible for the emergence of national identity among nineteenth-century European elites.[14] Regardless of whether or not Smith is correct in his argument, it seems unquestionable that the growing absence of the divine from the world, its *Entzauberung*, to use Max Weber's term, at least facilitates the continued maintenance of national identity and national self-assertiveness in the modern world. God's presumed

---

13  John A. Armstrong, *Nations before Nationalism* (Chapel Hill, NC: University of North Carolina Press, 1982); Benedict Anderson, *Imagined Communities* (London: Verso, 1983); Ernest Gellner, *Nations and Nationalism* (Ithaca, NY: Cornell University Press, 1983); Carlton Hayes, *Essays on Nationalism* (New York: Russell & Russell, 1966); Eric Hobsbawm, *Nations and Nationalism since 1780* (Cambridge, UK: Cambridge University Press, 1990).
14  Anthony D. Smith, *Theories of Nationalism* (London: Duckworth, 1971).

"death" has surely contributed to the growing emphasis on values that underline the human side of life. Human rights are in this sense an ersatz of sorts for the divine. Possibly even more powerful a substitute is the nation, or, until recently perhaps, the class. As many observers have noted, the fervor with which nationalists and communists have dedicated themselves to their groups has often resembled that of religious devotees in their common willingness to sacrifice their lives for the higher goal of an abstract ideal.

The connection between democracy and the nation is equally straightforward. Democratic regimes are self-styled popular regimes; they derive their legitimacy from the people and from their activity on behalf of the people. The American Declaration of Independence, in its insistence on government by, for and of the people is thus a classic nationalist document. Naturally, the people can be a multiethnic, indeed a multinational association. Yet it would appear to be highly likely, if not indeed inevitable, that in its appeals to the people, a democratic regime will either emphasize the national characteristics of that people if it is ethnically homogeneous, or will attempt to create more or less homogeneous characteristics if the people is ethnically heterogeneous. Legitimacy requires that a strong connection be established between government and "the" people: The logic of the situation demands that a people, or people in general, be transformed into a collectivity deserving of the definite article. The United States, with its constant emphasis on the American qualities of the people that inhabit the country, may serve as an example of the pressures faced by strongly democratic governments in multi-ethnic societies and of their tendency to adopt positions that lead to the creation of self-conscious cultural communities and an emphasis on national solidarity and national superiority.

The market, so goes the claim, is the best solvent of nationalism: It overcomes national differences, brings nations together, makes the state and, of course the nation-state superfluous. Contemporary Western Europe is supposed to be the prime example of the manner in which market relations overcome national narrowness, passions and emotionalism. Of course, one could point to just as many, if not far more, examples of how market relations also seem to have the radically opposite effect, leading to such phenomena as neo-Nazi attacks on racial minorities in Germany, Jean-Marie Le Pen's fulminations against immigrant threats in France, Jörg Haider's encouragement of *Ausländerfeindlichkeit* in Austria and Thatcherite economics in England. Theoretically, however, the important point is that markets place peoples into contact and competition. Nations that may have not known one another and thus, ipso facto, could not have been in conflict, are brought together under conditions that contribute little to peaceful resolutions of emergent problems.[15] What is more, the market has an inevitably differential impact on individuals and peoples. After all, it is in the very nature of market relations to reward efficient regions and to penalize inefficient ones. As Michael Hechter has argued, the market's accentuation of regional differences can create national differences, thereby not only leading to competition but also actually generating the drive toward independence as the only solution to the perceived inequities of capitalist relations.[16]

If these considerations are correct, we should expect "national liberation struggles" to multiply in Western Europe after 1992, with the creation of a unified market in a democratically ruled "Europe of regions." Not only will regionally-based national minorities assert their right to self-determination, but the dominant nations will likely experience a renewal of national pride, perhaps even hatred, toward these minorities, toward other nations and toward other states.

## The Modernity of the State

The future also looks good for the state, since the major features of modernity — the market, democracy and secularism — well-nigh require the continued existence of that institution. Although recent developments in a variety of countries represent something in the nature of a scaling down of the functions of the state, largely under

---

15  Karl Deutsch, *Nationalism and Social Communication* (Cambridge, MA: MIT Press, 1966).
16  Michael Hechter, *Internal Colonialism* (Berkeley, CA: University of California Press, 1977).

the guise of neoconservative justifications that emphasize the role of the market in creating social prosperity, it is equally true that countervailing pressures are pushing the state to assert itself in such areas as social policy, education, infrastructure and the like — precisely those spheres in which, as Adam Smith pointed out long ago, the market is perhaps inherently incapable of playing a decisive role. Seen in this light, the growing importance of communications to the industrial and postindustrial worlds means that the state will continue to exhibit a high profile in this sector for the foreseeable future. Roads, bridges, ports, satellites and other expensive public projects will long remain the preserve of the public institution par excellence, not of the market.

Perhaps more important, the market, while possibly the most efficient form of social production, is also unable to guarantee the just distribution of the social product, be it in the form of public services or social safety nets. Short of the realization of utopian socialist visions of the self-rule of autonomous workers, it is the state that will continue to be most responsible for the fair division of the social surplus and for the creation of conditions under which all individuals will be best able to pursue what they universally consider to be their entitlement — human rights. In current circumstances, the demand for social equality and economic and political justice can but enhance the role of the state, even if with a more human face.

Parliamentary democracy is also unthinkable without a strong state to act as its prop. Except in the tiny political settings that approximate Jean-Jacques Rousseau's utopian vision of direct democracy, in which the entire homogeneous people can deliberate over every issue, popular rule — the rule of the *demos* — necessarily entails institutions, organizations, groups, procedures and laws — in a word, a state. Strong institutions may be no guarantee of democracy, as too strong a state, one that is authoritarian or totalitarian, undermines democratic procedures and civil society. But weak institutions virtually ensure that democracy will function poorly and thus be prone to breakdown. Finally, secularism is premised on the division of authority between a ghettoized religious sphere and an ever-growing public sphere, a polity that exerts the authority formerly exercised by the religious. As the rule of the theocrats and gods is replaced with the rule of public servants, the state becomes a necessary condition for the grouping together of the secular holders of authority.

In addition to arguments concerning the continued vitality of the state's internal functions, the division of the world into states that claim to be, or by and large actually are, nation-states will continue to privilege the state as long as that division persists, which to all appearances will be a long time. States, after all, do not disappear easily. Not only are their resources generally far greater than those of their challengers within opposition movements, but the international system in general, and the great powers in particular, are usually opposed to the disappearance of states, at least since the Peace of Westphalia. Even under conditions of war, states are reluctant to see the complete eradication of their rivals and the emergence of successor states. The recent crises in the Soviet Union and Yugoslavia, whose republics appealed to the very right to self-determination that the West loudly proclaimed for several decades, were thus instructive, showing — once again — that Western states are still as concerned as ever with *raison d'état* and not the rights of individuals or of nations.

By the same token, the emergence of international organizations is not only not contradictory of the state, it is premised on the existence of states: It is states, after all, that are united in the United Nations, the European Community and so on. There is no transformation of quantity into quality at work here, inasmuch as sovereignty, the supreme authority that all states still claim to want to preserve, is something that states either possess or do not. However great their involvement in international organizations, therefore, states will continue to be the repositories of sovereignty until and unless they decide to self-destruct. By the same token, however great the autonomy of sub-state regions, their authority will always remain subordinate to that of the state and therefore not be supreme. To be sure, the growing role of international economic processes, of international organizations arid of non-state international actors will reduce the dominant position of the state on the world arena, and in this sense critics of realist theories may be right in hoping that the state will no longer have a monopoly on international affairs.[17] Perhaps, as they claim, wars will be less frequent and international harmony more likely. But even if this prognosis is correct, the state will continue to exist and will continue to be sovereign within the territory that it claims for itself. In becoming enmeshed in a greater variety of international networks, the state may therefore be tamed, humanized and reduced in stature — but, at home and within the very organizations that will hope to tame it, the state will remain of paramount importance.

If modernity truly promotes the nation and the state, and as most modern states are indeed nation-states — that is to say, not ethnically homogeneous polities, but merely the sovereign political organizations of particular cultural communities — then it follows that nation-states will continue to prosper. Their persistence, however, need not logically entail chauvinism or persecution of minorities. As I suggested above, the nation-state only facilitates interethnic animosities. It is in combination with other aspects of modernity, especially democracy and the market, that chauvinism may be inevitable. If I am right in thinking that modernity also fosters nations, states and nation-states, then it is obviously hopeless for policy makers and scholars to expect that chauvinism will disappear as modernity deepens. At best, while chauvinist attitudes will remain, actual conflict and violent behavior may be curtailed. Life, in other words, is rather tougher than Voltaire's Pangloss suspected.

## West European Exceptionalism?

But is not the state rapidly becoming passé? Does not the trend toward European integration suggest that the nation-state, if not the state, is becoming the least modern of contemporary political organizations? Is not the internationalization of human life and the creation of common homes, be they in Europe or in other parts of the world, irreversible and overwhelming? Once again, in

---

17   James Rosenau, *Turbulence in World Politics* (Princeton, NJ: Princeton University Press, 1990); Robert Keohane, ed., *Neorealism and Its Critics* (New York: Columbia University Press,1986).

evaluating what some might consider to be iron laws of development, we would do well to distinguish between rhetoric and reality. To be sure, the rhetoric suggests that Europe has now embarked on union, that wars have finally come to an end and that the millennium, indeed the end of history, are just around the corner. Still, we would not be remiss in being somewhat skeptical of such grandiose claims, surely not the first to herald the end of strife and the coming of paradise on earth. Neither would we be remiss in pointing to the fact that the euphoria of 1989 disappeared within a mere year. Nor would we be wrong to note that the key slogan of the 1970s and 1980s was Euro-sclerosis and not Euro-optimism and that all slogans—like proletarian internationalism, *die Neue Ordnung* and the new world order—appear to have a limited life span.

Rather than leaving the argument at the level of skepticism, however, I should like to refer to three rather more concrete factors. First, 1992 represents economic integration: There is no reason why a single European market should not exist side by side with the state or, indeed, with a strengthened state. Although politics and economics obviously intersect and overlap, the modern state and capitalism can and do occupy relatively autonomous spheres. Second, the underlying impetus for Western Europe's integration was, I suggest, the division of Europe into two spheres of influence and the concomitant elimination of European security concerns. The end of the Cold War, the unification of Germany, Eastern Europe's insistence on being accepted into a common European "home," and the disintegration of the USSR suggest that European integration will be extraordinarily difficult to achieve. Notwithstanding declarations to the contrary, West European states have very different interests, and these interests, be they geopolitical or economic, are unlikely to converge effortlessly in post-perestroika Europe.[18] Third, political unification would have to involve the voluntary, and not compulsory, abdication of sovereignty by decidedly sovereign, institutionally strong and resource-rich

---

18  For a particularly gloomy view, see John Mearsheimer, "Back to the Future," *International Security*, 15, no. 1 (Summer 1990) pp. 5-56.

European states. Because sovereignty is an all-or-nothing proposition — by definition, supreme authority cannot be "lessened" or "increased" by degrees — such abdication not only appears to have no precedents in history, but by necessarily involving the creation of a pan-European political organization with a monopoly of violence its chances of success seem minimal. Is "Europe" an exception, then? For better or for worse, no.

## The Modernity of Elites

Just as nations and states are necessary to nationalism, so too are national elites, who utilize the nation as a vehicle for advancing their political, material or cultural interests and launch struggles for independence, self-government or enhanced well-being.[19] Such a view of nationalism necessarily assumes that elites, not masses, are the key actors in history, that elites invariably pursue power and influence precisely because they are capable of doing so and that they can successfully mobilize masses by means of various strategies, some focused on rational calculations of means and ends, others centered on perceptions of status still others appealing to "constitutive myths," or mythomoteurs.[20] Can elites therefore create nations *ex nihilo*, or must specific ethnie be present out of which nations can then be forged? Do nations follow appeals to material self-interest or do symbols mean most to them? Different theorists provide different answers, but most, fortunately, premise their arguments on the centrality of elites and thus accept my basic point.[21]

Although elites may or may not be a given in all forms of social organization, it is surely the case that conditions of modernity

---

19  See Joseph Rothschild, *Ethnopolitics* (New York: Columbia University Press, 1981) and John Breuilly, *Nationalism and the State* (Manchester, UK: Manchester University Press, 1985).

20  See Michael Hechter, *Principles of Group Solidarity* (Berkeley, CA: University of California Press, 1988); Donald Horowitz, *Ethnic Groups in Conflict* (Berkeley, CA: University of California Press, 1985); Anthony D. Smith, *The Ethnic Origins of Nations* (Oxford: Basil Blackwell, 1988) p. 15.

21  See Paul Brass, "Language and National Identity in the Soviet Union and India," in Motyl, *Thinking Theoretically*, pp. 99-128.

virtually guarantee that ethnic majorities and minorities will possess them. The spread of education, urbanization and industrialization may or may not attenuate ethnic differences, as modernization theory at one time suggested, but they clearly function to produce strata that are socially mobilized, technically trained and thus ideally equipped to mobilize their nations for the advancement of their own or their nations' interests.

Not surprisingly, modern national elites have appropriated the language of human rights in general and of self-determination in particular. Indeed, the discourse of human rights exerts a hegemonic influence on contemporary thinking: Even dictators feel impelled to proclaim themselves solemn defenders of human rights. In and of itself, this hegemony does not suffice to propel elites onto the path of nationalism, but it greatly facilitates such a move. The championing of human rights literally invites elites to assert themselves. Moreover, it provides them with a universal language and with irrefutable arguments, so much so that even opposition to human-rights demands must also be couched in the language of human rights. The irony is that, because human rights have become the dominant discourse of Western states, politicians and statesmen are forced to pay homage to a principle that privyleges the sovereign individual or the sovereign group over the sovereign state and, if universally implemented, would lead to the destabilization of the international system and to the internal delegitimation of their own rule.[22]

Sufficing to push national elites toward the actual pursuit of states for their nations is—*horribile dictu*—democracy. Political freedom, party competition, voting and the like permit, encourage and compel elites to pursue their interests in the most efficient manner, and that means utilizing nations as vehicles of political and material power. Conditions of freedom remove whatever political obstacles there may have been to the pursuit of nationalism. Parliamentary competition accentuates the groupness of groups

---

22  Alexander J. Motyl, "Rites, Rituals, and Soviet-American Relations," in Robert Jervis and Seweryn Bialer, eds., *Soviet-American Relations after the Cold War* (Durham, NC: Duke University Press, 1991) pp.183-96.

and thus provides elites with ready-made vehicles for their ambitions. The imperative of popular legitimation forces elites to identify with the supposed repository of sovereignty and, in this manner, to be supporters of the nation. National elites in democratic settings, therefore, will both express nationalist sentiments and actually translate their beliefs into the pursuit of nation-states or self-government. Recent events in the postcommunist states of East Central Europe appear to substantiate the truth of this proposition. Whether or not nationalist elites then succeed in their endeavors is of course a wholly different question, one that depends on their ability to attract followers and overcome opposition.

## Whither Nationalism?

Far into the future, I suspect, is how long nationalism will persist. As I have argued above, nationalism is not some atavistic, premodern phenomenon that is slated to disappear with the growing modernity of the world. Quite the contrary: The things called nationalism are likely to intensify under conditions of modernity, which is the ideal breeding ground for chauvinism, national self-determination, national self-government and national identity. Modernity promotes nations, states and thus nation-states. We can expect nationalism, however defined, to grow in intensity as modern states become even more modern and unmodern states embark on the road to modernity. In short, *modernity breeds nationalism*.

Contrary to the Western assertion that nationalism is non-European, in being modern, nationalism is the most European of contemporary phenomena. The newly liberated peoples of East Central Europe are, as a result, faced with an insoluble conundrum. Being genuinely European by being nationalist will not get them admitted into "Europe." Rejecting European values and behaviors by not being nationalist, on the other hand, might get them admitted, but is probably a hopeless endeavor in a world of nations, state and nation-states. Cynics — or is it idealists? — might add that, in insisting on such rigorous entrance requirements, "Europe" has just this impossible dilemma in mind.

# 2

# Liberalism, Nationalism, and National Liberation Struggles*

This paper consists of three parts. Taking John Rawls's recently published *The Law of Peoples* as my starting point, I argue that the principles he enunciates and the definitions he employs necessarily endorse independence for liberal peoples in both a liberal and a not fully liberal world. I then examine the question of the compatibility of liberalism and nationalism, a compatibility that Rawls takes for granted in his discussion. I conclude that, although there is no definitive answer to the question, there are persuasive conceptual reasons for viewing liberalism and nationalism as compatible as well as eminently important practical reasons for attempting a reconciliation between the two. Finally, I argue that the national liberation struggles of liberal peoples in the former Soviet bloc either demonstrate empirically that liberalism and nationalism are compatible or, at the very least, raise important questions about the relationship of liberalism and nationalism that should concern liberals.

## I.

In *The Law of Peoples* John Rawls sets out the following agenda:

> By the "Law of Peoples" I mean a particular political conception of right and justice that applies to the principles and norms of international law and practice. I shall use the term "Society of Peoples" to mean all those peoples who follow the ideals and principles of the Law of Peoples in their mutual relations. These peoples have their own internal governments, which may be constitutional liberal democratic or nonliberal but decent governments. In this book I consider how the content of the Law of Peoples might be developed out of a liberal idea of justice similar to, but more general than, the idea I called *justice as fairness* [ital. in original] in *A Theory*

---

\* First printed in: *Hagar: International Social Science Review*, vol. 1, no. 2 (2001), pp. 135-143. Reprinted with permission of the original publisher.

of *Justice* (1971). This idea of justice is based on the familiar idea of the social contract, and the procedure followed before the principles of right and justice are selected and agreed upon is in some ways the same in both the domestic and the international case.[1]

The peoples that constitute Rawls's world are fivefold: 1) reasonable liberal peoples, 2) decent hierarchical peoples, 3) outlaw states, 4) societies burdened by unfavorable conditions, and 5) benevolent absolutisms. Reasonable liberal peoples will, argues Rawls, develop a Law of Peoples more or less identical to that reasonable individuals would have developed in the original position.[2] Rawls also believes that decent hierarchical peoples— "nonliberal societies whose basic institutions meet certain specified conditions of political right and justice"[3] —would consent to such a Law. The liberal and decent peoples united in the Society of Peoples may, Rawls continues, justifiably defend themselves against outlaw states and "owe a duty of assistance" to burdened societies. "The aim of the Law of Peoples would be fully achieved when all societies have been able to establish either a liberal or a decent regime, however unlikely that may be."[4]

My paper proceeds from Rawls's argument and discuss its implications for the ethnocultural communities known as nations and the claim, known as nationalism, that nations should be independent.[5]

---

1   Rawls, J., *The Law of Peoples* (Cambridge: Harvard University Press, 1999), pp. 3-4.
2   The Law of Peoples consists of eight principles: "1) Peoples are free and independent, and their freedom and independence are to be respected by other peoples. 2) Peoples are to observe treaties and undertakings. 3) Peoples are equal and are parties to the agreements that bind them. 4) Peoples are to observe a duty of non-intervention. 5) Peoples have the right of self-defense but no right to instigate war for reasons other than self-defense. 6) Peoples are to honor human rights. 7) Peoples are to observe certain specified restrictions in the conduct of war. 8) Peoples have a duty to assist other peoples living under unfavorable conditions that prevent their having a just or decent political and social regime" (Ibid., p. 37).
3   Ibid., p. 3, fn 2.
4   Ibid., p. 5.
5   Definitions of nations and nationalism are discussed in Alexander J. Motyl, *Sovietology, Rationality, Nationality: Coming to Grips with Nationalism in the USSR* (New York: Columbia University Press, 1990).

Let us assume that, at time *t*, the world consists of the five kinds of peoples Rawls identifies. Let us also assume that, due to the intrinsic reasonableness of liberalism on the one hand and the ability of liberal societies to promote liberalism and decency and to defend themselves effectively against outlaw states on the other, the world comes to consist of only liberal societies at time $t + n$. That is to say, every society that was formerly decent, burdened, absolutist, or outlawed comes to embrace a liberal order domestically and to subscribe to the Law of Peoples internationally. (I assume that such societies may consist of more than one people.) Would such a world be just? By Rawls's own logic, it could not and would not be just unless and until every individual people in the world subscribed to the Law of Peoples *as a people*.

The first principle of the Law of Peoples unequivocally states that "Peoples are free and independent, and their freedom and independence are to be respected by other peoples."[6] For the Law of Peoples to be a genuinely binding agreement between and among peoples, every people must subscribe to it. But in order to subscribe to the Law, every people must of course be free and independent. All liberal peoples are free in a world consisting of liberal societies, but they are not necessarily independent. Inasmuch as the Law of Peoples applies to peoples and not to states or societies, a liberal world order requires that all liberal peoples be free *and* independent.

But that is to say that a liberal world order would have to promote—indeed, it would be premised on—separatism. Where two or more liberal peoples inhabit, say, a formerly outlaw state or burdened society, they would have to establish their own liberal societies and their own instruments of self-rule. Then, and only then, could they, as free and independent peoples, subscribe to the Law of Peoples and partake on an equal and independent basis in the Society of Peoples.

There are at least three other reasons that a Rawlsian liberal world order would promote the independence of peoples. First is that every people must have a territory. Thus, Rawls argues:

---

[6] Rawls, *Law of Peoples*, p. 37.

> Unless a definite agent is given responsibility for maintaining an asset and bears the responsibility and loss for not doing so, that asset tends to deteriorate. On my account the role of the institution of property is to prevent this deterioration from occurring. In the present case, the asset is the people's territory and its potential capacity to support them *in perpetuity*; and the agent is the people itself as politically organized. The perpetuity condition is crucial. People must recognize that they cannot make up for failing to regulate their numbers or to care for their land by conquest in war, or by migrating into another people's territory without their consent.[7]

A liberal people inhabiting a formerly outlaw state, burdened society, benevolent absolutism, or decent hierarchical society will of course occupy a particular geographic and social place, but that place can function as a territorial asset only if it becomes the people's holding in perpetuity. Perpetual assets can be deemed such only if there is mutual agreement that the territory in question does indeed belong to this liberal people and not to that one. Otherwise, deterioration, even if unlikely, may occur, and the temptation to engage in war and/or migrate may, however improbably, emerge.

Second is that Rawls recognizes that each people has a "further interest"—namely, "a people's proper self-respect of themselves as a people, resting on their common awareness of their trials during their history and of their culture with its accomplishments. Altogether distinct from their self-concern for their security and the safety of their territory, this interest shows itself in a people's insisting on receiving from other peoples a proper respect and recognition of their equality."[8] Because this further interest is a perfectly legitimate feature of every liberal people, it follows that all liberal peoples will insist—albeit with, obviously, the civility and tact that necessarily characterize liberals and liberal peoples—on proper respect and recognition of their equality and, more important, be willing to reciprocate by granting respect and recognition to all peoples. But if membership in the Society of Peoples entails adherence to the Law of Peoples and adherence to the Law of Peoples entails freedom and independence, then it fol-

---

7   Ibid., p. 8.
8   Ibid., pp. 34-35.

lows that any self-respecting people will want to be independent. Moreover, every self-respecting people will want nonindependent liberal peoples to be independent and therefore self-respecting.

The third argument for independence is that, in a liberal world, there can be no liberal or geopolitical argument against it. If all societies are liberal domestically and adhere to the Law of Peoples internationally, if all societies reject war, annexation, and illegal migration, if all societies pursue trade, abolish armies, and are fundamentally decent, then there is no liberally grounded argument against national separation and the creation of an independent people with its own territory and government. In particular, private property will, *ceteris paribus*, be no obstacle to separation, as its status will remain sacrosanct regardless of the liberal territory in which it happens to be located. It may be the case that secession will entail discussion, disagreement, negotiation, and a redrawing of maps, but reasonable liberal peoples will surely be able to resolve all such contentious issues. By the same token, the creation of new governments may entail some costs, but material costs can be no argument against promoting freedom, independence, self-respect, and proper asset utilization. If money matters at this level of the analysis, then it would also have to be a factor in determining whether or not equal participation in a liberal domestic order is really worth the material costs. But no Rawlsian could possibly accept such a trade-off. Short-term transaction costs would be a small price to pay for the creation of a universal Society of Peoples.

In sum, Rawlsian liberals in a Rawlsian liberal world would have to be nationalists or nationalist sympathizers. Indeed, the willingness to accede to and promote secession would be the mark of a true Rawlsian liberal. A perfectly liberal world would therefore consist of a vastly larger number of self-governing units than today's system of states, but, as there is no argument against separation at any stage of the process and as the costs are likely to be minimal, nonexistent, or irrelevant, preventing or discouraging separation would be a profoundly illiberal policy. And there is no reason to expect such *matryoshka* nationalism to result in interethnic chaos and violence: reasonable liberal peoples who pursue trade and abjure war with one another have no reason to exchange insults, whip up passions, grab territory, and build armies.

Rawls's argument for a Law of Peoples has important implications for national liberation even before the world is uniformly liberal. Imagine the world as consisting of liberal peoples, decent hierarchical peoples, outlaw states, burdened societies, and benevolent absolutisms at any time before $t + n$. Why should a liberal people, A, *not* separate from a liberal society, B, and thereby join the Society of Peoples? If both peoples are truly liberal, then non-self-governing people A is entitled to self-respect, perpetual assets, and independence, while self-governing people B cannot possibly have any liberal, or even geopolitical, reasons to object. Trade would still continue, property would still remain in private hands, war would still be unthinkable, and relations would still be harmonious.

Now imagine that liberal peoples in all four nonliberal societies constitute underground liberal sub-societies. Such self-constitution is likely to be difficult, especially in outlaw states, but it is certainly possible and probably even desirable. After all, better pockets of liberal decency in nonliberal settings, than no liberalism at all. Would these liberally self-constituted societies be justified in pursuing secession? And would the eighth principle of the Law of Peoples—"Peoples have a duty to assist other peoples living under unfavorable conditions that prevent their having a just or decent political and social regime"—morally obligate existing liberal societies to help them?

The answer to both questions is "yes." If liberal peoples have a right to independence in a fully liberal world, then the reasons for independence would be no less, and probably even more, persuasive in a nonliberal setting. At the very least, if they attain independence, they can join the Society of Peoples and subscribe to its Law. Moreover, insofar as totalitarian outlaw states most nearly reproduce two of the defining characteristics of the original position—atomized individuals deliberating behind a veil of ignorance—one might even argue that liberal self-constitution under such conditions most closely approximates "true" liberalism and is thus most deserving of solicitude.

But there is another important argument for separation relating to the fifth principle of the Law of Peoples: "Peoples have the right to self-defense but no right to instigate war for reasons other than self-defense."[9] If independent liberal peoples have that right, even though outlaw states threaten them only "from outside," then nonindependent liberal peoples must have the same right, especially since they are subjected to continual attack by the outlaw state. Under conditions such as these, it is probably a moral obligation of independent liberal peoples to assist oppressed liberal peoples. Naturally, oppressed liberal peoples would have to acknowledge that non-self-governing liberal peoples have an equal right to equality and independence in the liberal societies that would arise if and when they, the oppressed liberal peoples, succeed in separating.

Things are somewhat more complicated with the other three nonliberal societies Rawls discusses. Chances are that decent hierarchical societies that are signatories to the Law of Peoples will not be engaged in a state of war with their minority peoples, but even so, the pursuit by such peoples of independence would appear to be a liberal good that should not be resisted. Leaving a benevolent absolutism is little different from the above two cases, while seceding from a burdened society should presumably be permitted if and only if it does not signally worsen the living standards enjoyed by the population that stays. The burden will not change if poorer or more or less materially equal peoples leave. On the other hand, richer peoples may presumably separate if they oblige themselves to assist their former fellows in the burdened society above and beyond what other liberal peoples might reasonably be expected to do.

## II.

Although Rawls evidently sees no difficulty in reconciling liberalism with nationalism, there are at least three arguments for accepting their compatibility:

---

9   Ibid., p. 37.

1. It is a historical fact that nationalists have espoused liberalism, democracy, authoritarianism, fascism, totalitarianism, and communism and that liberals, democrats, authoritarians, fascists, and totalitarians have espoused nationalism. It may therefore make sense to conclude, as does Mark Hagopian, that nationalism can be parasitic on all ideologies precisely because it is not an elaborate worldview, but an "ideal" or action program.[10] Admittedly, the empirical fact that liberal and nationalist individuals have been able to span the ideological spectrum does not prove that their views really were compatible with the ideologies they adopted. Contradictions may have been submerged or been deemed unimportant for tactical reasons. If so, although undeveloped nationalisms may be compatible with other ideologies, it could be the case that a fully developed nationalism would be tantamount to a political philosophy or ideology and thus be incompatible.

---

10 Mark Hagopian, *Ideals and Ideologies of Modern Politics* (New York: Longman, 1985).

2. Although contemporary liberalism generally opposes the nationalisms of nonindependent peoples, it is indifferent to and possibly even supportive of the successful nationalisms of independent peoples. That is to say, liberalism takes as its starting point the existing division of the world into self-styled nation-states.[11] Liberalism may criticize these states for the policies they pursue internally and externally, but it does not question the fundamental legitimacy of their existence—even though liberals fully appreciate that states are the products not of rarified social contracts but of wars and that boundaries are "arbitrary." Moreover, when peoples are the objects of genocidal or oppressive policies by outlaw states, liberalism is even willing to countenance secession. In other words, liberalism is comfortable with successful nationalisms and more or less at ease with tragically unsuccessful ones. The claim that liberalism must stand in opposition to striving nationalisms can therefore hold only if liberalism is defined as unconditionally privileging the state and ignoring all injustice short of mass murder. Needless to say, such a redefinition subverts liberalism. The only alternative to self-destruction is, I suggest, accommodation to that range of "normal" nationalisms found between the status quo and genocide.

---

11 See Margaret Canovan, *Nationhood and Political Theory* (Cheltenham: Edward Elgar, 1996).

3. The claim that liberalism and nationalism are always and everywhere intrinsically incompatible entails a view of both as consisting of changeless and timeless essences. Such a view reifies, decontextualizes, and dehistoricizes both liberalism and nationalism. Worse, it ignores the fact that, although any theory, philosophy, or ideology of liberalism and nationalism must entail a clear understanding of both concepts, there cannot be one, and only one, definition of any concept. All concepts are "essentially contested."[12] As a result, the question of whether or not liberalism and nationalism are compatible ultimately depends on how we define them. We can define them as being incompatible or we can define them as being compatible. Rawls, like Yael Tamir, Will Kymlicka, and many others, see no incompatibility mostly because both the liberalism and the nationalism they discuss are "soft."[13] Their versions of liberalism take it as a given that "individuals" are no less (or no more) of an abstraction than "nations" and that non-abstract individuals are concrete human beings with languages and cultures. In contrast, the liberal (as well as nationalist) argument for incompatibility entails "hard" versions of both liberalism and nationalism. According to the binary opposition favored by liberals, the really real individual confronts and brooks no compromise with the really unreal nation. Hard-boiled nationalists employ the same modifiers but in reverse order.

There is, *a priori*, no reason for preferring soft to hard or hard to soft definitions of liberalism and nationalism. The only way to answer the question of compatibility, therefore, is to say "it depends." Why might we prefer one version of liberalism and nationalism to another? Among other things, it depends on the project. If our hope is to promote liberalism in a nationalist world and if we expect the world to remain nationalist for some time to

---

12 Connolly, W., *The Terms of Political Discourse* (Lexington, MA.: Heath, 1974)
13 Tamir, Y. *Liberal Nationalism* (Princeton: Princeton University Press, 1993); Kymlicka, W., *Multicultural Citizenship: A Liberal Theory of Minority Rights* (Oxford: Clarendon, 1995).

come,[14] it makes sense to construct maximally compatible versions of both and then attempt to liberalize nationalism (or, possibly, to nationalize liberalism). Alternatively, if we are indifferent to the liberal project's impact on the world of genuinely concrete human beings and/or believe that nationalism is on its last legs anyway, then a maximalist liberalism probably makes more sense.

## III.

It is in fact the case empirically that liberal and decent peoples have pursued liberation from outlaw states by means of "national liberation struggles." The existence of such cases suggests that the issues discussed above cannot be divorced from consideration of concrete ethical choices facing liberals and nationalists alike. Solidarity, and the Estonian, Latvian, Lithuanian, and Ukrainian Popular Fronts were, I submit, just such national movements of liberal and decent peoples defending themselves against the predations of an unjust, repressive, and arguably genocidal regime—the Soviet Union. (Whether or not the independent states that emerged after 1989-1991 were also liberal is of course another question.)

Few would disagree with this characterization of the Soviet system. But it will be necessary to demonstrate just why I claim these movements may legitimately be said to have been representative of liberal and decent peoples. First, it is indisputable that all these movements enjoyed enormous popular support. Solidarity claimed a membership of ten million (about one third of the population) and, in the years after General Jaruzelski's crackdown in 1981, succeeded in creating a parallel society, effectively isolating the Communist regime and thereby laying the groundwork for its assumption of power in 1989. The Baltic popular fronts may have enjoyed even greater popular support; the Ukrainian Rukh appears to have been weaker than the others, but in 1989-1991 was

---

14 I make the argument for nationalism's likely longevity in *Revolutions, Nations, Empires: Conceptual Limits and Theoretical Possibilities* (New York: Columbia University Press, 1999), pp. 99-113.

still capable of bringing millions of supporters into the streets.[15] Second, the programs adopted by all these movements were either straightforwardly liberal or, at the very least, no worse than decently hierarchical.[16]

Do these two sub-claims justify the view that these were liberal and decent peoples engaged in resisting outlaw states? Had these movements been democratically elected, the answer, according to Rawls's criteria, would have to be a resounding "yes." That Solidarity and the popular fronts were not actually elected, however, only marginally weakens their representative credentials. Because democratic elections were impossible under outlaw state conditions, these movements' remarkable ability to mobilize mass support for several straight years—above ground in the case of the fronts, and both above and below ground in the case of Solidarity—was the functional equivalent of, to borrow from Ernest Renan, daily plebiscites.

Regardless of whether these movements, individually or collectively, brought down the Soviet empire, there is no disputing that they were implicated in the collapse of the USSR's brand of imperial totalitarianism.[17] In contrast, the Soviet and East European liberal-democratic dissidents who preceded the formation of Solidarity and the popular fronts were singularly unsuccessful in mobilizing popular opposition, even though they did provide a moral example and generate individual leaders, such as Vaclav Havel and Andrei Sakharov.[18] The national movements proved

---

15 For discussions of these movements, see Rein Taagepera, *Estonia: Return to Independence* (Boulder, Colo.: Westview, 1993); V. Stanley Vardys and Judith B. Sedaitis, *Lithuania: The Rebel Nation* (Boulder, Colo.: Westview, 1997); Juris Dreifelds, *Latvia in Transition* (Cambridge: Cambridge University Press, 1996); Bohdan Nahaylo, *The Ukrainian Resurgence* (Toronto: University of Toronto Press, 1999); Michael Bernhard, *The Origins of Democratization in Poland* (New York: Columbia University Press, 1993); Timothy Garton Ash, *The Polish Revolution: Solidarity* (New York: Vintage, 1985).

16 See Charles F. Furtado Jr. and Andrea Chandler, eds., *Perestroika in the Soviet Republics: Documents on the National Question* (Boulder, Colo.: Westview, 1992).

17 See Motyl, *Sovietology, Rationality, Nationality*.

18 See Ludmilla Alexeyeva, *Soviet Dissent* (Middletown, Conn.: Wesleyan University Press, 1985); Rudolf L. Tokes, *Opposition in Eastern Europe* (Baltimore,

stronger and more effective than the democrats precisely because the former were based on the nation while the latter were based on the individual. Individual democrats may have known what kind of societies they desired the Soviet Union and its satellites to be, but they had few ideas about how to replace imperial totalitarianism with democracy. For better or for worse, liberalism by its very "nature" has little to say about how to resist, how to mobilize, and how to overthrow an outlaw state. For one thing, liberalism is not about mobilization and it takes states as a given; for another, liberal individuals may be especially susceptible to free-riding and thus to undermining a movement's emergence and consolidation.

National movements, in contrast, have good answers to these questions. How to resist? By using the nation as an autonomous space beyond the reach of totalitarian and imperial control. How to mobilize and avoid free-riding? By drawing on national sentiment and national loyalty. How to overthrow an outlaw state? By creating an alternative society.[19] Because national movements can subvert outlaw states—surely the ultimate evil in Rawls's world order—there may be a case to be made for the claim that even illiberal or nonliberal such movements advance the cause of freedom. But when national movements enjoy enormous popular support and stand for genuinely liberal goals, thus having the right to call themselves the representatives of liberal peoples, the case for their being intrinsically supportive of liberalism becomes well-nigh irresistible. That many Western liberals and democrats either refused to support, or were embarrassed by, such movements in Eastern Europe and the USSR—at precisely the time when open support and non-embarrassment might have made a critical difference to their ability to promote freedom or resist repression—gets at the core of liberalism's (or is it liberals'?) problem with nationalism. By sacrificing genuine freedom on the altar of a hard liberalism's inflexible principles, liberals transform liber-

---

Md.: Johns Hopkins University Press, 1979); Bohdan Nahaylo and Victor Swoboda, *Soviet Disunion* (New York: Free Press, 1990).

19  I discuss these issues in *Sovietology, Rationality, Nationality*.

alism into a politically irrelevant philosophy and turn their backs on political projects that, like nationalism, may be in greatest need of—and be genuinely open to—liberalism's useful proddings and philosophical interventions.

# 3

# Inventing Invention
# The Limits of National Identity Formation*

## Loose lips sink ships.

According to Eric Hobsbawm, Benedict Anderson, and the "constructivist" school they have inspired, national identity, like the nation claiming it, is invented or imagined.[1] As a construct, it is neither natural or given — adjectives that might be favored by such currently unfashionable "primordialists" as Harold Isaacs and Clifford Geertz[2] — nor mythic or rooted, designations central to the "perennialist" thought of Anthony Smith and John Armstrong.[3] As I argue in this essay, the constructivists are

---

* First printed in: Ronald Grigor Suny and Michael D. Kennedy, eds., *Intellectuals and the Articulation of the Nation* (Ann Arbor: University of Michigan Press, 1999), pp. 57-75. Reprinted with permission of the original publisher. I thank Ron Suny, Michael Kennedy, Mark von Hagen, Jack Snyder, Stefan Cornelis, and Karen Ballentine for their criticism and comments.

1   Eric Hobsbawm, *Nations and Nationalism since 1780: Programme, Myth, Reality* (Cambridge: Cambridge University Press, 1990); Eric Hobsbawm and Terence Ranger, eds., *The Invention of Tradition* (Cambridge: Cambridge University Press, 1992); Benedict Anderson, *Imagined Communities* (London: Verso, 1983).

2   Harold R. Isaacs, "Basic Group Identity: The Idols of the Tribe," in *Ethnicity*, ed. Nathan Glazer and Daniel P. Moynihan (Cambridge, Mass.: Harvard University Press, 1975), pp. 29-52; Clifford Geertz, "The Integrative Revolution: Primordial Sentiments and Civil Politics in the New States," in *Political Development and Social Change*, ed. Jason L. Finkle and Richard W. Gable (New York: John Wiley and Sons, 1966), pp. 655-69. Donald Horowitz, *Ethnic Groups in Conflict* (Berkeley and Los Angeles: University of California Press, 1985), also comes close to making a primordialist case. Consider Jürgen Habermas's neoprimordialist explanation of recent events in West Germany: "[W]hat happened was that the floodgates of public opinion must have opened and changed the general climate to the point where stereotypes and opinions that had lurked beneath the surface ... now suddenly burst forth." "'More Humility, Fewer Illusions' - a Talk between Adam Michnik and Jürgen Habermas," *New York Review of Books*, March 24, 1994, p. 24.

3   Anthony Smith, The *Ethnic Origins of Nations* (Oxford: Basil Blackwell, 1986), and "The Nation: Invented, Imagined, Reconstructed?" *Millennium* 20, no. 3 (Winter 1991), pp. 353-68; John A. Armstrong, *Nations before Nationalism* (Chapel

persuasive only if invention and imagination are not taken seriously as concepts.[4] If they are, the constructivists are either trivial or unpersuasive. The problem with constructivism, therefore, is both self-imposed and conceptual. It follows that the constructivist project might be salvaged if the language of invention and imagination is modified or abandoned.

My discussion of the constructivist approach to national identity formation consists of four parts. The first unpacks the concepts of invention and imagination. The second examines what a nontrivial constructivist approach to national identity formation must entail. The third argues that the only conceptually consistent form of constructivism, one that sees national identity formation as the product of conscious elite invention and imagination, collapses under closer scrutiny. I conclude the essay with an alternative approach that retains many of constructivism's insights, while avoiding, I trust successfully, its mistake. In particular, I decouple national identity formation from elites engaged in conscious inventing and imagining and argue that national identity can emerge under conditions that, while more prevalent in modern times, could have existed in the distant past and can exist in the future. Nations, therefore, while historical and contingent, are not uniquely modern or, for that matter, necessarily transient.

## Constructivism's Concepts

Hobsbawm suggests that the scope of invention "includes both 'traditions' actually invented, constructed and formally instituted and those emerging in a less easily traceable manner

---

Hill: University of North Carolina Press, 1982), and "The Autonomy of Ethnic Identity: Historic Cleavages and Nationality Relations in the USSR," in *Thinking Theoretically about Soviet Nationalities,* ed. Alexander J. Motyl (New York: Columbia University Press, 1992), pp. 23-43.

4  Much of my thinking about concepts is drawn from Giovanni Sartori, "Guidelines for Concept Analysis," in *Social Science Concepts,* ed. Sartori (Beverly Hills, Calif.: Sage, 1984), pp. 15-85.

within a brief and dateable period."⁵ He also notes that invention is the "attempt to structure at least some parts of social life ... as unchanging and invariant."⁶ Anderson claims that the nation is *"imagined* because the members of even the smallest nation will never know most of their fellow-members, meet them, or even hear of them, yet in the minds of each lives the image of their communion."⁷

Hobsbawm's elaborations are confusing. Some reflection shows that construction, institution, emergence, and structuring are quite different concepts. Construction and structuring imply conscious activity of a directed and innovative kind; emergence suggests unwilled occurrences or processes; and institution implies an interaction between individual and mass human behavior. Anderson is closer to the mark in arguing that imagination involves not just an image, but an image of a nonexistent thing, the *communion* of the members of the nation. Yet he, too, leaves us without a dear sense of what imagination entails.

A closer look at invention and imagination might start with dictionary definitions: to imagine is "to form a mental image of (something not present)," and to invent is "to think up or imagine," "to create or produce for the first time."⁸ Regardless of what they denote, inventing and imagining clearly connote a bringing into being of something previously absent. But what, and how?

Consider the act of invention. Whatever its form and whatever the context, invention—or, more precisely, the inventor performing it—transforms the materials at hand into something qualitatively different and new. The invented thing is a novel entity, neither an agglomeration of previously given materials and, hence, merely the sum of its parts, nor something hidden

---

5   Eric Hobsbawm, "Introduction: Inventing Traditions," in Hobsbawm and Ranger, *The Invention of Tradition*, p. 1.
6   Hobsbawm, "Introduction," p. 2.
7   Anderson, *Imagined Communities*, p. 15.
8   *Webster's Seventh New Collegiate Dictionary* (Springfield: G. and C. Merriam, 1963), pp. 445, 416.

in these materials, something waiting for the inventor to set it free. Thus, a hammer is neither a piece of wood and a piece of metal, nor the external manifestation of the "hammerness" they embody, but a thing that, while consisting of wood and metal, represents an ontological reality different from theirs.

Imagination—or, again, the imaginer—works in the same way, juxtaposing or combining elements in novel ways that produce qualitatively new, because otherwise nonexistent, things or situations. I do not imagine the horse outside my window or the horns on the bull in my barn. But I do imagine a being that represents an amalgam of both—a unicorn. Likewise, I do not imagine the homeless in New York City— after all, I see them every day—but I might imagine a city without any poverty whatsoever. I imagine Utopia, *Schlaraffenland*, and many other such *imaginary* situations, just as I imagine similarly nonexistent entities, such as phoenixes, trolls, and fairies, although I can see their component parts—wings, fangs, and wands—in everyday life.

The point is that both invention and imagination presuppose preexisting building blocks on the one hand and their combination and subsequent transformation by inventors or imaginers into a novel end-product on the other. We cannot invent or imagine ex nihilo. Such an act should be called *creation*. Nor do we invent or imagine already existing things. Here, *remembrance* might be the more appropriate term. Nor, finally, can invention or imagination occur without conscious inventors and imaginers. It is not enough for images passively to "live," as Anderson puts it, in people's minds. Imagination, like invention, requires *active* imaginers and inventors. In sum, invention and imagination have three defining characteristics: building blocks, conscious human agency, and novelty. If any characteristic is absent, then invention or imagination cannot be said to have taken place.

This, I suggest, is a sensible way for the invention and imagination of national identity to be understood. If traditions are *not* invented and if communities are *not* imagined in such a precise manner, then invention and imagination are only metaphors of marginal relevance to rigorous social scientific enquiry. As metaphors, both terms might signify that something *like* actual invention and imagination is taking place. That something may involve active people or new things, but inasmuch as just about everything involves people or things, we are left with fuzzy variables that encompass most of life.

## Hard and Soft Constructivism

As with all schools of thought, constructivism is a nuanced intellectual undertaking. While all constructivists would agree that identity is the product of social and historical developments, they disagree, implicitly if not explicitly, on the manner in which construction takes place. "Hard" constructivists, such as Hobsbawm wants to be, emphasize conscious elite activity; "soft" constructivists, such as Anderson actually is, focus on mere human agency. In the first instance, elites rooted in concrete social and historical situations purposefully create identity; in the second, identity is created, emerging almost as an unintended consequence of the actions of human beings rooted in concrete social and historical situations.

Hobsbawm, typically, peppers his writings with examples of conscious activity, such as that of the "Hindu zealots [who] destroyed a mosque in Ayodhya, ostensibly on the grounds that the mosque had been imposed by the Muslim Moghul conqueror Babur on the Hindus in a particularly sacred location which marked the birthplace of the god Rama." And yet, as Hobsbawm notes, "nobody until the nineteenth century suggested that Ayodhya was the birthplace of Rama" and "the mosque was almost certainly not built in the time of Babur."[9] In contrast, Anderson locates national identity within a swirl of such grand historical forces as the rise of print capitalism and the threefold decline of a "particular script-language," Latin, of the "belief that society was naturally organized around and under high

---

9  Eric Hobsbawm, "The New Threat to History," *New York Review of Books*, December 16, 1993, p. 63

centres," and a "conception of temporality in which cosmology and history were indistinguishable."[10]

I suggest that the only conceptually consistent and theoretically coherent form of constructivism is, and must be, hard. If constructivism does *not* argue that elites create national identity consciously, if the nationalists of whom Ernest Gellner writes as the "historic agents" of nationalism "know not what they do,"[11] then we are, at best, left with the trivial conclusion that, since "men make their own history," as they obviously must for history to be more than the recording of natural events, everything in history is in some sense "made" — constructed — by men and women. At worst, we descend into self-contradiction and subvert invention and imagination semantically by depriving both of one of their defining characteristics: active inventors and imaginers. Constructivism, then, *must* argue that national identity can arise only if elites consciously take preexisting building blocks and transform them into national identity.

Let us unpack this proposition by examining, first, the elites. As noted above, the logic of invention and imagination as concepts implies only that they be self-consciously acting inventors and imaginers. No other characteristics are essential. Thus, elites may or may not be rich or poor, powerful or powerless, with or without status and influence. Inasmuch as they must be *self-consciously* involved in inventing and imagining, however, it is clear that elites will be a select, and probably fairly small, group of people with unusual cognitive and/or affective capacities. Intellectuals, writers, and political activists, precisely those individuals discussed by Miroslav Hroch, come to mind.[12]

Inventors and imaginers act on the preexisting materials or building blocks of national identity. What these building blocks are will depend on what national identity is or, more precisely, on how

---

10   Anderson, *Imagined Communities,* p. 40.
11   Ernest Gellner, *Nations and Nationalism* (Ithaca, NY: Cornell University Press, 1983), p. 49.
12   Miroslav Hroch, *Social Preconditions of National Revival in Europe* (Cambridge: Cambridge University Press, 1985).

it is defined, and the definition, clearly, may not logically entail either a confirmation or a refutation of constructivism's claims. Defining national identity as a set of beliefs—about the nation, its nationness, and so on—meets this condition. As such a set, national identity consists of *propositions* about life, statements of the "This is that" variety.[13] It follows that identity construction must be a form of belief construction and that a nation, a group of people with national identity, holds certain propositions about itself to be true. Hard constructivists must therefore claim that elites consciously attempt to persuade a population that a set of propositions—each of the form $A'=B'$, $A''=B''$ ... $A^*=B^*$—is true. These propositions need not actually *be* true: they need not correspond to empirical reality and therefore qualify as facts. Indeed, contrary to the view of national identity as irremediably bogus and backward, national propositions by their very nature as propositions need be neither more nor less true than nonnational propositions.

One logical consequence of defining national identity as a belief system is that the entity we call a nation need not call itself that as well. The term may be absent from the language of the people concerned—the Inuit are a case in point—and even if it were present, it might have a thoroughly different meaning from that we use or from those other nations use. For instance, Americans use the word *nation*—as in "this nation's capital"—to mean "country." There is, thus, no logical reason for nations not to have existed before the word *nation* or the doctrine of nationalism entered politics and the social-science discourse.[14] To suppose otherwise is either to conflate the etymology of the word *nation* with the origins of the phenomenon, as does Liah Greenfeld, or to reduce the phenomenon to a word or words, or

---

13 See Sartori, "Guidelines for Concept Analysis," pp. 81-82; Kenneth Russell Olson, *An Essay on Facts* (Stanford, Calif.: Center for the Study of Language and Information, 1987).
14 Many historians would of course strenuously disagree. See Hobsbawm, *Nations and Nationalism*, p. 14.

a "stance," as does Rogers Brubaker.[15] In either case, the implicit—and, to my mind, unwarranted—assumption is that language constitutes all of reality.

## National Identity and Lifeworld

If national identity consists of knowledge claims, then the preexistingmaterials, the building blocks that comprise national identity, must also consist of knowledge claims. What can they be? Consider first that national identity draws on only some materials from within a larger array of building blocks. Consider also that all of these materials havein common their potential utility as building blocks of national identity. It seems fair to conclude that preexisting materials form a coherent set and are not a mere agglomeration of randomly aligned elements. For the sake of convenience, let us call this set of propositional building blocks a "lifeworld"—the intersubjectively held knowledge claims that a group—any group—presumably takes for granted and that enables its members to communicate with one another. It is irrelevant for our purposes whether or not what I designate a lifeworld is identical with, or has all the theoretical overtones of, the concept discussed by Jürgen Habermas and other philosophers.[16]

National identity and lifeworld are distinct concepts with distinct referents. While national identity refers to a particular way in which people see themselves, lifeworld refers to the ontological and epistemological claims they share in order to contemplate seeing themselves in a particular way, say, as having an identity. To ask about the origins of national identity is, thus,

---

15 Liah Greenfeld, *Nationalism: Five Roads to Modernity* (Cambridge, Mass.: Harvard University Press, 1992), pp. 4-8; Rogers Brubaker, "Rethinking Nationhood," *Contention* 4 (Fall 1994), pp. 3-14.

16 On the concept of lifeworld, see Donald M. Lowe, "Intentionality and the Method of History," in *Phenomenology and the Social Sciences*, ed. Maurice Natanson (Evanston, Ill.: Northwestern University Press, 1973), 2:103-30; Aron Gurwitsch, *Phenomenology and the Theory of Science* (Evanston, Ill.: Northwestern University Press, 1974), pp. 3-32; Jürgen Habermas, *Legitimation Crisis*, trans. Thomas McCarthy (Boston: Beacon Press, 1975), pp. 10-11.

not to ask about the origins of lifeworlds. Human beings have been constructing ontologies and epistemologies since time immemorial, and although the question of why they do so is interesting, it is not one that we have to answer in order to get at the problem of national identity. We expect lifeworlds to occur, perhaps as a result of some inner need on the part of men and women to deal with the existential frailty of the human condition, to give shape to shapelessness in an effort to overcome, as Peter Berger and Thomas Luckmann put it, "chaos."[17] The search for meaning may therefore be immanent in the human condition; national identity, at least according to nonprimordialist assumptions, obviously is not.

We can express the relationship between national identity and lifeworld in the following manner, where N stands for national identity proposition and L for lifeworld proposition:

Na          Nb          Nc ...

 .           .           .


 . .       . .         . .

La   Lb    Lc   Ld    Le   Lf ...

Each N represents a novel amalgam of at least two L's. The diagram notwithstanding, it is not necessary that N propositions consist only of separate L pairs or that there be fewer N propositions than L propositions.

A closer look at the relationship between the set of L propositions and the set of N propositions leads to several important conclusions. First, and most obviously, we see that would-be inventors and imaginers are actually under severe constraints in their ability to invent and imagine. They may and do combine L propositions in novel ways to produce N, but they are confined to drawing on L and only on L. They cannot invent

---

17  Peter L. Berger and Thomas Luckmann, *The Social Construction of Reality: A Treatise in the Sociology of Knowledge* (Garden City, NY: Doubleday, 1966).

and imagine anything they wish; the sky, evidently, is not the limit.

Second, inventors and imaginers are constrained by more than just the field of L. Although there is no reason why N propositions cannot be constructed so as to contradict individual L propositions, it is unlikely that the "nation" intended to entertain contradictory propositions will be able to maintain such a balancing act for any meaningful length of time. We therefore expect the set of N propositions to be consistent with the set of L propositions, at least over time. By the same token, N propositions should be equally consistent with one another as well.

Third, the elites transforming L propositions into N propositions must be intimately familiar with the lifeworld. If they are not, they would be incapable of identifying its propositions and combining them in noncontradictory ways. But this requirement leads to a paradox. For if the elites *are* ensconced in the lifeworld, how could they, and why should they, invent or imagine N? Prenational elites have no reason even to suspect that L propositions could produce distinctly national N propositions. And even if they did, it is unclear why they should care. Inventions are useful things, but elites cannot know that N is useful before nations exist. Circularity seems to be unavoidable.

Fourth, even if elites could create N, how and why do these propositions come to be accepted by the target audience? We have no reason to think that people at large share elite preferences; indeed, if they did, elites would be irrelevant to national identity formation. If, alternatively, the people are assumed to be indifferent to, or ignorant of, elite preferences, then there is no reason to expect them to accept the veracity of propositions that represent novel additions to already functioning lifeworlds. Of course, elites might force these ideas on the masses, but such behavior decidedly is not what constructivists mean by construction.

In the final analysis, there appears to be no logically persuasive reason for national identity formation to occur as a result of conscious elite activity. Without introducing exogenous conditions into the argument, we cannot explain why elites should invent N or why masses should accept N. If some nations or a discourse of nationalism are assumed already to exist, then we might be able to provide nonnational elites with a motive to invent their own N propositions and masses with a reason to believe them, but this "solution" of the problem is, of course, merely a restatement of the problem.

## The Irrelevance of Elites

While accepting the logic of hard constructivism, the above analysis revealed that the centerpiece of that approach—the proposition that national identity is constructed by elites acting in a self-consciously constructivist manner is problematic. It will be worthwhile to pursue this point by examining whether all instances of the construction of N really require conscious elites. If even some N propositions can and do emerge without elites, then it logically follows that elites are not a necessary condition of their emergence.

The simplest way of addressing this issue is by identifying the kind of truth claims that can pass for national propositions. These may, of course, be abstract philosophical statements that would seem to require the creative intervention of intellectuals. More likely than not, however, national propositions will take the form of the myths, traditions, rites, and rituals that Hobsbawm carelessly dismisses as mere "custom."[18] Clearly, if national propositions can legitimately encompass so many disparate truth claims—and familiarity with any nation suggests that they surely can—then the view of national identity as an elite construct only is manifestly false.

Orally transmitted myths, such as epics, poems, and songs, are collective undertakings as much as they are the creations of a Homer or the preserve only of the actual storytellers. Their collective telling and retelling—and the listening to their telling and retelling—translate into a continual process of textual creation and recreation within which authors and readers are

---

18  Hobsbawm, "Introduction," p. 2.

more or less equally implicated. The following passage, narrated by the young Muslim protagonist of Kurban Said's remarkable novel, *Ali and Nino*, illustrates the point:

> It really was amazing, what wonderful liars these people were. There is no story they would not invent to glorify their country. Only yesterday a fat Armenian tried to tell me that the Christian Maras Church in Shusha was five thousand years old. "Don't tell such tall stories," I told him. "The Christian Faith is not yet two thousand years old. They can't have built a Christian church before Christianity was even thought of." The fat man was very hurt and said reproachfully: "You are, of course, an educated man. But let an old man tell you: The Christian Faith may be only two thousand years old in other countries. But to us, the people of Karabagh, the Saviour showed the light three thousand years before the others. That's how it is." Five minutes later the same man went on to tell me without batting an eyelid that the French General Murat had been an Armenian from Shusha. He had gone to France as a child to make Karabagh's name famous there as well. Even when I was just on the way to Shusha the driver of my coach pointed at the little stone bridge we were about to cross and said proudly: "This bridge was built by Alexander the Great when he went forth to immortal victories in Persia!" "1897" was chiseled in big figures on the parapet. I pointed this out to the coachman, but he only waved his hand: "Och, sir, the Russians put that in later, because they were jealous of our glory!"[19]

Like national myths, national traditions can also emerge without elites. Thus, some customary ways of doing things appear to be rooted in their functionality within a given material context, and what is functional—such as cattle grazing in a flatland or wine growing on a mountainside—then "becomes," for reasons that anthropologists may be better equipped to answer, natural, meaningful, symbolically inevitable, and profoundly national without the necessary intervention of elites. Other ways of doing things may appear to be, and may indeed be, materially dysfunctional, but can make perfect sense within a

---

19  Kurban Said, *Ali and Nino* (New York: Random House, 1970), 43-44. I am grateful to John A. Armstrong for bringing to my attention information that identified Kurban Said as one Essad Bey, an Azerbaijani Jew who converted to Islam and dropped his family name, Nussinbaum. After the Soviet takeover of Azerbaijan, he fled to Berlin, where he began his career as a writer. He moved to Vienna in 1933, where he stayed until 1938, emigrating after the Anschluss to Italy, where he died.

cultural matrix that well-nigh demands such traditions for the sake of internal consistency and coherence. Human sacrifice may seem to be an odd way of overcoming droughts or economic distress, until it is recognized that appeasing angry gods who brought about the calamity requires an especially precious offering. Ritual sacrifice may be a logical consequence of a worldview whose assumptions are that emotional deities run the world and are wont to wreak havoc upon it.

Finally, some rites — such as church rites — may be dated to the creative intervention of a St. Basil, but we should beware of falling into the genetic fallacy by assuming that Basil the Great is the cause of the continued maintenance of currently existing rites among, say, Orthodox Serbs or Ukrainian Uniates. He may have institutionalized the rites, but he is not responsible for the existence of the institution. Who or what, then, is? Religious elites foster riles, but so do churchgoers who partake of the rituals. But — and, I know, this verges on circularity — so does the institution. Patterned behavior assumes a life of its own, independent of the volition of the individuals involved in its structures. Put another way, institutions, as types of structures, involve people in predetermined relations that, in turn, determine the overall pattern of their behavior.[20]

Evidently, there can be national propositions without elites. And if elites are not a necessary condition of national identity formation, then their being or not being conscious of identity construction is obviously a moot issue. Equally important, however, the above examples suggest that even generalized consciousness of construction may not be necessary for construction to occur. Many established elites, the office holders, construct identity simply by "doing their job," by "mindlessly" following the rules, patterns, habits, and procedures prescribed by institutions. By the same logic, ordinary people may also have an incremental impact on national identity formation. We do not

---

20 The "new institutionalist" literature is enormous. For a summary of its basic arguments see Douglass North *Institutions, Institutional Change, and Economic Performance* (Cambridge: Cambridge University Press, 1990).

suppose that the development of agriculture or art required premeditated invention; so, too, it should be possible for national "self-awareness," although admittedly different from agriculture and art, to be generated "unconsciously," by the force of numerous cumulative acts with unintended consequences.

In light of these conclusions, the appropriate research question is neither, as hard constructivism would have it, "Why and how do elites construct national identity?" nor, as soft constructivism would ask, "Is national identity constructed historically?" but, "Why and how can the construction of national identity take place?" In other words, what are the conditions that make national identity possible?

## Conditions of National Identity Formation

To ask such a question is to embark on a *conditional* argument. That is to say, we want to isolate the necessary, facilitating, and sufficient conditions of national identity formation. Without necessary conditions, national identity formation cannot occur. With facilitating conditions, it is more likely to occur. And with sufficient conditions, it must occur — but only if necessary conditions are present as well.

Conditional arguments resemble, but emphatically are not, soft constructivist or "conjunctural" in nature.[21] Conditional arguments do not merely assert that things happen in history because people act; nor do they claim that the chance coming together of certain things brings about other things. Rather, conditional arguments claim to be able to illuminate the logic or pattern underlying the occurrence of phenomena. They do this by rigorously isolating not concrete, and hence unique, historical phenomena, but abstract causal variables, or conditions, that must

---

[21] Note Theda Skocpol's definition of conjuncture as the "coming together of separately determined and not consciously coordinated ... processes and group efforts." *States and Social Revolutions* (Cambridge: Cambridge University Press, 1979), p. 298.

be present and related to one another in a specific way, as necessary, sufficient, and facilitating.[22]

This essay has gone to some pains to point out that one condition of national identity formation is unnecessary—elites—and one necessary—a lifeworld. If there is no lifeworld at hand, there can be no national identity, regardless of whether or not inventive or imaginative elites are present. Unpacking national identity will help us isolate additional conditions, including the elusive sufficient condition.

Regardless of its particular relationship with a lifeworld, a distinctly *national* belief system has to be a special kind of set of intersubjectively held propositions. Otherwise, classes and other kinds of identity groups could also be nations, and we do not want to say that. Rather than filling the notion of nation with positive content, however, and thereby suggesting that nations have essences, I propose that national identity be seen as a coherent package of propositions relating to origins and boundaries. Origins provide a nation with historical authenticity, while boundaries grant it present-day distinctiveness. The inspiration is, of course, Anthony Smith and Fredrik Barth. The former's focus on *mythomoteurs* alerts us to the importance of a nation's having a place in time, while the latter's discussion of boundaries underscores a nation's difference from "the other" and hence its place in space.[23]

At the very least, therefore, nations are groups of people who believe in two things: that their group, as a group, comes from somewhere, and that their group differs from other groups in other ways besides origins as well. A nation's claims to origins and otherness maybe "objectively" false, although there is no reason to think they must be so. Nor is there any reason to insist that such claims must be made in the modern language of the

---

[22] See Ernest Sosa and Michael Tooley, eds., *Causation* (Oxford: Oxford University Press, 1993), pp. 5-8.

[23] Smith, *Ethnic Origins of Nations*; Fredrik Barth, *Ethnic Groups and Boundaries* (Boston: Little, Brown, 1969). See also Crawford Young, *The Politics of Cultural Pluralism* (Madison: University of Wisconsin Press, 1976), pp. 41-44.

nation: clearly, one can believe in origins and otherness without resorting to a nationalist discourse.

The existence of two sets of propositions, one relating to a group's origins, another to its otherness, is another necessary condition of national identity formation, and not an exhaustive list of the defining characteristics of a nation. A complete definition would entail more particulars about origins and otherness. Even so, this protodefinition has its uses. In particular, it permits us to differentiate nations from classes, as well as to underscore the former's kinship with religious and ethnic groups. The propositions characteristic of classes distinguish them from other classes but, as a rule, do not root them in originary myths. In contrast, religious identity shares both characteristics with national identity, and it is, as a result, no surprise that the overlap between religious groups and nations is and has been historically great.[24] Positioned in between classes and religious groups are ethnic and kinship groups, which generally possess a weaker sense of the other and a vague sense of origins.

If a national identity must consist of both sets of propositions, it can do so if and only if they fit together in a single propositional package. If propositional sets are at odds with each other, then, as I argued above, the protonation will be unable to sustain both for any meaningful length of time. Sooner or later, one set will have to be abandoned or modified. The sufficient condition of national identity formation, therefore, must be the logical *compatibility* or *complementarity* of propositions regarding a nation's historical origins on the one hand and its relationship with "the other" on the other hand. Thus, national identity is possible if a lifeworld is present and if there exist propositions relating to a group's place in time and space. National identity is inevitable if both sets of propositions are complementary. A nation, then, exists, or comes into being, when people sharing a lifeworld believe in a set of logically complementary propositions regarding origins and otherness.

---

24  See Pedro Ramet, ed., *Religion and Nationalism in Soviet and East European Politics* (Durham, N.C.: Duke University Press, 1989).

Consider the following example. Contemporary Ukrainians trace their origins as a nation to the state of Kievan Rus', founded some onethousand years ago. They also define themselves in contrast to their quintessential version of "the other," the Russians. Both propositional sets complement each other perfectly. By claiming Rus' and Kiev for themselves, Ukrainians challenge the prevailing Russian originary myth and exclude the Russian other from their past and from their pre sent. By differentiating themselves from the Russians, they perforce reject the Russian rejection of Ukrainian historicity and thereby claim historical legitimacy for themselves. Inasmuch as these two complementary propositional sets exist in contemporary Ukraine and are believed by its inhabitants, they make of their believers a nation even if, as is indeed the case, many "Ukrainians" might dispute their own nationhood or prefer the term *narod* to *natsiia*.[25]

## Explaining (Sort of) National Identity

National identity exists wherever and whenever such compatible propositions arise and are believed in. To some degree, complementarity, like spontaneous combustion, may be serendipitous. But inasmuch as we expect N propositions to be as consistent with one another as with L propositions, the process by which N propositions are constructed "naturally" facilitates national identity formation. There is, thus, a self-propelling dynamic built into propositional construction, once that pushes N propositions toward complementarity. *Attaining* complementarity, however, is an entirely different matter, one that is not a logically necessary consequence of this dynamic.

What, then, is? *I do not know.* As I have argued in this essay, however, I do claim to know that complementarity can come about as a result of elites *and* nonelites, acting and speaking as nationalists *and* as nonnationalists. The construction of national

---

25 Alexander J. Motyl, *Dilemmas of Independence: Ukraine after Totalitarianism* (New York: Council on Foreign Relations, 1993), pp. 76-103.

identity cannot therefore be confined to some historical period or to certain social actors. While this insight does not permit us to predict instances of national identity formation, it does lead us to conclude that national identity is, ceteris paribus, always and everywhere possible. This, I submit, is a truly radical claim of the historicity and contingency of nations, one that goes far further than Anderson and Hobsbawm can go because of their insistence on imagination and invention.

There is, as a result, no reason to expect national identity formation not to have taken place before, say, 1789. The ancient Israelites, whose national belief system provided them with a distinct place in time and space, were as much of a nation as most contemporary nations. The Romans, especially during the republic, appear to have fit the definitional requirements as well. So too did the Greeks, whose myths provided them with origins and whose distaste for "barbarians" testified to their refined sense of "the other." These examples notwithstanding, it goes without saying that nations have been far more common in recent centuries than in the distant past. But to put the issue in this manner is to embark on a search for those conditions that *facilitate* — that is to say, make more likely — national identity formation. Two such conditions come to mind.

Modernity — by which I mean both the secular and rationalist ethos of the Enlightenment and the material trappings of the modern world — facilitates the emergence of national identities in two ways that directly address the question of origins and place. First, as a set of ideas regarding the worldly rootedness of humanity and its ability to determine its own destiny according to this-worldly needs, modernity translates into a sense of history, of human historicity, and thus encourages a concern with secular origins. To understand better where we are and where we are going, we want also to understand where we came from.[26] And second, technology, urbanization, communications, "print capita-

---

26 For a fascinating discussion of these issues, see Zygmunt Bauman, "Soil, Blood, and Identity," *Sociological Review* 40, no. 4 (November 1992): pp. 675-701.

lism," and industrialization bring disparate peoples together, compel them to interact and communicate with one another, and thereby enhance awareness of "the other" and, possibly, the creation of boundaries.[27]

Modernity has also produced an ideology—nationalism—that explicitly argues for the complementarity of these two propositional sets and proposes that the existential needs of nations demand their conjunction with states.[28] More exactly, not modernity per se, but modern-day intellectual, cultural, and political elites invented and imagined nationalism—and *not*, as I have argued, tradition or communities. While nationalism's emergence as a zeitgeist clearly facilitates national identity formation, the two phenomena are, no less clearly, ontologically independent of each other. There can be nationalism without nations and nations without nationalism—a proposition that rests on a crucial distinction between identity and ideology that constructivism has failed to appreciate.

Finally, there is the state. By its very existence, a territorially defined state "imposes," though not in any remotely constructivist sense, physical unity—that is, both territorial and conceptual boundaries—on a population. A modern bureaucratic state goes even further and imposes administrative unity on some territorially bounded population. If complex, such a population would, as Gellner notes, interact more effectively and efficiently if united in a belief system endowing it with an overarching identity.[29] Where a complex (i.e., modern) population exists within a unified political-spatial setting, such as that which the state defines, a national identity functions to overcome the cleavages dividing the population and to provide it with the ability to communicate more effectively, to act more efficiently, to *live* more meaningfully and easily. At the very least, shared beliefs

---

27 Joseph Rothschild discusses these points in *Ethnopolitics* (New York: Columbia University Press, 1981).
28 On the connection between nationalism and modernity, see Greenfeld, *Nationalism;* and Alexander J. Motyl, "The Modernity of Nationalism," *Journal of International Affairs* 45 (Winter 1992): pp. 307-23.
29 Gellner, *Nations and Nationalism*, pp. 19-52.

facilitate cooperation by reducing, if not eliminating, the "free rider" problem and associated transaction costs.[30] The resulting identification of the nation with the state also contributes to originary enquiries hoping to root the latter, and hence also the former, in a historical past connoting naturalness and legitimacy.

These reflections suggest an interesting corollary. We know that people can attain a sense of overarching groupness and share in its propositions by means of the actions of a charismatic warrior, a priestly caste, a "barbarian" invader, itinerant bards and poets, or, even, themselves. Naturally, there are physical limits to how many people can be brought together under an overarching identity in ancient or premodern times. In contrast, modernity and the state increase exponentially the number of people that national identity can encompass. As a result, we correctly expect the communities sharing a national identity to have been, in general, substantially smaller in the past than in the present. Inasmuch as largeness is not a defining characteristic of nations, however, there is, *pace* Anderson, no reason why the "members of even the smallest nation" could *not* know "most of their fellow-members, meet them, or even hear of them." Such familiarity may be unlikely, but it is not impossible.

## Rights and Wrongs

Not accidentally, constructivism's current popularity is a reflection of primordialism's unpopularity. Despite their having become thoroughly unfashionable in most academic circles, however, primordialist views are not as unreflective as their unquestioning supporters, most run-of-the-mill nationalists, frequently are. Sophisticated nationalist thinkers, such as Maurice Barrès and Dmytro Dontsov, understood that their ontological assumptions reflected such philosophical currents as essentialism and realism.[31]

---

30 For a "soft" rational-choice interpretation of nationalism, see Alexander J. Motyl, *Sovietology, Rationality, Nationality: Coming to Grips with Nationalism in the USSR* (New York: Columbia University Press, 1990).
31 John A. Armstrong, "Collaborationism in World War II: The Integral Nationalist Variant in Eastern Europe," *Journal of Modern History* 40 (1968),

Nationalists and primordialists can, without too much difficulty, claim continuity with the ideas of, among many other philosophers, Plato, Kant, and Hegel. Forms, the Truth, and the Spirit all reflect the belief that appearances are only surface phenomena and that the reality lies somewhere below, in the essence or essences that presumably encapsulate it. How one approaches the question of national identity—construction versus presence—is not, thus, really an empirical issue that more research, or less nationalism, can resolve. Bridging so deep a philosophical divide may be impossible.

Sharing the assumptions of postmodernism, much contemporary social science concludes that nonessentialist and nominalist perspectives are singularly correct. Such a view is not unpersuasive, but the very spirit of postmodernism also cautions us against being too dogmatic in our judgements. After all, the relativism underlining postmodernism, must grant essences a hearing as well. George Steiner, for instance, accepts the ultimate validity of the deconstructionist message but still believes it possible to insist that an appreciation of art, a genuine understanding of the creative act itself, necessitates some belief in a "real presence"—a God—that our postmodern convictions actively strive to deny.[32] In similar fashion Charles Taylor argues that the modern search for personal authenticity must presuppose some standards to be meaningful.[33]

My point is as little that primordialism is *right* and constructivism is *wrong* as that constructivism is *right* and primordialism is *wrong*. Here, as elsewhere, it all depends. As Arthur Danto reminds us, good arguments are good, not because they alone are in possession of the truth, but because they are crafted

---

pp. 396-410; Alexander J. Motyl, *The Turn to the Right: The Ideological Origins and Development of Ukrainian Nationalism, 1919-1929* (Boulder, Colo.: East European Monographs, 1980); J. S. McClelland, ed., *The French Right* (New York: Harper and Row, 1970), pp. 143-211.

32  George Steiner, *Real Presences* (Chicago: University of Chicago Press, 1989).
33  Charles Taylor, *The Ethics of Authenticity* (Cambridge; Mass.: Harvard University Press, 1992).

well.[34] And a well-crafted argument is one that, at a minimum, is sensitive to conceptual clarity and rigor. Constructivism can be persuasive if it abandons the language of invention and imagination and the unwarranted theoretical claims they imply. Like any set of propositions, constructivism fails when it ignores the building blocks of its own knowledge claims.

---

34  Arthur C. Danto, *Narration and Knowledge* (New York: Columbia University Press, 1985).

# 4

# Imagined Communities, Rational Choosers, Invented Ethnies[*]

Social scientific theories of nations and nationalism are usually divided into two sets of rival camps. The first set opposes constructivism, according to which nations are invented, imagined, or mobilized, that is, humanly constructed, to primordialism, according to which nations are historically given entities. The second set opposes modernism, which claims that nations are only modern,[1] to perennialism, which sees them as premodern. Because constructivists tend to be modernists and primordialists tend to be perennialists, the two binary oppositions are usually superimposed on each other. Constructivism and modernism thus appear to be natural allies against the no less naturally allied primordialism and perennialism.

This division is both profoundly misleading and highly illuminating. Although attractive in its simplicity, the rivalry between modernism and perennialism rests on questionable conceptual and theoretical grounds. Despite the intellectual proclivities of individual scholars, constructivism can be just as easily perennialist as modernist, while primordialism can accommodate modernism by engaging in creative conceptual tinkering practiced by all theories. Expanding the range of constructivism and primordialism to encompass both modernism and perennialism has important implications for theories of nations and nationalism.

---

[*]  First printed in *Comparative Politics*, vol. 34, no. 2 (January 2002), pp. 233-250. Reprinted with permission of the original publisher.
[1] This usage of modernism is derived from Anthony D. Smith, *Nationalism and Modernism: A Critical Survey of Recent Theories of Nations and Nationalism* (London: Routledge, 1998). It is important to appreciate that, in the sense used in this article, modernism is not antithetical to or does not precede *post*-modernism, which is simply a special kind of constructivist claim.

The rivalry between constructivism and primordialism is equally misleading because it conceals the diversity of theories clustered under both genera. There are at least three different species, which may be termed extreme, strong, and weak, of both constructivism and primordialism.[2] Each version of constructivism and primordialism has its scholarly representatives, and, despite the three constructivisms' current ascendance, the varieties of primordialism are no worse intrinsically than their counterparts.[3] Constructivism looks manifestly superior to primordialism only if the former appears in its accommodatingly weak form, insisting only that nations are historical constructs, and the latter appears in its uncompromisingly extreme form, claiming that nations are natural entities with no history. By the same token, a weak primordialism that modestly countenances only the possibility of historically stable nations easily trumps an extreme constructivism that recognizes only the reality of words.

The binary opposition between a monolithic category called constructivism and another called primordialism is also illuminating. Despite the diversity of approaches, the extreme and strong species of constructivism and primordialism rest on obviously incompatible assumptions and as such are irreconcilable. Exceedingly weak forms of both would be less at odds, but, here, too, there are built-in limits, rooted in the axiomatic foundations —

---

2   Alexander J. Motyl, *Revolutions, Nations, Empires: Conceptual Limits and Theoretical Possibilities* (New York: Columbia University Press, 1999), p. 84. Both primordialism and constructivism differ on the cause of nations, the time during which they arise, and their properties: for extreme primordialism, immanent, transcendent, and immutable; for strong primordialism, conjunctural, historical, and permanent; for soft primordialism, indeterminate, recurrent, and conceptual; for extreme constructivism, discursive, ahistorical, and discursive; for strong constructivism: elites, contemporary, and malleable; and for weak constructivism, human activity, modern, and constructable.
3   Two recent examples of primordialism are Samuel P. Huntington, *The Clash of Civilizations and the Remaking of the World Order* (New York: Simon and Schuster, 1996) and Daniel Jonah Goldhagen, *Hitler's Willing Executioners: Ordinary Germans and the Holocaust* (New York: Vintage, 1996). Two recent examples of constructivism are Rogers Brubaker, *Nationalism Reframed: Nationhood and the National Question in the New Europe* (Cambridge: Cambridge University Press, 1996) and Geoff Eley and Ronald Grigor Suny, eds., *Becoming National: A Reader* (Oxford: Oxford University Press, 1996).

the "hard core" in Imre Lakatos's terminology[4] — of these approaches, to convergence. Constructivism and primordialism are not, and cannot possibly be, the "flips sides of one coin" or the "two faces of Janus."[5] Although the quest for an all-embracing "theory of everything" that would accommodate both constructivist and primordialist assumptions about reality is understandable, it results in self-contradiction and thus is a theory of nothing.[6]

Although Benedict Anderson and Anthony D. Smith do not embody either polar opposite, the former's work leans toward constructivism and the latter's inclines toward primordialism. Anderson's *Imagined Communities* has had an especially powerful impact on the study of nations and nationalism. While suggesting that both emerged from a peculiar conjunction of historical forces several hundred years ago, it implied with the word "imagined" that nations could simply be conjured up by imaginers and inventors. The book thereby resonated with the emerging postmodernist *Zeitgeist* and inspired much of the current constructivist literature.[7] Smith, meanwhile, after an early flirtation with the idea that nationalism was the product of crisis-ridden intellectuals interacting with the "scientific state," eventually came to argue in *The Ethnic Origins of Nations* that nations are entities with long historical roots in, among other things, myths or, as he prefers to call them, *mythomoteurs*.[8] David D. Laitin is rather more difficult to pin down. A wide-ranging scholar who has written about Africa, Spain, and the former Soviet Union, Laitin has progressively moved from a culturalist perspective to one rooted in rational

---

[4] Imre Lakatos, "Falsification and the Methodology of Scientific Research Programmes," in Imre Lakatos and Alan Musgrave, eds., *Criticism and the Growth of Knowledge* (Cambridge: Cambridge University Press, 1970).
[5] David D. Laitin, *Identity in Formation: The Russian-Speaking Populations in the Near Abroad* (Ithaca, N.Y.: Cornell University Press, 1998), p. 20.
[6] See John D. Barrow, *Theories of Everything: The Quest for Ultimate Explanation* (New York: Fawcett Columbine, 1991).
[7] Benedict Anderson, *Imagined Communities* (London: Verso, 1983).
[8] Anthony D. Smith, *The Ethnic Origins of Nations* (Oxford: Basil Blackwell, 1986).

choice.⁹ These competing loyalties are evident—indeed, they clash—in the book under review.

## Imagined Communities

The essays collected in Anderson's latest volume, *The Spectre of Comparisons*, may disappoint readers expecting theoretical breakthroughs. To be sure, such expectations are unwarranted, as *Imagined Communities* did not really proffer a rigorous, conceptually coherent explanation of a set of phenomena, or a theory.[10] Although the book has been interpreted in this fashion, it claims only that nations emerged in the eighteenth and nineteenth centuries as a result of various forces—print capitalism, the decline of Latin, a new conception of time—that came together at that time. Such a conjunctural argument may be powerful historically, but it cannot be a theory if it fails to suggest, in terms that are not specific to this historical period, what makes these factors converge at this time.

Anderson's main contribution to the study of nations and nationalism may be the term "imagined community." The theoretical limitations of the concept, which have been the subject of an excellent essay by Yael Tamir, are obvious.[11] The view that imagining suffices to make nations of communities seems at best a gross overestimation of the power of imagination. That nations, unlike other entities such as classes and electorates, are especially susceptible to imagination, seems wrong. And that nations are, like all socially constructed entities, imagined seems trivial. The term also has severe conceptual limitations. A closer look at Anderson's famous definition of the nation as "an imagined political

---

9   David D. Laitin, *Hegemony and Culture* (Chicago: University of Chicago Press, 1986) and *Language Repertoires and State Construction in Africa* (New York: Cambridge University Press, 1992).
10  Giovanni Sartori defines a theory as a "body of systematically related generalizations of explanatory value." See his "Guidelines for Concept Analysis," in Giovanni Sartori, ed., *Social Science Concepts* (Beverly Hills, Calif.: Sage, 1984), p. 84.
11  Yael Tamir, "The Enigma of Nationalism," *World Politics*, 47 (April 1995), pp. 418-40.

community—and imagined as both inherently limited and sovereign" reveals these limitations.[12]

Is the nation, according to this definition, a community, a group of people? Or is it really the image of a community, the image of a group of people? Is *Imagined Communities* thus about the emergence of peculiar sets of people or about the emergence of a peculiar idea about sets of people? The difference between these two positions is enormous, the first aligning Anderson with modernist approaches to the nation, the second with decidedly postmodernist ones. Moreover, is not the term "limited," used by Anderson to suggest that nations are never coterminous with all of humanity, superfluous, except in the trivial sense that all communities are limited in comparison to all of humanity? Is not the term "sovereign" misplaced as well, especially because it refers, as Anderson points out, to the "sovereign state" and not to the nation?[13] Worse, is not such a definition of the nation merely a restatement of the nationalist view of the nation as necessarily conjoining nationality with statehood? All that is left is Anderson's definition of the nation as an imagined political community. What, exactly, does he mean by "imagined" in conjunction with "community"?

To charge Anderson with theoretical weakness and conceptual sloppiness is, to some degree, an injustice. An anthropologist and a historian, Anderson, especially in *The Spectre of Comparisons*, is mostly interested in telling richly textured stories about texts, people, culture, Indonesia, and the Philippines. The fourth essay of the book, "A Time of Darkness and a Time of Light," tells the story of Soetomo, a leading Indonesian nationalist, in light of and in relation to his memoirs, *Kenang-Kenangan*.[14] The fifth essay, "Professional Dreams," dissects two masterpieces of Javanese literature, the *Serat Centhini* and the *Suluk Gatholoco*, and situates both poems in the context of social, cultural, and national devel-

---

12  Anderson, *Imagined Communities*, p. 15.
13  Ibid., p. 16.
14  Benedict Anderson, *The Spectre of Comparisons: Nationalism, Southeast Asia, and the World* (London: Verso, 1998), pp. 77-104.

opments in emergent Indonesia.[15] Sometimes Anderson employs such neoessentialist terminology so beloved of post-modernism as seriality, governmentality, hybridity, and universality to make—or to obscure—his point.[16] Most of the time he talks simply, and mercifully, of classes, violence, and elections. Indeed, the most remarkable thing about the book may be how little it reflects, and need reflect, a view of nations as imagined or invented. Such essays as "Gravel in Jakarta's Shoes," "Withdrawal Symptoms," "Murder and Progress in Modern Siam," and "Cacique Democracy in the Philippines" are fairly conventional, if invariably interesting and elegantly crafted, analyses that deal with a multiplicity of factors such as class, ideology, politics, and imperialism.[17]

Its empirical bent notwithstanding, *The Spectre of Comparisons* does not get off the theoretical hook quite so easily. A closer look reveals that Anderson makes claims that in effect, if not intent, amount to a theory. Only the first three essays—out of seventeen—concern nationalism in general and explicitly build on some of the themes enunciated in *Imagined Communities*, particularly the spread of capitalism and print technology and the role of the state in promoting "official nationalism." The third essay, "Long-Distance Nationalism," is perhaps most explicit in weaving these strands into a theoretical argument. It argues that, just as the "essential nexus of long-distance transportation and print-capitalist communications" made it possible for colonists to the Americas to identify their "real" homelands as England or Spain, so too the "transnationalization of advanced capitalism and … the steepening economic stratification of the global economy" have resulted in the "ethnicization of political life in the wealthy, postindustrial states" and in "long-distance nationalism."[18] Assimilation has become more difficult just as the long-distance promotion of nationalist projects in putative homelands by individuals resident elsewhere has become more common. Indeed, long-distance nationalism is,

---

15  Ibid., pp. 105-30.
16  See in particular chapter 1, "Nationalism, Identity, and the Logic of Seriality," of Anderson, *Spectre of Comparisons*, pp. 29-45.
17  Ibid., pp. 131-226.
18  Ibid., p. 67.

according to Anderson, a "probably menacing portent for the future."[19]

These three essays argue in the same conjunctural vein as *Imagined Communities*. They effectively elevate conjuncture from a singular historical occurrence to a theoretical claim. Once Anderson pushes the argument of *Imagined Communities* past the conjuncture of capitalism, printing, and the state in the eighteenth and nineteenth centuries and even projects it into the future, then what originally appeared to be a unique concatenation of forces achieves implicit theoretical status. What sort of theory is it?

*Imagined Communities* had suggested that a "strong case can be made for the primacy of capitalism" in explaining why nations became "so popular."[20] The centrality of capitalism to much of the argument in *The Spectre of Comparisons* suggests that it should figure as the *spiritus movens* of subsequent phases of national development as well. Such an explicitly Marxist turn is both defensible and possible. In its acceptance of the causal power of the economic substructure, however, such a move runs the risk of subverting Anderson's notion of the imagined nation as possessing a superstructural reality all its own. If capitalism is always the culprit, nations may "in the final analysis" somehow be reducible to capitalism. In particular, long-distance nationalism, as an artifice of the imagination wholly unconnected to the territory, state, or economy of the homeland, does not sit well with the primacy of economic relations. At worst, therefore, Anderson's implicit theory of the nation rests on a contradiction. At best, his argument, in being only implicit, may be immune to criticism on theoretical grounds but would then be of marginal relevance to theories of nations and nationalism.

## Rational Choosers

Readers expecting to find a tightly argued theoretical argument in Laitin's *Identity in Formation* will also be disappointed. Laitin's

---

19  Ibid., p. 74.
20  Anderson, *Imagined Communities*, p. 41.

study of the Russian-speaking populations in Estonia, Latvia, Ukraine, and Kazakstan is full of stories, anecdotes, personal experiences, historical excursions, thick description, polemics, survey data, and disjointedly organized theoretical claims that appear to have been compiled and not written, and certainly not edited. (The book would have benefited from a radical shortening.) Worse, the data assembled by Laitin signally fail to support his theory, while his ad hoc attempts to salvage it succeed only in contradicting it.

Unlike Anderson, Laitin has been explicitly interested in theory in all his work. His current approach, rooted in rational choice and game theory, centers on the device of the tipping game, a construct that purports to be not just a metaphor, but an actual reflection of what goes on in people's minds when they make choices regarding language and identity. Laitin depicts such games in diagram form as consisting of two curves—a horizontally positioned S-shaped curve and its mirror image. The x axis represents the percentage of the population engaging in the activity represented by the curve, for example, choosing to speak either Russian or Estonian. The y axis represents the payoffs for speaking either language. At first, the payoff for speaking Russian may exceed that for speaking Estonian. As more people shift to Estonian, however, the payoff for Russian declines and that for Estonian grows. At some point, the tipping point where the two curves intersect, the payoff for Estonian begins to exceed that for Russian, and a "cascade" toward speaking Estonian may be expected.[21] Everyone living in a bilingual environment plays this game, but Laitin's primary focus is of course on the twenty-five million Russian-speakers (*russkoiazychnye*) resident in the so-called "near abroad," the ex-Soviet non-Russian republics. Formerly dominant, the Russian-speakers were transformed into "beached diasporas" after the USSR's collapse and the sudden emergence of

---

21 Laitin, *Identity in Formation*, pp. 22-24. Much of Laitin's thinking on these issues seems to be derived from the work of Thomas Schelling. See, in particular, Thomas Schelling, *The Strategy of Conflict* (Cambridge, Mass.: Harvard University Press, 1960).

independent non-Russian states with "nationalizing" agendas.[22] Will they become loyal citizens, disgruntled minorities, or fifth columns on the order of the Sudeten Germans in interwar Czechoslovakia?[23] By focusing on the payoffs involved in either switching to a titular language (Estonian, Latvian, Ukrainian, or Kazak) or retaining Russian, Laitin hopes to elucidate the prospects of their assimilating into the titular nationality, developing a "conglomerate" identity, or acquiring the identity of a distinct Russian-speaking nationality.

Several failings are immediately worthy of note. The first flows from Laitin's insistence that tipping games really motivate people: "The dilemma portrayed in this diagram [of a tipping game] reflects practical decisions that real people face."[24] Do human choices regarding language and identity really involve the conscious application of the tipping game model? Do people truly act primarily, if not exclusively, on the basis of the trade-offs the model implies? Are people even aware of these trade-offs? Or are tipping games a metaphor, a catchy "as if" device, or an algorithm for expressing general trends in aggregate human behavior? These questions cannot be brushed aside by asserting, as Laitin effectively does, that the model is plausible, that choices are made, and that the people he and his colleagues interviewed appear to have been motivated by it in making their choices.[25]

A second failing concerns Laitin's claim that language, while "only one element of a person's complex social identity,"[26] is the

---

22 Ibid., pp. 32-33, 93-104.
23 For a comparison of the Sudeten Germans and Russians, see Rogers Brubaker, *Nationalism Reframed: Nationhood and the National Question in the New Europe* (Cambridge: Cambridge University Press, 1996), pp. 160-78.
24 Laitin, *Identity in Formation*, p. 27. Similarly, Timur Kuran builds a seemingly powerful theory of revolution on the notion of "preference falsification." But if private preferences can be falsified and thus be at variance with publicly expressed preferences, then there is no basis whatsoever for thinking that scholars can see into the souls of preference-falsifiers and determine what they really think. See Timur Kuran, "Now out of Never: The Element of Surprise in the East European Revolution of 1989," *World Politics*, 44 (October 1991), pp. 7-48.
25 Ibid., pp. 3-10, 26-28.
26 Ibid., p. 22 fn.

most important. The book argues that language shifts portend "identity in formation." Laitin's case for associating language with identity rests, again, on an anecdote. The anecdote concerns Liuba Grigor'ev, who by deciding to study Estonian "lays the foundation for a constructed Estonian identity for her grandchildren,"[27] but makes a larger point, that language change now may make possible or facilitate identity change later. While this point seems indisputable, Laitin is explicitly concerned with the causal impact of choice. How can a conscious choice today to learn Estonian be causally related to a conscious choice two generations later to become Estonian? A choice made at time $t$ may be intended to influence the choice that will have to be made later at $t + n$, but intent and effect are two different things. The first choice may produce conditions that constrain the second choice, but so do millions of other choices, events, and developments that occur in the interim period. To isolate the casual impact of that first choice from the web of causes produced by everything else is probably an impossible task.[28] And even if some connection could be established, is today's choice a sufficient, necessary, or facilitating condition of the later choice?

A third failing flows from Laitin's use of rational choice theory. Even if we grant the appropriateness of the tipping game and the view that language shifts somehow imply identity shifts, Laitin's scheme founders on rational choice theory's inability to account for the preferences that underpin it. If rational choice theory assumes that all preferences at all times and at all places are exclusively material, then it is making a false and easily falsifiable claim that introduces contradiction into its theoretical core and thereby undermines its axiomatic foundations.[29] If, alternatively, rational choice theory admits the possibility of different kinds of preferences based on culture, history, and ideology, then it has no choice but to give theoretical priority to culture, history, or ideology

---

27 Ibid., p. 23.
28 I thank two anonymous reviewers for bringing these issues to my attention.
29 See Gabriel Almond, *A Discipline Divided: Schools and Sects in Political Science* (Newbury Park, Calif.: Sage, 1990), pp. 48-51, 117-35.

and thereby make itself redundant, especially as culture, history, and ideology also relativize the utility maximization (or risk minimization) strategy underlying the rational choice calculus.[30]

Laitin, to his credit, acknowledges that material benefit is not the only human preference. Languages, thus, can be adopted for reasons that also involve "in-group scorn" and "out-group acceptance."[31] Although seemingly neutral as terms, "in-group scorn" and "out-group acceptance" are loaded concepts that necessarily imply both a sense of identity, one that permits individuals to identify an in and an out group, and a sense of distinctly national, perhaps even nationalist, identity that permits individuals to prefer the pleasure of acceptance to the pain of scorn. But the whole point of the tipping game exercise is to show how language shifts can help us understand identity shifts. Language shifts are somehow supposed to "cause" identity shifts. But if identity underlies language loyalty in the first place, a point to which most nationalists and primordialists could easily subscribe, then the causal mechanism underlying the tipping game really amounts to a circle and Laitin's argument becomes an elaborate exercise in circular reasoning and an implicit endorsement of the givenness of nationhood.[32]

The final failing concerns the very notion of choice in post-Soviet circumstances. Is choice a meaningful notion under conditions of political, economic, and social disarray, on the one hand, and widespread confusion regarding identity, on the other? Laitin provides anecdotal evidence to support his argument, but the issue is rather more serious than he seems to believe.[33] Societal chaos implies that the information available to "choosers" is highly imperfect and possibly nonexistent; and even if such information exists, people concerned with survival in a social breakdown, as in

---

30  Alexander J. Motyl, *Sovietology, Rationality, Nationality: Coming to Grips with Nationalism in the USSR* (New York: Columbia University Press, 1990) makes the same mistake.
31  Laitin, *Identity in Formation*, p. 56.
32  Identical primordialist assumptions are evident in James D. Fearon and David D. Laitin, "Explaining Interethnic Cooperation," *American Political Science Review*, 90 (December 1996), 715-35.
33  Laitin, *Identity in Formation*, p. 114.

this case, have little time to acquire and digest it. Surely there are limits to how bounded rationality may be if it is to remain a useful theoretical device. Similarly, if there is widespread confusion about identity, to what degree is it possible for individuals to be motivated by in-group scorn and out-group acceptance? What is "in" and what is "out" in such circumstances?

These failings are minor in comparison to those that bedevil Laitin's theory as a whole. The core of that theory attempts to explain the different degree of "openness to assimilation" by Russian-speakers in Estonia, Latvia, Ukraine, and Kazakstan. Basing his conclusions on a sophisticated analysis of survey results, Laitin concludes that the mean index of openness to assimilation is highest in Latvia and Estonia (.67 and .53), third highest in Ukraine (.49), and lowest in Kazakstan (.31).[34] The finding is important, if only because it contradicts the conventional wisdom that the Baltic states are least receptive to Russians and that Ukraine, as a kindred Slavic state, is most receptive. With openness to assimilation as his dependent variable, Laitin then tries to account for the variation in terms of four sets of independent variables—demographic background variables, economic returns for assimilation, status variables, and titular accommodation to Russians.[35] But there are three, as Laitin puts it, "theoretical lacunae" in the model. Most important is its failure to answer "how and with what weight are the three elements of the language-utility function to be combined" and

---

34  Ibid., pp. 202-05.
35  Ibid., pp. 252-53. These sets consist of the following variables: demographic background variables (percentage who speak titular language; religious distance of titulars from Orthodoxy; linguistic difference of titular language from Russian; percent of Russians in capital city; percent of Russians in republic); economic returns for assimilation (job status explained on basis of knowing titular language; economic usefulness of learning titular language; mean quality of job for Russian in Russian guise less quality of job for Russian in titular guise; percentage of Russians in unskilled labor/ratio of percent of Russians in unskilled labor to percent of all respondents in survey); status variables (loss of in-group status in friendship for speaking titular language; loss of in-group status in respect for speaking titular language; gain in out-group status in friendship for speaking titular language; gain in out-group status in respect for speaking titular language); titular accommodation to Russians (percent of titular respondents who fully accept internationality marriage of son/daughter; citizen/job rights for Russian monolinguals).

"how are the opportunities and constraints set by the policies of the nationalizing state to be included."³⁶ The first lacuna is fatal to the model, it amounts to an admission that the theory is little more than a collection of variables. The second lacuna amounts to the remarkable claim that national-identity formation can be meaningfully studied in the absence of the state.³⁷ Finally, both lacunae are invitations to ad hoc interventions.

Since theoretically the payoff for any tipping game has to involve material benefit, in-group scorn, and out-group acceptance, Laitin's data should support the theoretical importance of the second and third sets of variables and not that of the first and fourth. However, the first set of demographic background variables does quite well, thereby suggesting that "a choice model [may not be] useful for studying assimilation." Laitin counters this problem by arguing that, while "cultural difference and demographics" may have accounted for language choice in Soviet times, conditions are different in the post-Soviet period, "because the language policies of the nationalizing states have raised the expected returns for speaking the titular language." As a result, "Russian-speakers need to calculate more consciously the potential payoffs for learning the titular language."³⁸ In other words, the choice model is useful precisely because—Laitin's earlier invocation of lacunae notwithstanding—current state policies really are relevant while historical and cultural legacies are not.

---

36  Ibid., p. 250.
37  In an excellent post-Sovietological study, for instance, Yitzhak M. Brudny shows how in the post-Stalin era intellectuals, policy makers, and propagandists promoted Soviet Russian nationalism on the basis of cultural traditions, ideological refinements, and their own interests: "In the postcommunist period Russian nationalist ideas were consistently embraced by those members of the Russian political elite who opposed the policies of Yeltsin's government. The reason for their embrace of the imperial, anti-Western, antimarket, and authoritarian vision of Russia is rooted in the fact that this vision constituted the only well-articulated ideological alternative to the process of political and economic reform currently underway in Russia." Yitzhak Brudny, *Reinventing Russia: Russian Nationalism and the Soviet State, 1953-1991* (Cambridge, Mass.: Harvard University Press, 1998), pp. 22-23.
38  Laitin., *Identity in Formation*, p. 253.

The second set of variables, economic returns for assimilation, provide no support for the model. Indeed, Laitin admits that, "if the tipping model relied solely on expected economic returns and probabilities for occupational mobility, these data present an insurmountable challenge."[39] The fourth set of variables, titular accommodation to Russians, also contravenes Laitin's expectations, with Ukrainians being most accommodating, Latvians second, Kazaks third, and Estonians fourth. Only the third set of status variables provides some consolation for the model. Those variables regarding in-group status lend it no support, while those regarding out-group status do, albeit indirectly. Do these findings corroborate Laitin's theory? The first set does, but should not. The second set should, but does not. The fourth does not, but we never learn why that does not matter. The third should, but only "half" does.

Undeterred by such recalcitrant data, Laitin still claims to snatch victory from the jaws of defeat. Although "Russian-speakers suffered a status loss among titulars for speaking in their titular guise" in all four republics, Laitin believes that assimilation is most likely where "Russians face the lowest status *dis*incentives to assimilate."[40] A dispassionate reading of all the data collected in Laitin's four sets of variables would suggest that disincentives are lowest in Ukraine and highest in Latvia and Estonia. Instead, Laitin chooses to place most emphasis on only two of fifteen variables, those regarding out-group status, which show that Russian-speakers attempting to speak titular languages appear to lose most status among titulars in Ukraine and least in Latvia and Estonia.[41] He then justifies this choice culturally and historically: "The relative contempt Ukrainian respondents showed for the Russian-speaker in her Ukrainian guise reflects the hostile face of Ukrainian nationalism."[42] Laitin reaches this conclusion from a highly selective reading of recent Ukrainian history: insignificant and isolated extremist groupings are interpreted as reflecting Ukrainian na-

---

39  Ibid., p. 254.
40  Ibid., pp. 255, 236.
41  Ibid., p. 252.
42  Ibid., p. 256 (emphasis in the original).

tionalism in its entirety. Moreover, his terminology betrays a strangely reified and indeed primordial vies of Ukrainians: "The West sees the civic face of Dr. Jekyll; the Russians are beginning to see the enraged one, Mr. Hyde."[43] In reality, contemporary Ukrainians, at least in their attitudes toward Russian-speakers, consist of very many Dr. Jekylls and very few Mr. Hydes.[44]

## Invented Ethnies

Like Laitin, Smith is explicitly concerned with theory construction. But unlike many rational choice theorists, Smith finds that each modernist theory, however different from his own, has weaknesses and strengths. All, including postmodernist theories, have made contributions. Indeed, there has even been theoretical progress. Can these competing theoretical approaches ultimately be reconciled? "Theoretical convergence" is possible, but only if, among other things, some variant of perennialism is adopted and the "close links between ethnicity and nations and nationalism" are recognized.[45] However, because the first condition is not as tough as Smith thinks, different theories can accept it and still remain quite different. And because the second condition may rest on a false distinction, acceptance of it only creates the illusion of convergence.

If genuine nations, however defined, could indisputably be identified perennially, some in ancient times, some in medieval times, and some in modern times, as John Armstrong suggests, would their existence vindicate primordialism?[46] Of course, it would not. The fact that nations existed several thousand years ago does not prove the central claim of primordialism, that the nations of today can be traced back thousands of years. The nations of yesteryear may have been completely different entities from the

---

43  Ibid., p. 102.
44  For a nuanced treatment of these issues, see Paul D'Anieri, Robert Kravchuk, and Taras Kuzio, *Politics and Society in Ukraine* (Boulder, Colo.: Westview, 1999), pp. 45-89.
45  Smith, *Nationalism and Modernism*, p. 226.
46  John Armstrong, *Nations Before Nationalism* (Chapel Hill: University of North Carolina Press, 1982).

nations of today. There may be no connection between the Hittites who inhabited ancient Anatolia and the Turks who venerate Ataturk. Whether or not there is such a connection, whether or not continuity can actually be established, are empirical questions that commitment to a primordialist or constructivist agenda cannot answer a priori. Indeed, a more or less dispassionate enquiry into the question of continuity would in all likelihood have to concede that, although nations may have existed then and do exist now, only very few of them can be connected in any meaningful way across the vast span of history. The Jews, Armenians, and Chinese might qualify and give temporary encouragement to primordialism, but so many other groups appear to be utterly unrelated as to provide little solace to those primordialists who happen not to be Jewish or Armenian or Chinese.

Would the existence of ancient and medieval nations refute constructivism? Of course, it would not. There is no reason for such nations not to have been constructed, either willfully and purposefully by self-conscious inventors and imaginers or historically and contingently by concatenations of events. If the case for imagining a nineteenth-century nation can be strong, then there is no reason that, a priori, the case for imagining a ninth-century nation cannot be equally strong. Indeed, if constructivists could show that even such seemingly continuous nations as the Jews were constructed at some time in the distant past—the argument that Moses was an inventor and imaginer of the first order is not unattractive—then their case would stand on especially strong grounds.[47]

If constructivism can be consistent with both perennialism and modernism, why is the possibility of premodern nations so controversial, especially among constructivists? Why is, as Smith's book demonstrates, so much scholarly labor expended on the argument that nations can only be modern? If the constructivist reluctance to acknowledge perennialism cannot be rooted in its implications for their theoretical project, then there must be nontheoretical reasons for such a stance. Perhaps politics holds the

---

[47] See Steven Grosby, "Religion and Nationality in Antiquity," *European Journal of Sociology*, 32 (1991), pp. 229-65.

answer. Historically, nationalists tend to be primordialists and nonnationalists or antinationalists—whether liberal or Marxist or postmodernist—tend to be constructivist. Acknowledgement of perennialism appears to give credence to nationalist claims of the inevitability of nations and thus to undermine the nonnationalist agenda. But here, too, the political connection is contingent, the result of historical conjunctions, and not theoretically necessary.

If it is perfectly possible to be a self-consciously constructivist nationalist, then it should also be possible to be a self-consciously primordialist or perennialist nonnationalist. There are many instances of nation-building elites who are fully aware of the fact that they are building and not reviving or awakening nations. Robert Paul Magocsi, for instance, has contributed enormously to the creation of a modern Ruthenian consciousness and is an unabashedly constructivist historian at the University of Toronto.[48] By the same token, one may recognize, as most people do, the more or less permanent reality of nations, just as one recognizes the reality of sexes and trees and stars, without necessarily endorsing the nationalist case for self-determination, nation states, and collective rights or disputing the possibility of gender, landscaped gardens, or astrology. The existence of nations may pose a problem for liberals and Marxists committed to the absolute primacy of the individual or of class. (Of course, the ubiquity of nations poses no problem for postmodernists enamored of diversity, decentering, and the ubiquitous Other.[49]) This impossibility of reconciling the claims of nations with those of individuals and classes hardly makes liberals abandon liberalism or Marxists abandon Marxism.[50]

---

48 See Robert Paul Magocsi, *Our People: Carpatho-Rusyns and Their Descendants in North America*, 3rd rev. ed. (Toronto: Multicultural History Society of Ontario, 1994). See also the unabashedly nationalist *A New Slavic Language Is Born: The Rusyn Literary Language of Slovakia* (Boulder, Colo.: East European Monographs, 1996).
49 See the essays in Eley and Suny, *Becoming National*.
50 See Will Kymlicka, *Contemporary Political Philosophy* (Oxford: Clarendon, 1990), Yael Tamir, *Liberal Nationalism* (Princeton, N.J.: Princeton University Press, 1993), Ronald Beiner, ed., Theorizing Nationalism (Albany, N.Y.: State University of New York Press, 1999), John Rawls, *The Law of Peoples* (Cambridge, Mass.: Harvard University Press, 1999), and John Rawls, *Political Liberalism* (New York: Columbia University Press, 1993). The works of Otto

Both groups may want to temper some of their hopes and expectations and they may decide to adopt a tragic pose, but there is no reason to discard either normative project just because nations were here, are here, and may never go away. If nations are perennial, both liberalism and Marxism retain as much attractiveness and power as they would if nations were not perennial. And nationalism, as a project of self-determination and the construction of nation states, is no less, and no more, plausible if nations are perennial or merely modern.

Of course, if nations are perennial, then hopes for a nonnational or nonnationalist world could be ephemeral. The opposition to perennialism may, thus, be rooted neither in theory nor even in politics. It may simply reflect a peculiar kind of teleology that embraces a vision of history that—inevitably, ineluctably, and irresistibly—must culminate in the triumph of liberalism or of Marxism. Such a belief, almost religious in its thrust and intensity, necessarily views complicating factors like nations as insurmountable obstacles to the realization of the vision. Nations, in this view, cannot be perennial, because perennialism means nothing less than the impossibility of liberalism's or Marxism's final and complete triumph. Whether the vision is Francis Fukuyama's or Karl Marx's, history cannot end as long as nations are around and mess things up.[51]

Ironically, although the theoretical reach of constructivism can easily be extended by perennialism, that of primordialism is threatened by modernism. Because primordialism must insist that nations are modern and premodern, modernism cannot, strictly speaking, be reconciled with primordialism. The only way in which this theoretical failing can be remedied is by introducing the concept of the "ethnie" as, simultaneously, a kind of nonnation and

---

Bauer, Vladimir Lenin, Rosa Luxemburg, and Iosef Stalin are the classic statements of the various Marxist positions on the national question.

51  Francis Fukuyama, "The End of History?" in Fareed Zakaria, ed., *The New Shape of World Politics* (New York: Foreign Affairs, 1997), pp. 1-25; For Karl Marx's most utopian vision of communism, see "The German Ideology," in Robert C. Tucker, ed., *The Marx-Engels Reader*, 2d ed. (New York: Norton, 1978), pp. 193-200.

protonation. Primordialism can thus acknowledge modernism while finessing its own limitations. Such conceptual massaging is, I stress, a perfectly legitimate as well as widely practiced means of coping with theoretical difficulties.[52]

Unfortunately, the conceptual differences between ethnies and nations are not obvious to the naked eye. Most scholars, as Smith observes, use ethnic groups and nations interchangeably, reflective perhaps of semantic sloppiness or of semantic proximity.[53] A large part of the problem is that ethnic groups are effectively defined as little more than premodern nations, i.e., as nations existing in premodern settings. Smith, for instance, insists that ethnies lack the following features of nations: "a clearly delimited territory or 'homeland', a public culture, economic unity and legal rights and duties for everyone."[54] Although important in their own right, these features are aspects of modern life and not of imagined or unimagined political communities. Because the defining characteristics of ethnies and nations remain unaffected by the modifiers "modern" and "premodern," premodern nations are still nations, just as premodern people are still people. Nations thus appear to be thoroughly modern ethnies and ethnies appear to be nothing more than premodern nations. Only the defining characteristics of their contexts are different, but their contexts, although relevant to the kind of causal propositions that can be made about nations/ethnies, are irrelevant to what nations/ethnies are.

The argument that ethnies cannot be nations because they lack states or territories is unpersuasive because the presence or absence of states is a characteristic, not of imagined communities, but of the setting within which they are imagined. The setting may promote such an imaginative undertaking, but it remains conceptually and causally distinct from the resultant community. Therefore, the Scots or Quebecois should not be demoted to ethnies even though they

---

52 Stephen Gaukroger, *Explanatory Structures* (Hassocks, Sussex, U.K.: Harvester, 1978), pp. 91-196.
53 Smith, *Nationalism and Modernism*, p. 45. Craig Calhoun, *Nationalism* (Minneapolis: University of Minnesota Press, 1997), pp. 29-50, expends an entire chapter on the supposed differences and fails to resolve the muddle.
54 Smith, *Nationalism and Modernism*, p. 196.

do not possess states. Nor would the Poles or Lithuanians have been demoted to ethnies after they lost their statehood to Nazi Germany. No less important, binding nations to states—as even Anderson does implicitly— accepts the nationalist definition of nations and states, whereby the only real nations are nations with states and the only real states are nation states. By the same token, insistence that only nations can inhabit delimited territories either lapses, once again, into the language and logic of nationalists (if the territory is tantamount to the state) or makes the mystifying claim that groups of people—ethnies—can really be imagined as living in placeless places. While diaspora peoples can live in many places— the Jews and the Roma and Sinti come to mind— all people, whether the individuals of liberalism, the classes of Marxism, or the nations of nationalism, must live somewhere.

Shifting focus to subjective differences between ethnies and nations is no less problematic. It is not sufficient to insist, as Smith does, that ethnic groups are not nations because "they have little or no collective self-awareness or sense of community and solidarity."[55] As Jan Assmann points out, all groups have some sense of collective self-awareness, if only in the sense of being "from here."[56] Insistence that groups can be nations only if they call themselves that name confuses the etymology of a term with the defining characteristics of a concept.[57] Finally, arguing that ethnies cannot be nations because a nation is the "largest community which, when the chips are down, effectively commands men's loyalty" falls squarely into the nationalist trap.[58] Why should anyone agree with a quintessentially nationalist definition? Postmodernists are surely right to argue that multiple identities are theoretically and empirically possible.[59] Why, then, can Italian Americans not be as much Italian as they are American? Except for nationalists, the

---

55  Ibid., p. 45.
56  Jan Assmann, *Das kulturelle Gedächtnis: Schrift, Erinnerung und politische Identität in frühen Hochkulturen* (Munich: C. H. Beck, 1997), pp. 34-37.
57  See Motyl, *Revolutions, Nations, Empires*, pp. 6-8.
58  Rupert Emerson, *From Empire to Nation: The Rise to Self-Assertion of Asian and African Peoples* (Boston: Beacon, 1960), p. 95.
59  See Geoff Eley and Ronald Grigor Suny, "Introduction: From the Moment of Social History to the Work of Cultural Representation," in Eley and Suny, eds., *Becoming National*, pp. 3-37.

coexistence of long-distance nationalism with "on-the-spot" nationalism cannot be excluded a priori.

If, alternatively, objective differences between ethnies and nations are emphasized, a host of formidable conceptual problems is encountered. Perhaps ethnies are significantly smaller. In that case, just how many people must nations encompass? Anderson assumes that nations must be large enough to enable imagination to do its work.[60] But how large is large enough? The reality of nations, which range from the tiny to the enormous, obviously suggests that they can span a wide range of numeric values. If, as Mao Zedong fantasized, several hundred Chinese could survive a nuclear holocaust, would "the" Chinese still not exist? Whatever the cut-off point, the numeric threshold for nationness can evidently be quite low. The only exit from this *cul de sac* is semantic. Although we may not be able to determine when a nation is, nations are not families or kinship groups or tribes, however large or small.[61] But this semantic distinction between nations and other groups is persuasive only because it rests on different combinations of conceptually delineated defining characteristics—A, B, C for nations as opposed to B, D, E for families and D, E, F for kinship groups and F, G, I for tribes and so on—and not on arbitrarily assigned numeric values.[62]

Do ethnies, unlike nations, lack urban elites? Are ethnies precluded from being nations because they consist only of peasants? This view is modernist, of course, but why should it be accepted? All masses, even the most rudimentary peasantry, are led by someone, and all elites, even the most cohesive, consist also of followers. Moreover, why should peasants not constitute nations before Fanonian intellectuals or *narodniki* discover them? It is not as if peasants are the inarticulate bumpkins Karl Marx made them out to be.[63] Nor are they, as James Scott tells us, unaware of their

---

60  Anderson, *Imagined Communities*, p. 15.
61  Walker Connor, "When Is a Nation?" *Ethnic and Racial Studies*, 13 (1990), pp. 92-103.
62  On defining characteristics, see Giovanni Sartori, "Guidelines for Concept Analysis," in Giovanni Sartori, ed., *Social Science Concepts* (Beverly Hills, Calif.: Sage, 1984), pp. 22-35.
63  Karl Marx, "The Eighteenth Brumaire of Louis Bonaparte," in Tucker, *The Marx-Engels Reader*, p. 608.

interests and indifferent to oppression.⁶⁴ Their culture, as anthropologists assure us, is no less vibrant than that of urbanites, while their social systems are hardly as uniform as the binary opposition between tradition and modernity, or between *Gemeinschaft* and *Gesellschaft*, suggests.⁶⁵ Finally, insistence that nations can exist only when modern elites are fused with modern masses under modern conditions amounts to a circular argument that modernity gives rise to nations precisely because they are modern and thus uniquely susceptible to causation by modernity.

Although the conceptual underpinnings of the distinction between ethnies and nations are weak, it does have a theoretical *raison d'être*. The distinction enables modernist scholars to endorse the spirit of perennialism while rejecting its letter, thereby avoiding what appears to be the slippery slope to primordialism. Whether or not this move is a progressive modification of either constructivism's or primordialism's research program is of course another issue. More important, perhaps, because perennialism can be as incompatible with primordialism as it can be compatible with constructivism, even this flimsy rationale falls away. It may be wiser to consign one of the two terms, perhaps ethnie, to the conceptual ash heap. Otherwise, scholars will have to establish better just how ethnies differ from nations and just why the differences matter.

Such a task is, in principle, perfectly possible. If nations are defined as a set of people with defining characteristics A, B, and C, where neither A, nor B, nor C is related to such aspects of modernity as the state, nationalism, or the word "nation", then ethnies would have to be a set of people with defining characteristics G, H, I. If nations, as clusters of A, B, and C, can be found in the real world, as can families (B, D, E), kinship groups (D, E, F), and tribes (F, G, H), is it possible also to find the cluster designated as an ethnie (G,

---

64 James C. Scott, *Weapons of the Weak: Everyday Forms of Peasant Resistance* (New Haven, Conn.: Yale University Press, 1985); James C. Scott, *Domination and the Arts of Resistance: Hidden Transcripts* (New Haven, Conn.: Yale University Press, 1990).

65 See the discussion of the Indonesian poem, "Serat Centhini," in Anderson, *Spectre of Comparisons*, pp.105-130. See also Clifford Geertz, *The Interpretation of Cultures* (New York: Basic Books, 1973).

H, I) or is it non-identifiable and therefore nonexistent? If the search for an ethnie is successful, then there is every reason to ask Smith's question concerning the relationship between nations and ethnies, but this time tautology would be avoided. Tautology would also be sidestepped if the existence of ethnies were posited first, before nations were sought.

## Primordial Theories?

Smith ends his book with a list of each theory's strengths and weaknesses. A disinterested observer might conclude that the theories he discusses, like the theories examined in this article, seem ultimately to be equally valid or equally invalid. Progress might be possible if each paradigm became more nuanced over time. But if all the paradigms proceed apace—and there is no reason to suppose that primordialist, constructivist, perennialist, and modernist theories could not—then it will be just as hard to choose among them later as sooner.

Notwithstanding Smith's hopes, I share John D. Barrow's doubts about the ability of any one theory to account for all conceptually possible and theoretically relevant ways in which propositional sets may be made or become coherent and complementary.[66] The same conclusion applies by logical extension to every other conceptualization of nations and nationalism. Indeed, it cannot even be stated with finality that nations are only constructed or that they only emerge. But why should this conclusion be surprising or distressing? After all, it is no easier to determine whether revolutions are made or come, whether wars are chosen or generated by anarchic systems, or whether agency trumps structure or structure, agency.[67] In all these pairings it is

---

66 Barrow, *Theories of Everything*.
67 See Theda Skocpol, *States and Social Revolutions* (Cambridge: Cambridge University Press, 1979); Said Amir Arjomand, "Iran's Islamic Revolution in Comparative Perspective," *World Politics*, 38 (April 1986), pp. 383-414; Kenneth Waltz, *Theory of International Relations* (Reading, Mass.: Addison-Wesley, 1979); Stephen Van Evera, *Causes of War: Power and the Roots of Conflict* (Ithaca, N.Y.: Cornell University Press, 1999); Anthony Giddens, *The Constitution of Society: Outline of the Theory of Structuration* (Cambridge: Polity, 1984).

possible to imagine both outcomes theoretically, and both are encountered empirically.

Is there a solution to this dilemma? Two partial solutions come to mind. First, theoretical pluralism could simple be accepted. It would be necessary to recognize that the explanatory power of all theories is limited and that the policy recommendations they generate can never be best, only less worse. Second, a modified theoretical agenda could be pursued. Theoretical pluralism implies, among other things, the impossibility of isolating the sufficient condition of anything. Although we may therefore never be able to determine what "the" cause of nations and nationalism is, there is still much for theory to explain. Rather than asking why nations emerge, their reality could be taken as given, and the focus could be changed to determining which condition or conditions make them possible and more or less likely. Which conditions are necessary to nations and nationalism, and which facilitate them? Here, too, there is no reason not to expect a variety of theoretically legitimate answers. However, if the field of inquiry is shifted from the impossible task of isolating only one sufficient condition to the possible task of identifying a variety of, possibly contradictory, necessary and facilitating conditions, then knowledge about nations and nationalism will, however imperfectly, be enhanced.[68]

How realistic are these solutions, in theory and practice? Since manifestly imperfect theories refuse to go away, adopting the first solution requires a small cognitive shift and not a leap of paradigmatic faith, with one significant exception. Rational choice theory will have to accept its own mortality and abandon its pretensions to exclusive scientific status. This adjustment will not come easily.[69] The second suggestion presupposes a willingness to countenance the possibility of perennialism. Although modernist theories can be refashioned to this end, it is hard to imagine that the political obstacles to such a shift will occur quickly, if at all. Like nations, theories may be constructed, but, ironically, attachments to both appear to be primordial.

---

[68] See Motyl, *Revolutions, Nations, Empires*, pp. 15-18.
[69] See Jonathan Cohn, "Irrational Exuberance: When Did Political Science Forget About Politics?" *The New Republic* (October 25, 1999), pp. 25-31.

# 5

# The Social Construction of Social Construction
## Implications for Theories of Nationalism and Identity Formation*

Although most contemporary theories of nationalism and identity formation rest on some form of social constructivism, few theorists of nationalism and identity formation interrogate social constructivism as a social construction—a social-science concept "imposed" on the non-self-consciously constructivist behaviors of people, who generally do not believe they are engaging in construction. Since social constructivism—unless it is a metaphysics about what is real—is really about the *concept* of social construction, the first task of constructivists is to ask, not how various populations have engaged in social construction, but how social construction should be defined. As this article shows, constructivism is at best a run-of-the-mill theoretical approach—perfectly respectable, but no different from any other theoretical approach in the social sciences. It is only when social constructivism makes outlandishly radical claims—that all of reality or all of social reality is constructed—that it is unusual, exciting, and wrong.

## What's in a Name?

Let us imagine three sets of people living many centuries ago. The first group calls itself the Herers. They live in a territory they call "here," they pursue a variety of simple economic activities, possess a coherent social structure, speak a language and practice a culture they call "ours," and are ruled by their elders. The

---

\* First printed in: *Nationalities Papers*, 38, no. 1 (January 2010), pp. 59-71. Reprinted with permission of the original publisher.

Herers love "here" and they cannot imagine life elsewhere; they also love what is "ours." They term the people who live "there" Therers and they recognize that Therer language and culture are "theirs" and definitely not "ours." The Therers actually call themselves something else—Pomos. They possess a strictly bounded territorial homeland, a language replete with abstruse terminology, a culture that mystifies the Herers, a coherent political order with genuinely participatory characteristics, and an elaborate system of myths, beliefs, and norms they consider to be the essence of Pomoness. Finally, there are the Rationalists, a fanatical sect of like-minded individuals dedicated to the exaltation of reason and the rational pursuit of individual utility. Utterly committed to these goals, they abandoned their homes and, although speaking different languages and possessing different cultures, established a liberally ruled "trading state," perhaps on an island or in some region tucked away beyond here and there.

Let us also imagine that all three groups have, up to this point in the thought experiment, been sealed off from the age of nationalism. They are, in other words, completely unaware of the nationalist terminology that is being crafted in Europe. Naturally, their innocence cannot last and, sooner or later, they, too, are exposed to the ideas circulating among self-styled nationalists. A particularly incendiary nationalist pamphlet appears in the Herer midst. The Herers are swept off their feet by its message. They see themselves mirrored in the analysis and decide forthwith to be a nation. Unfortunately, the age of print capitalism is not without its imperfections, and a typographical error mars the text: *natio* appears as *ratio*—Latin, evidently, is not quite dead—and *nationalist* appears as *rationalist*. Henceforth, the Herers call themselves the Herer *ratio* and the Herer elders call themselves rationalists.

The same pamphlet appears among the Pomos, but this one, a later edition carefully proofread by a meticulous nationalist, bears no typographical errors. The Pomos read the text; they, too, see themselves reflected in the analysis, but are aghast. Nations, they conclude, are absurd human constructions and nationalists are evil connivers. To make this point to the world they decide to abandon the Pomo name and describe themselves as the very antithesis of the age of nationalism. Henceforth, they will be known as the Antination and the Antinationalists.

The Rationalists are especially avid readers, mostly of economic texts, and one day they stumble upon a pamphlet that profoundly affects them. It is a carefully reasoned statement of their principles, a systematic compilation of all the beliefs they claim as their own. The Rationalists are both astounded by and immensely pleased with their own cleverness. Unfortunately, they, too, are the victims of the vagaries of print capitalism. A typographical error appears in the pamphlet: *ratio* – this author, evidently, also had a penchant for Latin phrases – appears as *natio* and *rationalism* appears as *nationalism*. Puzzled, but also persuaded that changing their appellation holds no costs and may offer some benefits – perhaps a free subscription to subsequent pamphlets – they proceed to call themselves a *natio* as a group and *nationalists* as individuals.

Of the three imagined communities described above, which are the nations and the nationalists and which are not? The Herers possess many of the "objective" characteristics of nationhood — common territory, economy, language, and culture – but they call themselves rationalists, not nationalists. The Pomos possess both the "objective" and "subjective" characteristics of a nation, but they insist on calling themselves an Antination. Finally, the Rationalists, who appear to be anything but a nation, call themselves just that.

Clearly, if a group can be a nation only if it explicitly terms itself a nation, then the Herers cannot be a nation, even though their style of life and their explicit commitment to the ideas of nationalism would appear to qualify them for national status. If the explicit acceptance of nationalist ideology is a necessary condition of nationhood, then the Pomos, although satisfying most definitions of a nation, cannot be one. Last but not least, if a group is a nation once it conceptualizes itself as a nation — that is, if the appellation is a sufficient condition of nationhood — then the Rationalists are a nation, even though they explicitly reject everything that real nationalists stand for. By this logic, even the Pomos might have to be deemed a nation on the grounds that an antination is just an awkward terminological variant of a nation.

The moral of this exercise in imagination is, I suggest, that the terms employed by nations and nationalists are at best of marginal relevance to theories of nations and nationalism. Nations may call themselves blue or they may follow Nelson Goodman's terminology and call themselves "grue" (*Fact, Fiction, and Forecast*); nations may be for or against nationalism; and nonnations may call themselves a *natio* or they may call themselves a *ratio*. Why certain groups call themselves this or that may be interesting and important questions if, like Leah Greenfeld, we are interested in how and why words circulate or how and why people appropriate terms and to what ends. But a focus on the actual names tells us little about whether the groups involved should be viewed as constituting nations. Only students of nations and nationalism—the scholars, and not the nations or the nationalists—can answer that question (just as they, the scholars, typically define every other social-science term). If a nation, according to our definition, is a set of people with defining characteristics A, B, and C, then any set of people with just these characteristics is a nation, regardless of how it calls itself and what its elites think. By this standard, the Herers appear to be a nation, the Pomos are definitely a nation even though they would prefer to think of themselves as something else; and the Rationalists remain rationalists even though they call themselves nationalists.

This argument has important implications for the study of nations and nationalism. If the term *nation* is irrelevant to answering the question of whether or not a set of people is a nation, then there is no reason to think that nations must be confined to the age of nationalism that burst on the world in—take your pick—1688, 1776, or 1789. Because nations exist whenever a set of people can be identified as having defining characteristics A, B, and C, then nations can in principle exist before, during, or after the term *nation* and the language and logic of a worldview called *nationalism* exist. Did group X in the year 1000 possess characteristics A, B, and C? Did group Y in the year 1900 possess these same characteristics? If yes, then X and Y are nations. If no, then they are not.

Abandoning the stipulation that entities can be nations only if they use the language and logic of the age of nationalism has two important side benefits. First, we avoid falling into the nationalist trap. By consciously rejecting nationalist assumptions regarding nations and states, we avoid thinking, however inadvertently, as nationalists and thereby remain open to a variety of theoretical perspectives. Second, we also avoid violating the most rudimentary rules of concept formation and theory building. Building causal propositions into definitions and then using the latter to prove the validity of the former is an exercise in circularity. If nations can be defined only in terms of the age of nationalism, we should not be surprised to learn that they can be explained only in those terms as well.

Rather than constructing one's own definitions, why not just appropriate those used by historical agents in general or nations in particular? There are two reasons that make such an approach impossible. First, this approach assumes that social scientists, in some specific here and now, can come to understand all the concepts employed by historical agents—in some other there and then. Although approximations are surely possible, complete comprehension is impossible, as we can never fully penetrate the linguistic world of others. Because we can never imagine what it was like to be a statesman in nineteenth-century Europe or a nationalist in twentieth-century Africa, the turn to historical agents inevitably results in concepts that are no less fuzzy and inexact than those employed by the social scientists who reject this technique. Moreover, as Arthur Danto points out, the more the lifeworlds of the others approximate ours, the more likely—and less necessary—is comprehension, while the less their lifeworlds approximate ours, the less likely—and more necessary—is comprehension (287-297). In other words, we can understand what we understand anyway, and we cannot understand what we cannot understand anyway.

Second, the turn to historical agents is also premised on the belief that, in order to understand or explain certain social facts (the state, the nation, etc.), the discourses employed by the people implicated in those social facts are best suited to such an undertaking. It is unclear why that should be the case. Naturally, if our goal is to understand their discourses, then it makes sense to employ as much of their discursive terminology as possible. If the goal is to understand their actions in terms of their discourses and other social facts, then again it makes sense to use their terminology. But if the goal is to explain how discourses affect social facts or how social facts affect discourses, then there is simply no alternative to employing concepts (for instance, such as "discourse" and "social facts") that are ours and not theirs. In any case, regardless of the theoretical undertaking, it is impossible not to employ our own concepts at some point. We could, for instance, employ the definition of nation or of sovereignty of historical agents, but sooner or later those definitions will have to be supplemented with such concepts as discourse and identity. We could perform the maneuver once again and use their definitions of discourse and identity, but then again, sooner or later, our own language and our own concepts would creep in—perhaps in the form of speech or self-definition. But these two notions are also ours, and not theirs, and so we would presumably have to embark upon a further translation and contextualization. And so on. Even if we stop short of infinite regress, sooner or later definitional circularity will set in as later concepts are based on earlier concepts.

In sum, the conceptual apparatus of historical agents, even if fully understood, can be employed only if embedded in the language of contemporary social science. For the turn to historical agents to work, one would have to adopt their entire language and understand it, and all its cultural and social and other nuances and connotations, completely. But that is as impossible as to imagine what it would be like to have been a nineteenth-century peasant or, for that matter, a bat—even if we possessed perfect knowledge of the past.

## The Ideal Chronicle

Let us engage in a thought experiment inspired by Danto. In *Narration and Knowledge*, he imagines an ideal chronicle that consists of descriptive present-tense sentences regarding every event in history (149–182). Would such a chronicle make history superfluous? After all, it contains all the facts about everything. What else is there for a historian to do? Paradoxically, Danto concludes that the historian's task would be unaffected, precisely because the historian interprets the past in light of the future. As a result, an exhaustive collection of present-tense sentences would serve only as raw material for the historian writing from the perspective of the future.

Let us imagine that the ideal chronicle is even more exhaustive that Danto's. Let us imagine that it consists not only of a complete description of every event in every place and every time; let us also imagine that it consists of every statement uttered by every person in every place and every time. And let us also imagine that the ideal chronicle also consists of every thought had by every person in every place at every time. In short, the ideal chronicle would amount to a completely exhaustive data bank — one including information of interest to all social scientists, from those inclined to natural-science explanations to those inclined to constructivist explanations. Would such a wealth of data validate or invalidate any of the extant approaches? More generally, what implications would such a data bank have for the different approaches?

Several conclusions suggest themselves. First, and foremost, all our social scientists would find themselves in exactly the same position as Danto's historians. This massive amount of present-tense data would still have to be ordered in some way in order to produce something in the nature of either a "significant narrative," to use Danto's term for a historical account that provides some explanation for events, or a "theory" — a more rigorously constructed series of causes and effects. The ideal chronicle in and of itself would just be a mountain of inert data. The task of the social scientists would therefore begin after their encounter with the mountain. They would still have to "scale" it.

Second, there is no reason to think that they could not all scale it. With such an enormous mound of data, one can easily imagine that any number of perfectly persuasive theoretical accounts would be possible—no less possible than now, under conditions of scarcity of data. In other words, the absence of reliable data has nothing to do with the fact that there are many different theories that account for them more or less equally well. Indeed, theoretical pluralism would be unavoidable under conditions of perfect information, because it is just then that every possible causal connection and correlation could be demonstrated and every possible anomaly or deviance could be explained away.

Third, a perfect data bank would have one equally important implication for all social-science approaches. Under conditions of perfect information, no approach could possibly make any headway without clear and distinct concepts. If we agree with Philip Kitcher and think of theories as maps, then concepts are the units into which maps are divided—be they states or geographical zones or transportation networks or population centers. In this sense, a map can work, and serve its purpose as a map, if and only if the units are clearly defined and delineated, so that we can tell where one unit ends and another begins. In other words, the units of a map, like concepts, are about boundaries, about distinguishing one object from another object, about telling where one object ends and another begins.

Seen in this light, the two most popular theoretical approaches in today's social sciences—rational choice theory and social constructivism—would have to proceed along the same exact lines before they would be able to do anything with the reams of data they confront. Both would first have to develop their own *language*. Only then would they be able to make the data "talk." Rational choice theory, for instance, would do exactly what it does now—use the language of individuals, preferences, utility maximization, collective action, free riders, and the like. Some of these terms will of course be found within the ideal chronicle: after all, it will encapsulate everything said and thought by rational choice theorists of the past and immediate present. But the important point is that, while rational choice theory can draw on some of this social-scientific language to refine its concepts, it will have to develop an intersubjective language of its own—one understood by rational choice theorists here and now and one enabling them to comprehend the data contained in the ideal chronicle. That language will probably have to be refined as the data bank grows—as it does with every second—and the current language of rational choice theory enters the bank and becomes part and parcel of the raw data. But the important point is that, at any time, rational choice theorists will have to have a language of their own appropriate to the task of explaining the data contained in the ideal chronicle.

Constructivist theorists—and especially those who employ the social-constructivist conventional wisdom in their theories of nations, nationalism, and identity formation—will face the same exact challenge. Thus, their language, like that of rational choice theory, is theirs and not that of the people they are studying. Terms such as discourse, identity, social construction, inside-outside, polity, norms, and the like are intrinsic to their language, and as such are no less of an imposition on the discursive practices of the agents they are studying than the language of rational choice theory is an imposition on the strategic choices made by the individuals it is studying. Just as most people at most times do not consciously set out to maximize utility, so, too, they do not consciously set out to transform their identities into discursive practices. People may believe all sorts of things about their beliefs and behaviors, but there is no reason whatsoever to suppose that they are self-consciously engaging in "social construction." Indeed, it would be utterly bizarre if the hundreds of millions of people who have lived on earth—from peasants to workers to intellectuals to capitalists to socialists to fascists to Muslims to Catholics to Jews—actually believed that they were "socially constructing" anything at all. It takes very self-conscious and very self-reflexive intellectuals to believe that about themselves, and, even then, I wager that the vast majority of such intellectuals do not believe—or are completely unconscious of—engaging in social construction for most of their waking days.

No less important, constructivism faces an especially difficult task—one even more complex than that faced by rational choice theory—inasmuch as it must maintain the integrity of the discourse of agents while employing its own language to pull off the trick. After all, one of constructivism's central claims is that agents construct their own social reality. But how can constructivism go beyond this bald assertion of a metaphysical possibility to an actual demonstration of the claim? How can constructivism demonstrate that the language of agents—whether now or in the past, whether here or elsewhere in the world—actually constructs their world, and not our interpretation of their world, without using the language of interpretation, construction, and the like to make the claim? The answer, of course, is that constructivism cannot. In that sense, constructivism resembles a dog chasing its own tail. Constructivism claims that agents construct reality in their language, but the assertion of this claim and the demonstration of this claim can only be effected by the use of constructivist language, which by definition is alien to the language of the agents concerned and could not possibly have figured in their construction of social reality.

The conundrum of theories of social constructivism is that social construction is a social construction, that is to say, a social-science concept "imposed" on the non-self-consciously constructivist behaviors of people, who by and large do not believe that they are engaging in construction. Social constructivism—unless it is a metaphysics about what is real—is thus really about nothing more than a concept, in this case, the concept of social construction, as it applies to social reality. If that is indeed the case, then the first task of constructivists is to ask, not how various populations have engaged in social construction, but how should social construction be defined. And that means that their focus should be on the traditional tasks of analytic philosophy. Indeed, seen in this light, constructivism is transformed into a run-of-the-mill theoretical approach—perfectly respectable, but no different from any other theoretical approach in the social sciences. It is only when social constructivism makes outlandishly radical claims—about all of reality being constructed or all of social reality being constructed—that is it unusual and exciting and, of course, absurd.

## The Social Construction of What?

In a nutshell, social constructivism argues that, of all the entities that exist in the world, a certain class thereof is created by human beings. As products of some kind of human process, these humanly constructed entities may be referred to as artifacts. But which of the many entities that exist in the world are artifacts? If we assume for the sake of argument that there exist non-humanly constructed entities—let us provisionally call them "nature"—then socially constructed artifacts encompass everything else—from paintings to cars to stone axes to languages to culture to concepts to games. In a word, everything that is not specifically a part of nature is an artifact and everything is therefore socially constructed. If we assume, as some idealist scholars do, that even reality is a construct of human thought, then the realm of socially constructed artifacts expands to fill the entire known universe. What seems at first glance to be a triumph of constructivist thought turns out, on closer examination, to be a fatal flaw. At best, the concept of social construction helps differentiate the world of nature from the world of humanity—a distinction that is obvious and which could surely have been made without the assistance of the concept of social construction. At worst, social construction is just another word for the universe. Either way, the concept is much too broad to be of any use to theorizing about the world.

Is there any way of redeeming the concept—perhaps by narrowing its scope or differentiating among its referents? We can follow Ian Hacking's example and ask about "the social construction of *what?*" It is clear from the above discussion that artifacts—that is, humanly constructed entities—can be found in at least four realms of reality. I shall call the first *theory*, the second *discourse*, the third *social facts*, and the fourth the *natural world*. In making these distinctions, I am not, at least for the time being, suggesting that these four areas are or are not causally related. Nor do I wish to suggest that these four realms are completely independent of one another or that they suffice to describe all of reality. This fourfold division is a crass and crude simplification, but some such simplification and division—and this one has the merit of corresponding to social-scientific use and common sense—is imperative if the concept of social construction is to be rescued from oblivion.

By theory I mean nothing more than the concepts that social scientists, social scientists, philosophers, critics, and other professional thinkers employ in their attempts to explain or understand the world. By discourse—a term I employ without any of the Foucaldian baggage that is usually attached to it—I mean only the way in which entities in general or specific entities in particular are thought and talked about in some society. By social facts I mean all human institutions, organizations, and behaviors, from war to marriage to money to ordering beer in a French café. The natural world, if one exists independently of human thought, consists of those entities identified in the natural sciences and ranging from the things we call trees to the things we call galaxies. Naturally, the concept of social construction obviously refers to the first three sets of entities and, depending on the extent of one's commitment to the constructionist program, possibly even to the fourth.

Further distinctions with a difference are also possible. One may believe that all, some, or none of the content of any realm of reality is socially constructed. It is perfectly possible, for instance, to believe that all of theory, much of discourse, some social facts, and no part of the natural world is socially constructed. It is just as possible to insist that all four realms are constructed to an equal degree—all, some, or not at all—or to variable degrees. Naturally, there are internal limits to the number of possible permutations and combinations, as it may indeed be the case that the degree of social construction at one level presupposes a minimal degree of social construction at another level or levels. The most obvious example of this would be the claim that the natural world is socially constructed. Such a claim would appear to be absurd without the concomitant claim that theory, discourse, and social facts are also socially constructed. By the same token, the claim that social facts are socially constructed presupposes that theory and discourse be also, at least to some degree, socially constructed. Note, however, that the social construction of social facts need not presuppose—while certainly accommodating—the social construction of the natural world. In sum, a claim of extensive social construction for any realm appears to presuppose claims of social construction for the realms "above"—but not "below"—it. Thus, theory may be socially constructed, but, if it is, none of the other three levels need be as well. Alternatively, if the natural world is believed to be socially constructed, then the three levels above it—theory, discourse, and social facts—must be socially constructed as well. Each level is, thus, embedded or nested in the ones that follow it.

To say that the realms of reality are logically connected in terms of social construction is not to say that they are causally connected. That is to say, although the social construction of, say, discourse presupposes at least some social construction of theory, there is no reason to think that either realm causes or brings about the other realm. For all we know, theory, discourse, social facts, and the natural world may arise for any number of natural or political, social, cultural, economic, religious, or ideological reasons—only one of which could be social construction by human agents. Indeed, there is no way of claiming a priori that social construction is, or must be, the sole cause of any realm. That may be the case, but that is a claim that has to be demonstrated and not assumed. We can of course define theory as being inseparable from discourse and both to be inevitably "instantiated" in just these social facts and no others, but such a definition is, as I have already suggested, tantamount to saying that the entire world is socially constructed and is thus useless.

Moreover, we also have no way of knowing a priori whether or not theory, discourse, social facts, and the natural world are or are not causally related. It may be the case that there is one and only one casual arrow moving, say, from theory to discourse to social facts to the natural world. It may be the case that only pairs of these realms are causally related. It may also be the case that some causal connections exist between and among all four realms—but only in addition to any number of other causal factors, to be found within realms. And, of course, it may be the case that there are no causal connections between and among these realms. A priori, therefore, it is an open question of just how these four realms are causally related. What is clear from these reflections, however, is that the number of possible causal connections is enormous.

All of this is obvious, of course. We know that reality is complex. My reason for stating the obvious is, however, to emphasize the following points. First, to claim that theory, discourse, social facts, and the natural world are all the product of one particular kind of social construction or that any one component of some realm is necessary and sufficient for all the others is an exceptionally strong and radical claim, one that is tantamount to a "theory of everything." But the problem with theories of everything is that, in claiming to have discovered some one factor that accounts for all of reality—i.e., everything—they become tantamount to either natural laws or metaphysical beliefs. They cannot be natural laws—partly because there do not seem to be any such claims in the social sciences and mostly because such a status can be attained only after, and not before, extensive empirical testing and flawless corroboration. They can be belief systems—something on the order of basic ontological assumptions or religions—but then they are not theories, and however interesting it may be for some people to believe such things, there is little point in debating the content of the belief. Constructivism therefore fails if it hopes to explain all of reality. On the other hand, there is no reason that constructivism could not be useful in explaining any one realm—theory, discourse, social facts, or the natural world. (Natural scientists would of course dispute the ability of constructivism to say anything meaningful about the natural world.) That is, constructivism may work, if it is modest; constructivism fails, if it is bold.

But even if we grant that a modest constructivism may be useful, is it the case that constructivism is really about the social construction of reality? Peter Berger, Thomas Luckmann, and John Searle really do talk about how reality is constructed originally, as it were in the time before institutions existed. Their intellectual experiments relate to the emergence—i.e., the actual construction—of social reality under conditions in which social reality was absent. In the world inhabited by constructivists and all other scholars, on the other hand, social reality already exists. Inasmuch as reality already exists, it is false to say that agents are, at any time after its original construction, actually constructing it. Rather they may be engaged in one of two possible alternative modes of behavior: reproduction or alteration. That is to say, after time $t$, when reality was constructed, all that we can do is either reproduce that reality or change it. But these are very different things from actually constructing reality. Reality construction involves, presumably, just those kinds of inter-human, inter-subjective engagements discussed by Berger and Luckmann and Searle. There is no reason to think, a priori, that a similar kind of process is involved in reproducing and changing reality. Of course, it may just be the case that construction, reproduction, and change involve the exact same processes. But that is a question that cannot be assumed; it has to be demonstrated, either theoretically or empirically.

## Can Constructivism Be Salvaged?

Social constructivism is obvious. The fact that artifacts are socially constructed—and not eternally present or natural occurrences—is obvious. After all, that is the very premise of the social sciences. Hence, to make the claim for constructivism is uninteresting—until and unless one also answers two more important questions: 1) what is constructed? and 2) how is it constructed? The first question is obviously logically prior. It permits several simple answers: everything, including the world of nature; everything but the world of nature; or some, but not all, artifacts. The first view is obviously the most radical, and it entails a rejection of the mind-independent reality of the real world: it is akin to Goodman's radical endorsement of "ways of worldmaking." The second view insists that all social reality—everything, that is, that is not strictly speaking physical, biological, chemical, and so on—is constructed socially. The third would limit social constructivism to only some area within the social universe.

The second question—how are things constructed socially?—is equally important, and it, too, permits of several answers. The first, and the most radical, is that consciously and willfully acting constructivist elites construct reality. The second is that elites construct reality, but that they do so unconsciously and unwillfully. The third is that "people"—or agents in general—construct reality. And the fourth insists only that social forces, historical forces, and the like somehow construct social reality. We can combine both questions to produce a matrix.

**Forms of Social Construction**

|  | Conscious Elites | Non-conscious Elites | People | Forces |
|---|---|---|---|---|
| Natural+Social |  |  |  |  |
| Social |  |  |  |  |
| Some Social |  |  |  |  |

As I have argued elsewhere, the only theoretically interesting claim concerns the first column, the action of conscious elites (89–94). Forces, people, and non-conscious elites are all agents of sorts, but they are really tantamount to life, to history, or to some such generality. As such, while non-conscious elites, people, and forces are to be legitimately distinguished from forces of nature and hence from the claim that social reality is the natural product of forces of nature, these three factors do little to make the claims of constructivism interesting. Indeed, inasmuch as these three factors do not act consciously to construct reality, they resemble forces of nature and, in this sense, give the alternative view some consolation and legitimacy. Thus, unless we argue for the primacy of consciously acting elites engaged in construction, I submit we are pursuing trivialities and restating the obvious—that people matter, that history matters, and that life is the product of living people living.

So, what exactly can self-consciously constructivist elites do? That they may be able to reproduce or change some artifacts would appear to be beyond dispute. That they reproduce or change *all* artifacts, on the other hand, is an unsustainable claim — as a quick look at social behaviors and cultures suggests. Some things do, after all, just happen. Do self-consciously constructivist elites also reproduce or change natural reality? Or, to put the question differently, is there a natural reality that is not socially constructed, and if there is, is it possible that it has some impact on social reality — the realm that is more obviously under the influence of human constructivist efforts? One can of course withdraw into a stubborn insistence that nothing exists outside of one's mind, and one can even insist that nothing has ever existed in the past, but such a move seems at best inutile and at worst ridiculous. It is useless because it logically implies either silence – something social constructivists never engage in — or no difference from a world that would be objectively real. It is ridiculous because it seems absurd to deny the reality of the objects and the people around us. Again, there is no ultimately absolute reason for not engaging in such radical skepticism, but there are also no good or even bad reasons for engaging in it. At best, a skeptic's world looks exactly like this one, except of course that it is not really real; at worst, the skeptic is just plain wrong.

The more important point is this. Once we accept the reality of a mind-independent reality, we cannot a priori claim that all social reality is exclusively the product of social construction. After all, that natural reality could in fact be producing some of the social reality we encounter all around us. It may be doing so directly or indirectly, but we have no way of being able to exclude that possibility. Michel Foucault's claim that man is an invention may therefore be true if and only if by man one means the concept of man or the concept of person or some such thing (307–319). That concept surely is a human invention and a social construction just like every other concept. If, alternatively, one believes that "man" as homo sapiens is an invention, then one is either making a statement of faith — something along the lines of man being created in the image of God — or one is plain wrong. Wrong, that is, if one believes in a real world and the capacity of some of the social sciences to produce meaningful generalizations about the entities and processes that occur within it. For man to be an invention, we would have to deny modern genetics, modern microbiology, and all the other natural sciences. And no amount of insisting that the body is the field on which social forces inscribe themselves can change the fact that, even if that claim is true, the underlying reality is that the body is also a biological organism subject to certain kinds of biological, neurological, and physical laws. We can deny that too, of course, but then we may as well deny that there is any reality at all and, to be consistent, should also deny the possibility of airplanes, medicine, and promotion the next time we need to travel, our heads hurt, and tenure is at stake.

In sum, constructivism appears to be useful if it is about self-consciously constructivist elites engaging in the reproduction or alteration of some human artifacts. But who could possibly disagree with the observation that there are indeed self-consciously constructivist elites who engage in the reproduction or alteration of some human artifacts? Indeed, it is unclear what the alternative to constructivism, as construed in this minimal manner, can possibly be. If constructivism is not a theory, but an "approach" that can be utilized by every theoretical perspective, then constructivism amounts to little more than the injunction that attention should be paid to people and ideas and culture and the large social entities in which they are embedded. Once again, who could possibly disagree?

## Understanding National Identity

I began this article with comments on Herer, Therer, and Pomo national identity, and it may be appropriate to end with some theoretical reflections on identity — all the more so as identity figures prominently in the constructivist literature and in contemporary theories of nations and nationalism. It is not hard to see why. Once we stipulate that people consciously construct reality, it is imperative that they have something resembling a blueprint according to which that reality will be constructed. If they desire to transform X into Y or A into B, they need to "see" X and A, desire Y and B, and believe that X and A can in fact be transformed into Y and B. That is to say, people need to know what they want and how to get it, and that is, in essence, what many theorists seems to believe that identity is—the norms, values, and beliefs of actors that impel them to construct reality in the same way that Goodman's concepts lead him to engage in worldmaking. But such a view of identity is grossly inadequate. I am not disputing the importance of norms, values, and beliefs, but it is important to realize that identity is presumably about those norms, values, and beliefs that pertain to "who I am." I may have many norms, values, and beliefs—and all of them may figure in my attempts to construct reality—but it is only those norms, values, and beliefs that actually define me in some way that actually relate to my sense of identity.

I submit that identity in general and national identity in particular is nothing other than the answer to the question: Who am I? Naturally, that question does not emerge in a vacuum. It may be posed by what I call an interrogator; it arises and is answered within a certain kind of social context; and it is presumably reflective of certain features that I do indeed possess or believe I possess. That last point is, as we shall see, critical. For imagine that my identity is exclusively a function of interrogator and context: were that the case, then it would change with every minute of every day. Surely, it makes no sense to call all those millions of different combinations of interrogator and context different forms of identity—if only because that would reduce, necessarily, the notion of multiple identities and malleable identities to the absurd. However we imagine it, the concept of identity has utility only if it is something that persists. If so, then it cannot only be a function of interrogator and context. Identity has to be a persisting quality or dimension of me, as I am, and not as I am defined by others or as I appear to them in different contexts.

Is identity therefore some kind of essence? That would be a simple solution to the problem, but if we want to avoid essentialism, it seems clear that identity must be, first and foremost, a function of something like a repertoire of possible identity-features that we possess independently of others and other contexts. These identity-features cannot, in the final analysis, merely be functions of the same cultural background or social setting or some such contextual feature, as that would bring us back to the dead end that we had just evaded. These features could be the product of certain physical or biological factors—genetic codes, chromosomal characteristics, and the like come to mind—or they could be the product of cultural, social, political, and economic settings that molded me as the "person" I am. That is to say, my identity repertoire (IR) at any time $t$ consists of the following repertoire of potentially usable features: B(iological) + C(ultural) + S(ocial) + E(conomic) + P(olitical). Biological features are presumably constant, but all the others are presumably the accumulated results of years of socialization and growth starting at birth (0) and ending with time t. Thus, $IR/t = B + (C+S+E+P)/0\text{-}t$.

If identity is then the product of interrogator and context and features, then, at time t+1, my identity represents some amalgam of $B+(C+S+E+P)/0\text{-}t$ as they are reinterpreted and selected and mixed *by me* in response to the interrogator and context at t+1. At t+n, the reinterpretation and selections that took place at t+1 become part of the identity repertoire. In this way, we can reconcile continuity and persistence with the originary importance of self-identifying features and the importance of interrogators and contexts. Identity is thus a lasting, if not actually permanent, self-definition. I am X if and only if I define myself as X for a lengthier period of time.

Note that, if this account is persuasive, it means that identity, while malleable, is malleable only within limits. If identity changes, it does so only over time and in response to both external stimuli and internal realignments. And, last but not least, some elements of my identity, those designated as biological, do not change. There are, in sum, real limits to identity change and to the extent of identity change. Identity is thus situational, but rooted in certain intrinsic characteristics that are not situational. The answer to the question of who I am cannot be provided in the absence of an interrogator and a context. At the same time, the question cannot be answered in the absence of a repertoire of possible answers at the person's disposal. We cannot therefore be anything at any time or at any place. We can be different things, but we can only be those things that are designated as possible by the identity repertoire. Thus, I cannot claim to be a 3,000-year-old giraffe; nor can I claim to be a Hungarian prima ballerina. As much as I might want to be either or both of these things, they are simply not within my repertoire and thus beyond my reach.

Are there hierarchies of identities? The approach outlined above suggests that the answer has to be yes—unless we assume that identities are inert and have no impact on behavior. If, alternatively, identities do matter to living, then it makes little sense to think that a person with a bounded identity repertoire and facing a limited set of contexts and interrogators—and a person will always face a limited, if not indeed very limited, set of contexts and interrogators—will not persistently favor certain identites over others in the arduous task of living. People do not actively engage in every form of politics implied by their many possible identity configurations. That is, if a person has $n$ possible identities, that person does not pursue with equal vigor and dedication $n$ forms of political activity. Quite the contrary, the forms of political activity one pursues is usually some number far smaller than $n$, and even that number, $n\text{-}x$, is usually arranged in some order of priority: one pursues $a$ above all, then $b$, and then perhaps $c$. How can we account for such behavior? Obviously, if political action is exclusively a function of context, then we would expect equally engaged action to take place in every context. But, of course, it does not. If action is a function only of identity, then here, too, we would expect as much engagement as there are identities; but this, too, is not the case.

There are only two ways of accounting for the hierarchy of action and the limited number of actions. First, it might be that some identities are more intensely held or felt or rooted than others, and it might then be the case that we act on just those more intensely held identities. Second, it might be that some identities are more prone to activation by the context or interrogator. The result in both cases is a strategic hierarchization of identities. Holders of a repertoire of potential identities either evaluate them and come to the conclusion that some matter more than others—which is to say, an ordinal ranking takes place very similar to that presupposed by rational choice theory's ordinal ranking of preferences—or holders of the repertoire take note of how contexts or interrogators activate and rank-order identities. In both instances, some kind of more or less self-conscious ranking appears to take place, and identities do not automatically arrange themselves in some hierarchy.

We are now in a position to answer the question of whether self-consciously constructivist elites construct—that is, reproduce or change—identity. A radical constructivist would say: yes, always and everywhere and to any extent desirable. My answer is: no, they can affect the interrogator or the context or the repertoire, but only partially, only marginally, and only fleetingly. By the same token, can I—as a putative member of some self-consciously constructivist nationalist elite—construct my national identity? I may be able to rank order my repertoire, but I am unlikely to be able to affect the interrogator and context to any significant degree. In a word, yes—but only up to a point.

## The Social Functions of Social Constructivism

The concept of social construction is a social construction that is largely confined to the realm of theory. One is hard-pressed to find instances of social construction-speak in institutional sites that are not dominated by social scientists. Why would radical versions of an otherwise banal theoretical approach be so appealing to so many scholars? I suggest that the answer lies in radical constructivism's claim to be a theory of everything. On the one hand, radical simplifications are appealing because they promise immediate and comprehensive solutions to the world's many ills, about which intellectuals are genuinely concerned. On the other hand, radical simplifications that emphasize discourse are especially appealing to intellectuals in general and modern intellectuals in particular. Lacking prestige, wealth, and power, unlistened to and ignored by the population in general and policy makers in particular, intellectuals have a strong interest in ideologies that position them at the center of the universe, trumpet their ability to speak arcanely above everything else, endow them with esoteric knowledge, and explain their inability to communicate with people in terms of the people's false consciousness. Constructivism is, in brief, the opiate of the intellectuals.

## References

Berger, Peter L., and Thomas Luckmann. *The Social Construction of Reality*. New York: Doubleday, 1966.

Danto, Arthur. *Narration and Knowledge*. New York: Columbia UP, 1985.

Foucault, Michel. *The Order of Things*. New York: Vintage, 1973.

Goodman, Nelson. *Ways of Worldmaking*. Indianapolis: Hackett, 1978.

Goodman, Nelson. *Fact, Fiction, and Forecast*. Cambridge: Harvard UP, 1983.

Greenfeld, Leah. *Nationalism: Five Roads to Modernity*. Cambridge: Harvard UP, 1992.

Hacking, Ian. *The Social Construction of What?* Cambridge: Harvard UP, 1999.

Kitcher, Philip. *Science, Truth, and Democracy*. New York: Oxford UP, 2003.

Motyl, Alexander J. *Revolutions, Nations, Empires*. New York: Columbia UP, 1999.

Searle, John. *The Construction of Social Reality*. New York: Free Press, 1995.

# 6

## Why Is the "KGB Bar" Possible?
## Binary Morality and Its Consequences*

This article asks why a popular bar named after a criminal Soviet secret police organization has not provoked the outrage of the developed world's intellectual and artistic elites, who would surely condemn an SS Bar. It attributes this moral blindness to the Holocaust's centrality in Israeli, German, and American national discourse and the resultant binary morality that ascribes collective innocence to all Jews at all times and in all places and collective guilt to all Germans—and potentially to all non-Jews—at all times and in all places. The moral logic of the Holocaust thus transforms Jews into victims and non-Jews into victimizers; the moral logic and reality of the Gulag transform everybody into both victim and victimizer. The binary morality of the Holocaust insists that all human beings be heroes; the fuzzy morality of the Gulag recognizes that all humans are just humans constantly confronted by moral ambiguity. But because the Gulag's moral ambiguity concerns non-Jews *and* Jews, the Gulag undercuts binary morality. The Holocaust and the Gulag are not just incompatible moral tales; they are incompatible *and* intersecting moral tales. As a result, they cannot co-exist. We therefore fail to respond to the KGB Bar because to recognize the Gulag as a mass murder worthy of categorical moral condemnation would be to challenge the sacred status of the

---

* First printed in: *Nationalities Papers*, 38, no. 5 (September 2010), pp. 671–687. Reprinted with permission of the original publisher. I wish to thank Elizabeth Hull, Adrian Karatnycky, Nadieszda Kizenko, Sayres Rudy, Timothy Snyder, Bohdan Vitvitsky, and two anonymous reviewers for their excellent comments on earlier drafts of this article. A Ukrainian-language version of an early draft of this paper appeared as Oleksandr Motyl', "Chomu mozhlyvyy bar 'KGB'?" *Krytyka* June 2008: 10-15. A German-language version of a much shorter draft appeared as Alexander J. Motyl, "Warum ist die KGB-Bar möglich? Binäre Moral und ihre Konsequenzen." *Transit* (Summer 2008), pp. 104-122.

Holocaust. Ironically, the KGB Bar is possible *precisely because* an SS Bar is impossible.

The KGB Bar is located on the second floor of a shabby townhouse in New York's East Village. As its web site coyly puts it (Woychuk): "KGB has become something of a New York literary institution. Writers hooked up in the publishing world read here with pleasure and without pay to an adoring public over drinks almost every Sunday evening (fiction), Monday evening (poetry), and most Tuesdays, Wednesdays and Thursdays. The crowd loves it. Admission is free, drinks are cheap and strong, and the level of excellence is such that KGB has been named best literary venue in New York City by New York Magazine, the Village Voice, and everyone else who bestows these awards of recognition."[1]

The website fails to mention that the KGB Bar's namesake is a notorious secret police organization with blood on its hands. Established in 1954, the real KGB—the Committee for State Security—traces its roots to 1917, when Vladimir Lenin founded the Cheka, the All-Russian Extraordinary Commission for Struggle against Counterrevolution and Sabotage. The Cheka and all subsequent versions of the Soviet secret police terrorized, tortured, killed, and imprisoned millions in the vast system of concentration camps that came to be known as the Main Labor Camp Administration or Gulag. After most of the camps were closed down after Joseph Stalin's death, the KGB focused on repressing thousands of dissidents and maintaining extensive espionage networks at home and abroad. KGB agents were fully aware of their lineage and

---

[1]  The owner clearly chose the name KGB intentionally (Woychuk): "But what do you call a place that's almost impossible to find without special knowledge or a guide, a place with a history of left wing radicalism, which I intended to establish as a legitimate counter-culture venue? KGB seemed my obvious choice. I called the Department of State in Albany and told them I wanted to register a new corporation. 'KGB!' the clerk on the line replied. 'You can't call a corporation KGB, not in New York State. Not KGB, FBI, CIA, or even GAY. You can't just pick a name out of a hat. You have to justify, give a good reason for whatever name you choose.' He was wrong as a matter of law but you don't argue with clerks at the Department of State. 'Okay,' I said. 'I want to call it Kraine Gallery Bar, after my gallery of the same name.' 'That you can do,' he replied reluctantly. And so Kraine Gallery Bar, d/b/a KGB Bar, was legally born."

proudly referred to themselves as *chekisty*, or members of the Cheka.

One such proud chekist is Vladimir Putin, Russia's former president. Putin resolved to join the secret police in the 1970s, a few years after Soviet tanks crushed the Prague Spring in Czechoslovakia, and during one of the largest KGB crackdowns on Soviet dissent (Jack 46–67). This kind of past should raise eyebrows. Instead, policy makers, scholars, and journalists accept Putin's choice as if it were merely a career move. They shake his hand at summits; they gladly let themselves be photographed in his presence; they attend elaborate meetings with him in Valdai. Some even rationalize Putin's choice by pointing out that he spent many years in Dresden and, hence, was presumably not involved in the repression taking place in the Soviet Union. How that gets Putin off the hook is unclear, if only because East Germany, with its own notoriously efficient version of the KGB, the Stasi, was no less repressive than the Soviet Union.

Imagine if a leader with a long and distinguished career in the Gestapo or SS were to become head of state. He would automatically become an international *persona non grata*. Just that fate befell Kurt Waldheim, former secretary general of the United Nations and president of Austria. Waldheim served in the German Wehrmacht as an officer and was apparently implicated in actions against Jews in the Balkans. Putin's moral guilt is surely comparable, if not identical, to Waldheim's, and yet the former president of Russia has been the target of no opprobrium whatsoever. Waldheim was shunned by Americans and Europeans; Putin hobnobs with presidents and prime ministers on both continents. German Chancellor Gerhard Schröder went so far as to call Putin a "real democrat" at the height of Ukraine's Orange Revolution in late 2004, when the possibility of Russian intervention against the popular uprising was all too real. French President Jacques Chirac went ever further, bestowing his country's prestigious Grand-Croix de la Légion d'Honneur on Putin on September 23, 2006.

## Indifference to the Gulag

According to most estimates, Stalin's brutal rule produced some twenty million deaths (Malia 263; Applebaum 584; Courtois 4). This number includes those who perished in the concentration camps or in exile, who died while being deported, who were executed and dumped in mass graves, and who starved during the Great Famine of 1933 in Ukraine and during collectivization in other parts of the Soviet Union (Libanova). Even if halved, this number is staggering. And it takes very little imagination to appreciate that it stands for real human lives that were unnecessarily and cruelly extinguished. As John Gray notes, "communism must be judged radically evil, despite the fact that its crimes did not include racial extermination of the kind committed by the Nazis" (Gray 39).

We live in an age of human rights, civil rights, women's rights, men's rights, minority rights, and animal rights. We are attuned to reacting to the slightest injustice in the world. We respond with horror to news report of senseless attacks on Iraqis, Israelis, and Russians. We cannot fathom the ethnic cleansing in Bosnia or the mass murders in Rwanda and Darfur. How then is it possible that the KGB Bar and what it stands for, the "Gulag" — I use the term as shorthand for the totality of Soviet crimes — should elicit no outrage among the developed world's intellectual and artistic elites, who share so many normative beliefs with respect to human and civil rights?

Many of the KGB Bar's patrons are young and may not know better. They may be genuinely ignorant of the KGB and its crimes (the bar was established in 1993, two years after the Soviet Union's collapse). And their generation's hipster penchant for irony and detachment may even explain their tendency to view Soviet-era leaders and memorabilia as absurd, campy, or cool. But many of the KGB Bar's patrons, like many of the writers, poets, and artists who perform there, are neither young nor ignorant. These globally connected intellectual and artistic elites consist of educated, informed, and mature individuals who read, analyze, and create for a living. They include journalists, professors, pundits, analysts, and artists working for the media, universities, think tanks, and a range of other institutions. These global intellectual and artistic elites rarely refrain from adopting clear normative and political positions on the issues of the day. They write articles, books, letters to the editor, and op-ed pieces; they produce critical artwork; they make appearances on radio and television; they contribute to the Internet. They are continually in touch with one another—closely following, commenting on, and responding to what their counterparts in other countries are writing, saying, thinking, and creating. And they have all been to New York, know its cultural and intellectual scene, and speak English. And yet not a single prominent or even semi-prominent intellectual, commentator, pundit, blogger, artist, website, magazine, newspaper, or radio or television station has reacted with outrage at the naming of a popular bar after a criminal organization. If an important artistic venue in an important city bore the name of the Gestapo or the SS, the response would be immediate. The developed world's intellectual and artistic elites would loudly condemn such a callous disregard for basic human decency.

Consider as a case in point the "Hitlers' [sic] Cross" restaurant that opened in a Mumbai suburb on August 18, 2006. The Indian Jewish Federation and the Israeli Embassy protested, as did individuals from Germany and Israel. Less than one week later, on August 24, the owner Punit Sablok changed the name to "Cross Café" and agreed to remove Hitler's name and the swastika from the billboard and menus ("Cross Café"). A similar fate befell the "Hitler TechnoBar & Cocktail show" in Pusan, South Korea. After an international uproar, its owner, a Mr. Hong, changed the name to "Ditler" and then to "Caesar."[2] There are apparently several

---

[2] Mr. Hong subsequently wrote (Lebow): "Dear foreign customers, I am the owner of 'Adolph Hitler Bar'. I've been snubbed by some foreign customers ever since I opened a cocktail bar named 'Hitler'. But I couldn't answer their questions nor explain my thoughts because of the difficulties of different languages. I'd like to say that I don't believe that Hitler was a good person either. I can totally understand why foreigners are upset. I've learned his brutalities against the peace of the world from books, TV and movies. As you know, Korea had a similar situation with Japan during WW2. I have upsetting feelings about what Japanese did to Korean as well. If I saw a bar name 'HiroHitto' in other countries, I should feel the same way. I am not a Nazi, the

other Hitler-themed bars in provincial South Korean cities that, while drawing critical attention on the Internet, have escaped the kind of international opprobrium that led to the renaming of the Mumbai and Pusan establishments. That these bars and restaurants have managed to survive is surely a function of their being simple eateries catering to run-of-the-mill customers in decidedly obscure towns in distant South Korea. None of them has the international stature of the KGB Bar, which is known to, frequented, and revered by intellectuals and artists throughout the world.

Indifference to the KGB Bar's association with the Gulag cannot be due to ignorance about the Gulag and its perpetrators, as the literature on the Soviet secret police, the concentration camps, and Soviet repression is substantial and easily available. Jonathan R. Adelman, Martin Amis, Anne Applebaum, John Barron, Robert Conquest, David Dallin, Amy W. Knight, Borys Levytsky, Roy Medvedev, Barrington Moore, Jr., and many others have written substantive studies. Stephane Courtois published the definitive account of Communist crimes in 1999, *The Black Book of Communism*; Avraham Shifrin compiled *The First Guidebook of Prisons and Concentration Camps in the Soviet Union* in 1982. Russian and non-Russian authors, witnesses, and survivors—Alexander Dolgun, Evgeniya Ginzburg, Petro Grigorenko, Nadezhda Mandelshtam, Valentyn Moroz, Mykhaylo Osadchy, and Aleksandr Solzhenitsyn, to name just a few—have left a wealth of memoirs and literary accounts. Since the collapse of the Soviet Union and the partial opening of Soviet archives, vastly more information has come to light. Nor is the Soviet Union—or its successor state, the Russian Federation—an obscure country of little interest to intellectual and artistic elites. There is a large non-academic literature on both countries, and the journalists, diplomats, and policy makers who

---

bar name came out at a meeting with interior designer. We just wanted a name that can be related to or represent Germany, easy to remember and easy to design the interior with. We couldn't think about the history point of view when picking the name. The name 'Hitler' was totally meaningless, it was nothing more than a material for the business. I feel shame and I'd like to make a sincere apology for using the name without being able to consider how foreigners might feel. I also thank to Mr. Lebow and his wife for letting me know my big mistake and giving me the chance to publish a written apology."

write these books invariably draw some attention to the Soviet Union's repressive apparatus and Russia's repressive history (Smith; Remnick; Kempe; Handelman; Matlock). Ignorance may therefore excuse the general public and the KGB Bar's youthful clientele, but it cannot excuse the developed world's intellectual and artistic elites. If nothing else, some of them surely must have read Anna Akhmatova's great poem, "Requiem".

Perhaps the developed world's intellectual and artistic elites know but are unfazed by so much suffering? They might, for instance, believe that the KGB's actions were not criminal or that the KGB's victims were expendable. Unreconstructed Stalinists, fanatical believers in progress, and Russian fascists might hold the first belief. Stalinists would claim that Communism was a higher good, and that the price of building it, even if in millions of innocent lives, was worth it. Believers in progress might hold that the opponents of Communist modernization stood in the way of the Soviet Union's transformation into a modern state and, however regrettably, had to be swept away. Russian fascists might view the grandeur and power of the Russian state as worthy of all sacrifice. Needless to say, while unreconstructed Stalinists might still haunt Left-Bank cafes, worshippers of progress might still be found on some campuses, and Russian fascists may feel at home in St. Petersburg and Moscow, their numbers among the developed world's intellectual and artistic elites today are decidedly smaller than those of champions of human rights.

A more persuasive explanation might consider the fact that, despite rhetorical concern for human rights, we live in a time in which wars, genocides, atrocities, ethnic cleansings, and mass killings are actually business as usual. Seen in this light, indifference to the KGB Bar and the Gulag would only be reflective of moral exhaustion. Alternatively, it might be the case that Western intellectual and artistic elites overlook the KGB Bar and the Gulag precisely because they are all too uneasily aware of the atrocities, genocides, and mass killings perpetrated by the "civilized" nations of Western Europe and North America during the age of colonialism and imperialism, the two world wars, the cold war, and the war on terror.

The case for moral exhaustion and moral unease is not unpersuasive—Who has not experienced some sense of jadedness in response to the next newsworthy atrocity? Which European or American does not feel uneasy talking about European colonial crimes in Africa or the obliteration of Hiroshima and Nagasaki?—but it fails with respect to the KGB Bar on two counts. First, even if we are all morally exhausted, it is unclear just why outrage at the KGB Bar should be completely absent among the developed world's intellectual and artistic elites. And second, even if we are all morally uneasy, it is unclear just why we would not want to satisfy our sense of moral outrage by pointing a finger at an easy target involving no European or American complicity.

If these mindsets do not explain indifference to the KGB Bar, then perhaps some moral myopia, some inability to *see* the suffering of the Gulag holds the key. Worldviews, cultures, discourses, ideologies, and the like can structure perceptions of reality in ways that make certain things visible and important and others invisible and unimportant. Much of Western culture, for instance, used to relegate—and perhaps still does—not-Western peoples to the margins of history (Said). Mainstream economists lacked the theoretical and conceptual apparatus to see world-economic crises of the sort that struck the world in 2008 (Krugman). Communism's obsession with class blinded it, and its believers, to the importance of ethnicity, with the result that Friedrich Engels could casually categorize Eastern Europe's small nations as "trash peoples" (*Völkerabfälle*). Conversely, feminism made us "see" women, even though they had always been manifestly present in all historical processes.

Similarly, the Gulag could be ignored or overlooked without the risk of moral opprobrium if it had no place in some discourse that defined good and evil. Does such a Gulag-negating discourse exist? And if it does, what exactly is the logic behind its negation of the reality of the Gulag?

To answer these questions, I shall focus exclusively on morality, logic, and discourse in general and the moral logics of discourses in particular. Although I will make occasional reference to countries and people, I will investigate, not concrete individuals and institutions and the way they form or sustain discursive practices, but the logics of these discourses especially as they pertain to moral judgments of good and evil. Such an approach obviously assumes that discourses, morality, and logic can be considered independently of individuals and institutions. Although social historians, anthropologists, and other students of concrete human beings are unlikely to agree with this assumption, suffice to say that it is both intellectually respectable as well as ontologically, epistemologically, and methodologically possible. One can, after all, investigate how the logic of Marxism negated the nationality question, just as one can examine how the logic of mainstream economics negated global financial crises. Whether or not such an assumption leads to interesting and useful analyses is a question that can only be answered after the analysis is made.

An emphasis on discourse, morality, and logic inevitably begs the question of *whose* discourse, morality, and logic. It is unquestionably the case that there are always many competing discourses, moralities, and logics in every society. But it is also unquestionably the case that, under certain conditions, dominant or even hegemonic discourses, moralities, and logics can emerge. Marxists might ascribe hegemony to the power of the ruling class. My approach in this paper is rather less deterministic. I shall suggest that a particular "Holocaust-affirming" and "Gulag-negating" discourse, morality, and logic achieved hegemony as a result of a confluence of circumstances. First, the Holocaust became the cornerstone, not just (as one would expect) of Jewish/Israeli collective national identity, but (as one would not expect) of German collective national identity. And second, the Holocaust's prominence in Jewish/Israeli and German collective national identity logically dovetailed with the geopolitical importance of both Germany and Israel to the United States, thereby complementing and reinforcing the discourse of American exceptionalism. The result was a way of seeing the world that demanded condemnation of the Holocaust and permitted indifference to the Gulag.[3]

## The Sacred Status of the Holocaust

The Holocaust is unique—in one way that is commonly acknowledged and one way that is not (Rosenbaum). The Holocaust is unique in the ghastliness of its clinically industrial approach to the killing of all Jews, but it is also unique in being the only mass murder to have acquired an extraordinary discursive status. The apotheosis of the struggle between pure good and pure evil, the Holocaust has become a transcendental grand narrative and a sacred text not just for Jews and Israelis—as one would expect—but for *everybody*—as one would not.

The objective reality of the Holocaust could not have produced sacred status; no reality can. After all, if objective reality were sufficient to produce sacredness, then the Holocaust would be remembered as a Jewish-Roma catastrophe, since the Roma, like the Jews, were slated for extermination by the Nazis and, like the Jews, suffered horrific losses. Instead, the Roma generally figure as a footnote to the Holocaust narrative (Lewy). Nor can the intensity of Jewish commemoration of the Holocaust account for this status. Just as Jews view the Holocaust as uniquely terrible, so too Roma, Poles, Kurds, Armenians, Cambodians, Crimean Tatars, Ukrainians, Tutsis, and many others view their catastrophes as uniquely catastrophic. Many of them also have elaborate institutional vehicles for remembering their catastrophes, but their exhortations to the world have not succeeded in ascribing sacred status to theirs. Nor, finally, could the power of some "vast Jewish conspiracy" or "Israel Lobby" have foisted the Holocaust on the world's imagination.

---

3  One of my anonymous reviewers noted that there exists a "UDBa Bar" in central Belgrade and a "Goli otok" decoration in some Bosnian restaurant. UDBa was the Yugoslav secret police and "Goli otok", or "Naked Island." was the site of, as the reviewer put it, the Yugoslav Gulag. I submit that the fact that both these establishments have escaped international criticism has something to do with the indifference with which we "see" Soviet and, thus, Communist crimes.

The Holocaust acquired such universally sacred status because of a unique and historically contingent concatenation of discursive developments. I submit that a mass killing or other human catastrophe can acquire such transcendent status only by passing through four logically connected steps. The first two steps are empirical conditions, while the next two are their logical consequences under conditions of national-identity formation.

1. Both victims and victimizers recognize the mass murder as a crime. The victims condemn it and the victimizers accept responsibility for it.
2. The mass murder becomes the central defining characteristic of the national identities of both victims and victimizers. The victims view their victimhood at the hands of the guilty victimizers as the core of their national identity, and the victimizers see their victimization of the innocent victims as the core of theirs.
3. The victims view themselves not just as innocent, but as collectively innocent, while the victimizers view themselves not just as guilty, but as collectively guilty.
4. Collective innocence, like collective guilt, is projected into the past and future of the entire nation.

Steps 1 and 2 need not occur, but, if and when they do, they lead to steps 3 and 4 under conditions of collective identity formation. Collective innocence and collective guilt (step 3) therefore follow from steps 1 and 2 precisely because national identity is a collective self-definition; as a result, the primary component of that identity — the mass murder and the questions of innocence and guilt that it raises — will also become collectivized. Step 4 follows from steps, 1, 2, and 3. Since nations are always conceived of as transgenerational entities, collective guilt and collective innocence come to characterize both actual victims and victimizers as well as their ancestors and children.

Thus, if, first, both victims and victimizers recognize the mass murder as a crime and, second, the mass murder becomes the central defining characteristic of the national identities of both victims and victimizers, then it follows — logically and therefore necessarily, precisely because national identity is a collective self-definition—that, third, collective innocence and collective guilt will take hold and, fourth, collective innocence and collective guilt will be projected into the past and future of the nations concerned.

The upshot of this four-step process is a "binary morality" that posits that one nation consists always and everywhere only of innocent victims and the other consists always and everywhere only of guilty victimizers. It is a short step from here to the proposition that, since one nation consists always and everywhere of victims, all other nations with which it comes into contact always and everywhere are *potential* victimizers. The Holocaust's sacred status thus entails acceptance of a moral system based on the transferability of the collective innocence and guilt incurred by some people at a particular time and place to all people at all other times and places. Such a moral logic denies the relevance to moral judgments of individual choice or the existence, in morally complex situations, of many possible choices. The distinctions between criminal, political, moral, and metaphysical guilt drawn by Karl Jaspers would also be inadmissible in the moral universe of binary morality.

## The Uniqueness of Germany

It makes perfect sense for a catastrophe of such enormity as the Holocaust to have become a cornerstone of contemporary Jewish/Israeli national identity. Catastrophes often serve as the foundation stones of national identities—such as Kosovo Polje for the Serbs, the Holodomor for Ukrainians, and the Genocide for Armenians. In the regnant, implicitly or explicitly Zionist, discourse, the Holocaust serves as the culmination of Jews' long history of persecution and the ultimate proof that a Jewish state is imperative. Moreover, all Jews *were* potential if not actual victims in the Holocaust, and from the viewpoint of the persecuted, all Germans were persecutors, at least to some degree.

The remarkable thing about the Holocaust is that the German discourse fully agrees with this interpretation. No other perpetrators of genocides have acknowledged their collective guilt. In the

United States, the descendants of slaveholders have yet to register unease for the crimes of their ancestors. The destruction of Native Americans is of interest primarily to scholars (Barkan). Turkey continues to dismiss the Armenian Genocide as a side effect of war (de Bellaigue). Hutus only grudgingly admit some guilt for the murder of Tutsis. Pol Pot's supporters have melted away. China's Communists still venerate Mao. Serbs reject any guilt for ethnic cleansing in Bosnia (Hayden). Ukrainians are silent about the mass killing of Poles in wartime Volhynia (Popovych 2-3, Hrytsak 14, Snyder 167-173). The Japanese are still reluctant to acknowledge guilt for atrocities committed during World War II (Buruma). And the Gulag remains a crime without acknowledged perpetrators, except perhaps for long-dead Communists.

The unwillingness to accept responsibility for crimes is the historical norm. Despite our current obsession with remembering, people throughout history have consistently forgotten, or were encouraged to forget, past crimes and catastrophes. They may have been remembered in songs, poems, and other texts, but active, institutionalized remembering of the kind that we see most visibly with respect to the Holocaust is the exception, not the rule. Indeed, that kind of remembering may be the sole exception to this rule.

Only in the Holocaust have the victimizers accepted responsibility for the crime. Even more astounding, the Holocaust has become the cornerstone of German national identity in a fashion that exactly complements its role in Jewish national identity. When large events are commemorated, it is usually for different reasons by different sides. Victors remember something as a grand and glorious event in their people's history; losers remember it as a tragedy. The Holocaust is the only instance of a catastrophe that has been embraced as a national catastrophe by both the victims and victimizers—and for the exact same reasons. Not surprisingly, the official version of German national identity— if not, obviously, all Germans—has also embraced collective guilt and binary morality.

Germany's adoption of the Holocaust as the central element of its modern national identity was not the culmination of some historically necessary teleology but the result of a historically contingent political process. As Bernhard Giesen points out (236–255), the attempt to construct a German political identity as a *Reichsnation* (empire nation), which had begun with the creation of the Reich in 1870, had been discredited by Nazism and World War II. That left two alternatives, both the logical products of Germany's division into two states and its frontline status in the cold war. The first, which went back to the pre-1870 roots of German identity, was to ground it in the notion of a *Kulturnation* (culture nation). This was the option generally favored by left-wing intellectuals who wanted to regenerate the German nation by purging it of everything that they believed had led to the catastrophe of World War II—militarism, anti-Semitism, Americanism, capitalism, and statehood. From their perspective, the Holocaust served as the ideal starting point from which a new type of German nation—or what Giesen terms a *Holocaustnation* (Holocaust nation)—could be built. The Holocaust both symbolized everything that had been wrong with the past and it supposedly pointed in the direction—peace and socialism—in which Germany should evolve in order to leave that awful past behind.

The second alternative, generally favored by conservative political forces and the middle class, grounded German national identity in the post-war economic miracle, or *Wirtschaftswunder*. The alternative was thus the *Wirtschaftswundernation* (economic miracle nation), which could emerge from the ruins of the war by promoting economic growth, opposing socialism, supporting the United States, and willingly building a capitalist society permeated with American products and values. This concept of the German national identity did not entail denial of the Holocaust, but it did imply relegating it to a corner of German history, transcending the German past, and focusing on the present and future.

For much of the 1950s and 1960s, the *Wirtschaftswundernation* model seemed to be taking root. Most Germans were preoccupied with economic recovery. Questions of identity and responsibility primarily concerned small groups of intellectuals aghast at the fact that, despite some de-Nazification in the late 1940s and early 1950s, the vast majority of Nazi party members and state functionaries had been reintegrated into society, oftentimes acquiring important positions in the process. That Germany's post-war governments were led by Christian Democrats reinforced this social division. It was small wonder that, for about two decades after World War II, Germans also examined their role in the Holocaust reluctantly and half-heartedly.

The *Wirtschaftswundernation* project broke down in 1968. Germany's youth and Germany's left—and very often they were the same people—used history, memory, and responsibility to discredit and delegitimize their political opponents, who had witnessed or participated in World War II. Left-wing student rebels pointedly asked their parents where they had been during the war, thereby using the Holocaust and the question of Germany's past to assert themselves politically and to set the national agenda. Had such questioning been confined to students, it might not have captured the national discourse. But the late 1960s and early 1970s saw the political tide turn as well, with Social Democratic governments, under Willy Brandt and Helmut Schmidt, coming to power. The students were the natural ideological, if not always electoral, allies of the Social Democrats, and the question of responsibility for the Holocaust became a convenient political weapon both in defining the Social Democratic alternative and in attacking the conservative opposition. Collective guilt could be appropriated precisely because it targeted conservatives with deadly accuracy. Brandt's falling on his knees in 1970 at the Warsaw memorial to the Jewish Ghetto Uprising represented the left's symbolic appropriation of the Holocaust. The post-1968 "march through the institutions" by the generation of 1968 effectively led to the dissemination and institutionalization of these views. The triumph of the left, and its subsequent penetration of German society, signaled the triumph of the *Holocaustnation*.

The creation of a *Holocaustnation* necessarily made collective guilt the core of German national identity. Some left-wing activists genuinely believed in such a proposition. Most Germans might have disputed the very legitimacy of collective guilt, preferring instead to speak of collective responsibility, but their need to resort to euphemisms masked the reality that they had effectively, if unwillingly and unconsciously, adopted the thesis of transgenerational collective guilt. The collapse of the German Democratic Republic reinforced this tendency. Its disappearance both enabled West German elites to extend the *Holocaustnation* project to a society that had hitherto denied any responsibility for the Holocaust and introduced a new form of moral myopia—that represented by the East Germans' *Ostalgie* (nostalgia for the East).

## The Hegemony of Binary Morality

If only Jews remembered the Holocaust, it might have remained just another genocide. If only Germans remembered it, it might have quickly receded into the past. It is precisely because both victims and victimizers incorporated the Holocaust into complementary transcendental national narratives, accepted collective expressions of innocence and guilt, and embraced binary morality that the Holocaust became unique and sacred—for them (Motyl, "Inventing Invention"). Were Israel and Germany insignificant countries of little interest to the United States, the sacred status of the Holocaust would have concerned only Germans, Israelis/Jews, and some of their neighbors. But Israel and Germany are the strategic allies of a superpower and leader of the "free world" and both played, or still play, key roles in two of the twentieth century's longest conflicts.

The Federal Republic of Germany was on the front line of the American struggle against the Soviet Union and Communism. Indeed, Germany arguably was the *raison d'être* of the cold war. The United States had to defend Germany, but defending Germany meant defending the German nation and its conception of national identity. Defending Germany's sovereignty thus entailed accepting Germany's appropriation of collective guilt and the binary morality that it implied. A similar logic held for U.S. policy toward Israel. A friend of the United States since its founding in 1947, Israel came to enjoy unconditional U.S. support after the 1967 Six Days' War. U.S. acceptance of Israel as a strategic ally and its commitment to Israel's sovereignty and right to exist entailed U.S. endorsement of Israel's view of itself as a haven for all the world's Jews and of their national identity as resting on the antithesis between collectively innocent victims and collectively guilty actual and potential victimizers.

The Holocaust came to have sacred status in the United States—not because the "Israel Lobby" exerts invidious influence on American foreign policy (Mearsheimer and Walt; Massing), but because the two countries that collaborated to create the narrative, Germany and Israel, happened to matter enormously to the United States and because the institutions and individuals in or associated with the "Lobby"—many of whom are prominent representatives of the developed world's globally connected intellectual and artistic elites—could articulate that importance in binary terms that intersected with America's exceptionalist national self-definition as a beacon of freedom and a defender of the weak. Although American elites had long since conceptualized their country in such terms, the competition with the Soviet Union and its proxies—and especially the Middle Eastern nationalists and terrorists who opposed Israel's right to exist—easily lent itself to binary us vs. them thinking (Rudy). Because the USSR was an "evil empire" long before President Ronald Reagan termed it as such, and because Israel's opponents appeared to be fanatics, anti-democrats, and anti-Semites, the United States could only be their opposite—a good and selfless nation committed to human rights and democracy.

The defense of two states under siege from the forces of evil—Communism and anti-Semitism—fit into and reinforced the larger American self-image, thereby becoming a moral imperative for a strategic goal. John Fousek puts it well (191):

> The ideology of American nationalist globalism, which defined international reality in terms of a Manichean struggle between the U.S.-led 'free world' and Soviet-controlled communist totalitarianism, served to justify the expansion of U.S. power throughout the world while obfuscating the enormous complexities of a world experiencing the final collapse of European colonialism. It enabled most Americans to feel pride in being citizens of a great nation that wanted only to protect its own way of life and to defend 'free peoples everywhere' from totalitarian aggression.

The Holocaust could thereby move from a source of self-identity for two nations implicated in a terrible human tragedy to a source of self-identity and a defining characteristic of the foreign policy of a superpower. Once that discursive shift took place, the United States effectively became complicit in reproducing and sustaining the Holocaust's sacred status. As Roger Cohen puts it (3), the United States became "the global custodian of the memory of the Holocaust."

In contrast to the Holocaust, which has gone through all the stages of acquiring sacred status, the Gulag has not even passed through the first: for both victims and victimizers to recognize the Gulag as a crime. The victims of Soviet crimes know they are victims and, like Jews, have developed elaborate moral-historical accounts of their victimhood at the hands of the Soviet regime, the Communist Party, and the secret police. But the victimizers have thus far refused to make an equivalent admission of guilt. Members of the KGB, such as Putin, insist they were only doing their jobs. Members of the Soviet Communist Party claim that they believed in a good cause, and that the Stalinists, most of whom are conveniently dead, were responsible. Foreign Communists wash their hands entirely of the matter. And the Russians insist that they were as victimized as the non-Russians. The result is a paradox. Soviet crimes appear to have produced millions of victims, but no victimizers.

## The Moral Lessons of the Gulag

We know from our daily lives that there are degrees of guilt—that all who fail to resist evil may bear some moral culpability, but that they bear different degrees of culpability. Binary morality fails to distinguish between venial sins and mortal sins and between sins of omission and sins of commission, but they are critical for any appreciation of how real people confront real moral dilemmas in real lives. James C. Scott has written of the "weapons of the weak"—the small forms of protest, such as graffiti, songs, work slowdowns, and the like, that the powerless adopt in order to protest their condition. According to binary morality, the weapons of the weak are not weapons but forms of surrender.

We commonly apply just this kind of complex moral logic to the Gulag. The scholarly literature on Soviet crimes, for instance, is nuanced in its evaluation of the moral choices facing both victimizers and victims. The former are often characterized as true believers in the glorious communist future or as ex-peasants who were particularly susceptible to cults of the personality. Although they may also have been perpetrators of horrific crimes, we know they were human and therefore imperfect. They joined the Party because it was a good career move for ambitious peasants. They supported Stalin because they believed in the shining future he promised. They failed to resist mass murder because they had children. They looked the other way because resistance was futile. They informed because they feared losing their careers (Fitzpatrick, Kotkin).

We know that resistance to Stalinism would have been an option for very few, and we accept that the vast majority of Soviet people at most times tried to live their lives with some dignity and some concern for their neighbors. We acknowledge that such behavior was reasonable, even if cowardly, precisely because the circumstances surrounding them—a police state, a massive repressive apparatus, almost certain imprisonment and death for oneself and for one's loved ones—forced people to act in non-heroic ways. Should one resist if resistance is certain not to produce any results? Should one resist if resistance is certain to provoke reprisal—against oneself and one's loved ones? Is there no middle ground between active resistance (taking up the gun in a hopeless cause) and active collaboration (consciously choosing to support a criminal regime)? "At what point," asks István Deák (62), "must one take a stand against oppression even at personal peril?"

When it comes to Nazism, however, all such considerations are dropped and we insist that Eastern Europeans living in German-occupied territories should have actively resisted Hitler— even though we know that such resistance would have resulted in death. That non-resistance may have also been a function of the mind-boggling devastation wrought by Stalin's revolution from above, that it may have also been a rational response to the awful dilemmas posed by occupation by competing totalitarian regimes, is irrelevant from the perspective of binary morality (Berkhoff). The sad fact is that the moral "gray zones" Primo Levi spoke of with reference to Auschwitz-Birkenau exist in all totalitarian settings that force ordinary people to choose between collaborating or dying (53).

Not surprisingly, there is also no room within binary morality for the ordinary Jews who lacked the strength not to collaborate with the Nazis (Petropoulos and Roth). According to Idith Zertal's depiction of how their experiences were received in Israel (87–88):

> This Holocaust literature, this record of the complexity of human existence and its negation in the cataclysmic situation of the camps was not handed down because it embodied—and still does—a vast threat, emanating from the very triviality of the "crimes" exposed and the banality of the people who committed them; ordinary Jews, everyday people, who might well have been us; individuals trapped in insoluble dilemmas with no way out except suicide; who, for one brief moment outside of "normal" time, turned into persecutors, beating, slapping, whipping, and torturing other people for more food, less work, less suffering, to save themselves—thereby forfeiting their place in the world. And because these accounts deal with ordinary, normal people, and expose the fragility and imperceptibility of the line between good and evil, right and wrong, and the leakage—invisible at the time—from one side of the line to the other—their troubling message could not be compulsory material for a nation establishing and defining itself as absolute good against the Holocaust's absolute evil.

## Challenging Binary Morality

The Gulag's lack of sacred stature may explain why a KGB Bar is not, like an SS Bar, impossible, but it does not explain why it is possible. To get at that question requires taking a closer look at the radically different moral logics embodied in our understandings of the two mass murders. The Gulag's moral logic is messy, while that of the Holocaust narrative is crystal clear. The Gulag shows that Jews, like everyone else who lived through the Nazi and Soviet regimes, faced moral choices, that some Jews made bad choices, and that some were even victimizers. The Gulag also shows that non-Jews faced moral choices, that some non-Jews made bad choices, and that, while some were victimizers, others were victims. The Gulag therefore challenges binary morality in four ways.

1) We know that some non-Jews bear responsibility for the Gulag, but, as Yuri Slezkine reminds us, so too do some Jews. According to Slezkine (254–255):

> the Soviet secret police — the regime's sacred center, known after 1934 as the NKVD — was one of the most Jewish of all Soviet institutions. In January 1937, on the eve of the Great Terror, the 111 top NKVD officials included 42 Jews, 35 Russians, 8 Latvians, and 26 others. Out of twenty NKVD directorates, twelve (60 percent, including State Security, Police, Labor Camps, and Resettlement [deportations]) were headed by officers who identified themselves as ethnic Jews. The most exclusive and sensitive of all NKVD agencies, the Main Directorate for State Security, consisted of ten departments: seven of them (Protection of Government Officials, Counterintelligence, Secret-Political, Special [surveillance in the army], Foreign Intelligence, Records, and Prisons) were run by immigrants from the former Pale of Settlement. Foreign service was an almost exclusively Jewish specialty (as was spying for the Soviet Union in Western Europe and especially in the United States). The Gulag, or Main Labor Camp Administration, was headed by ethnic Jews from 1930, when it was formed, until late November 1938, when the Great Terror was mostly over.[4]

That Communism, like Zionism, should have been an attractive option for the oppressed Jews of Eastern Europe is fully understandable. Both offered equality and freedom from anti-Semitism — Zionism by means of establishing a Jewish homeland in Palestine, Communism by means of transforming the countries in which Jews resided. Even so, joining Communist parties or secret police agencies for noble or understandable motives does not absolve those individuals who chose to join — whether Jewish, Russian, Ukrainian, French, or American — of some moral complicity in the crimes those parties or those secret police agencies committed. It should, I trust, be obvious that to make this claim is not to blame Communism on "the Jews" or on a Jewish conspiracy or to absolve German and other anti-Semites of their anti-Semitism.

---

4   I emphasize that the overrepresentation of Jews in the NKVD does not mean that "the Jews" bear some special responsibility for the Gulag. It means only that some Jews were implicated in Soviet crimes. By the same token, it cannot be right to argue, as so many historians do, that Austrian overrepresentation among concentration-camp staff proves that "the Austrians" were especially prone to be Nazis. They may have been, but that particular statistic cannot and does not establish any such proclivity.

2) The Gulag challenges the Holocaust's binary morality in another sense as well. Since binary morality claims that all Jews were only victims, in both the Holocaust and the Gulag, it is easy to conclude that all non-Jews, like all Germans, must have been only victimizers. But the reality is that, just as Jews were victims and victimizers in the Gulag, so too were non-Jews (Snyder, "Holocaust"). Russians, Ukrainians, Latvians, and all other Soviet nations including Jews were victims and victimizers, repressors and repressed, colonizers and colonized—although not necessarily to the same degree. Ukrainians, for instance, played an important role in the party and state, especially after World War II. But they also suffered terribly during the famine of 1933 and in the Stalinist purges and terror, and were overrepresented in the dissident movement (Motyl, Sovietology 153–157). Jews were overrepresented in the secret police apparatus until World War II, but they were also the targets of severe discriminatory measures in the 1940s and after. A similar balance sheet could be drawn for every other nation in the Soviet Union and Eastern Europe.

3) Even more of a challenge to binary morality is the fact of non-Jewish victimhood under the Nazis. Slavs were *Untermenschen* (subhumans) slated for slavery and eventual eradication by the Nazis. Slave laborers in the German Reich were overwhelmingly Ukrainians, Poles, Russians, and Belarusians. So, too, prisoners of war were subjected to inhuman conditions (Dallin; Snyder, "Holocaust"). Millions of Slavs died as the front passed eastward in 1941–1942 and then westward in 1943–1944. To be sure, Slavs also committed anti-Semitic atrocities (Dobroszycki and Gurock); thousands served in the German *Polizei* or as concentration camp guards; hundreds of thousands joined military units such as the Russian Liberation Army or the Waffen SS (Andreyev). But their actions cannot negate the enormity of the suffering that millions of their innocent compatriots endured. Nor can their actions justify that suffering.[5]

---

5   Consider Claus Leggewie's astounding claim (4) that "Those who mobilize the 'GULag memory' often overlook, again consciously or unconsciously, that victims of Stalinism were often former collaborators of National Socialism."

4) By showing that binary morality breaks down in the Soviet Union and Eastern Europe, both for Jews and non-Jews, the Gulag suggests that binary morality may also be inappropriate to comprehending the Holocaust. If even some Jews could have been both victims and victimizers at some place and in some time, then it may not be unreasonable to surmise that some Germans could also have been victimizers *and* victims in some place and in some time. We know from Günter Grass and W. G. Sebald that some German victimizers were also victims of terrible and militarily unnecessary bombings in Hamburg, Dresden, and other cities. And we surely know, even without reading anything, that German children could have been only victims.

Such small distinctions raise the possibility that German victimizers may have been variably guilty. In line with binary morality's expectations, a German could only have joined the Nazis or the anti-Nazi resistance. In reality, he could also have joined the Wehrmacht, as a perceived lesser of two evils. He could have joined some Nazi civic organization. He could have not joined, but shown his loyalty, whether real or feigned, by enthusiastically participating in rallies and meetings. He could have refrained from taking part in such meetings and rallies, while remaining more or less loyal. He could have kept his disloyalty to himself and his friends. Or he could have grumbled in the kitchen (Evans 60). And so on. We know that there is always a plethora of choices in any morally complex situation, ranging from active support to active resistance and everything in between. And we should know that these choices entail different degrees of innocence or guilt.[6] The controversy over Günter Grass's revelation in August 2006 that he served in the Waffen SS as a youth shows as much. As even his critics appreciated, that choice was a moral lapse, but not a crime. And the more

---

Since Leggewie cannot not know that the vast majority of Stalinism's victims were killed or sent to camps in the 1930s—before collaboration with National Socialism was possible—his statement can only mean that the possibility of future collaboration justifies present murder—a terrifying moral proposition to say the least.

6   The life of Ernst von Salomon, the morally tainted author of the remarkable *Der Fragebogen*, perfectly illustrates these complexities.

significant moral failing was his silence about this lapse. As the Grass controversy demonstrated, there are differences between concentration camp executioners and cynical spies such as Putin and between them and average citizens who make bad choices or who fail to make good ones.

## Why the KGB Bar Is Possible

The moral logic of the Holocaust transforms Jews into victims and non-Jews into victimizers; the moral logic and reality of the Gulag transform everybody into both victim and victimizer. The binary morality of the Holocaust insists that all human beings be heroes; the fuzzy morality of the Gulag recognizes that all humans are just humans constantly confronted by the "fragility and imperceptibility of the line between good and evil, right and wrong." But because the Gulag's moral ambiguity concerns non-Jews *and* Jews, the Gulag undercuts binary morality. The Holocaust and the Gulag are not just incompatible moral tales; they are incompatible *and* intersecting moral tales. As a result, they cannot co-exist. Only one can be "correct."

We fail to respond to the KGB Bar because to recognize the Gulag as a mass murder worthy of categorical moral condemnation would be to challenge the sacred status of the Holocaust. The Gulag's messy moral system threatens the binary moral clarity of the Holocaust and, thus, its importance to German, Israeli/Jewish, and American identity. To express outrage at the Gulag is to recognize the historically contingent and politically constructed nature of binary morality and to admit the moral inappropriateness of notions of transgenerational and transhistorical collective innocence and collective guilt. To question the discursive hegemony of binary morality is also to undermine the legitimacy of German, Israeli, and American national identity and thus of Germany, Israel, and the United States. Like all Americans, the developed world's intellectual and artistic elites are caught in the discursive webs of this logic and cannot *see* the Gulag. Ironically, the KGB Bar is possible *precisely because* an SS Bar is impossible.

# References

Adelman, Jonathan R., ed. *Terror and Communist Politics: The Role of the Secret Police in Communist States.* Boulder, CO: Westview, 1984. Print.

Amis, Martin. *Koba the Dread: Laughter and the Twenty Million.* Toronto: Knopf, 2002. Print.

Andreyev, Catherine. *Vlasov and the Russian Liberation Movement.* Cambridge: Cambridge UP, 1987. Print.

Applebaum, Anne. *Gulag: A History.* New York: Anchor, 2003. Print.

Barkan, Elazar. *The Guilt of Nations: Restitution and Negotiating Historical Injustices.* Baltimore, MD: Johns Hopkins UP, 2000. Print.

Barron, John. *KGB: The Secret Work of Soviet Secret Agents.* New York: Bantam, 1974. Print.

Barron, John. *KGB Today: The Hidden Hand.* New York: Readers Digest, 1983. Print.

Berkhoff, Karel C. *Harvest of Despair: Life and Death in Ukraine under Nazi Rule.* Cambridge, MA: Harvard UP, 2004. Print.

Buruma, Ian. *The Wages of Guilt: Memories of War in Germany and Japan.* London: Phoenix, 2002. Print.

Buruma, Ian. "Why They Hate Japan." *New York Review of Books,* 21 Sept. 2006. Web. 26 March 2010. <http://www.nybooks.com/articles/article-preview?article_id=19300>.

Cohen, Roger. "German Normality Is Not Quite Normal Enough." *The Atlantic Times,* August 2006: 3. Print.

Conquest, Robert. *The Great Terror: Stalin's Purges of the Thirties.* New York: Collier, 1973. Print.

Conquest, Robert. *Kolyma: The Arctic Death Camps.* New York: Penguin, 1978. Print.

Conquest, Robert. *Inside Stalin's Secret Police: NKVD Politics, 1936-39.* Stanford, CA: Hoover Institution Press, 1985. Print.

Conquest, Robert. *Harvest of Sorrow: Soviet Collectivization and the Terror-Famine.* New York: Oxford UP, 1986. Print.

Courtois, Stephane et al, eds. *The Black Book of Communism.* Cambridge, MA: Harvard UP, 1999. Print.

"Cross Café." Web. 3 March 2010. <http://en.wikipedia.org/wiki/Cross_Cafe>.

Dallin, Alexander. *German Rule in Russia, 1941-1945: A Study in Occupation Policy.* London: Macmillan, 1957. Print.

Dallin, David and Boris Nicolaevsky. *Forced Labour in Soviet Russia.* London: Hollis & Carter, 1948. Print.

Deák, István. "Scandal in Budapest." *New York Review of Books*, 19 Oct. 2006. Web. 26 March 2010. <http://www.nybooks.com/articles/article-preview?article_id=19460>.

de Bellaigue, Christopher. "Left Out in Turkey." *New York Review of Books*, 14 July 2005: 43-47. Print.

Dobroszycki, Lucjan and Jeffrey S. Gurock, eds. *The Holocaust in the Soviet Union: Studies and Sources on the Destruction of the Jews in Nazi-Occupied Territories of the USSR, 1941-1945.* Armonk, NY: M.E. Sharpe, 1993. Print.

Dolgun, Alexander. *Alexander Dolgun's Story: An American in the Gulag.* New York: Random House, 1975. Print.

Evans, Richard J. "How Willing Were They?" *New York Review of Books*, 26 June 2008: 59-62. Print.

Fitzpatrick, Sheila. *Everyday Stalinism: Ordinary Life in Extraordinary Times.* Oxford: Oxford UP, 2000. Print.

Fousek, John. *To Lead the Free World: American Nationalism and the Cultural Roots of the Cold War.* Chapel Hill: U of North Carolina P, 2000. Print.

Giesen, Bernhard. *Die Intellektuellen und die Nation: Eine deutsche Achsenzeit.* Frankfurt: Suhrkamp, 1993. Print.

Ginzburg, Evgeniya. *Journey into the Whirlwind.* New York: Harcourt, Brace & World, 1967. Print.

Grass, Günter. *Crabwalk.* New York: Harcourt, 2003. Print.

Gray, John. "Communists and Nazis: Just as Evil?" *New York Review of Books*, 8 April 2010: 37-40. Print.

Grigorenko, Petro. *Memoirs.* New York: W.W. Norton, 1982. Print.

Handelman, Stephen. *Comrade Criminal: The Theft of the Second Russian Revolution.* London: Michael Joseph, 1994. Print.

Hayden, Robert M. "Genocide Denial" Laws as Secular Heresy: A Critical Analysis with Reference to Bosnia." *Slavic Review* 67, 2008: 384-407. Print.

Hrytsak, Yaroslav. "Nashe i duzhe nashe hore." *Krytyka* July-Aug. 2003: 12-14. Print.

Jack, Andrew. *Inside Putin's Russia: Can There Be Reform without Democracy?* Oxford: Oxford UP, 2004. Print.

Jaspers, Karl. *Die Schuldfrage.* Heidelberg: n.p., 1946. Print.

Kaminski, Andrzej J. *Konzentrationslager 1896 bis heute.* Munich: Piper, 1990. Print.

Kempe, Frederick. *Siberian Odyssey: A Voyage into the Russian Soul.* New York: Putnam, 1992. Print.

Knight, Amy W. *The KGB: Police and Politics in the Soviet Union*. Boston: Unwin Hyman, 1988. Print.

Kotkin, Stephen. *Magnetic Mountain: Stalinism as Civilization*. Berkeley: U of California P, 1995. Print.

Krugman, Paul. "How Did Economists Get It So Wrong?" *New York Times* 2 Sept. 2009. Web. 3 March 2010. <http://www.nytimes.com/2009/09/06/magazine/06Economic-t.html>.

Lebow, Jeff. "A Visit to the Hitler Bar." Web. 3 March 2010. <http://www.pusanweb.com/feature/hitlerbar/>.

Leggewie, Claus. "Equally Criminal? Totalitarian Experience and European Memory." *Eurozine*. Web. 26 March 2010. <http://www.eurozine.com/articles/2006-06-01-leggewie-en.html>.

Levi, Primo. *The Drowned and the Saved*. New York: Summit, 1988. Print.

Levytsky, Borys. *The Uses of Terror: The Soviet Secret Police, 1917–1970*. London: Sidgwick and Jackson, 1971. Print.

Lewy, Guenter. *Nazi Persecution of the Gypsies*. New York: Oxford UP, 2001. Print.

Libanova, Ella and Nataliia Levchuk, Emel'ian Rudnitskii, Nataliia Ryngach, Svetlana Poniakina, and Pavel Shevchuk. "Ukraina stradaet ot chrezmernoi smertnosti naseleniia v trudoaktivnom vozraste." Web. 21 April 2008. <http://www.polit.ru/research/2008/04/15/demoscope327_print.html>.

Malia, Martin. *The Soviet Tragedy: A History of Socialism in Russia, 1917–1991*. New York: Free Press, 1994. Print.

Mandelshtam, Nadezhda. *Hope Against Hope*. New York: Random House, 1999. Print.

Massing, Michael. "The Storm over the Israel Lobby." *New York Review of Books*, 8 June 2006: 64–73. Print.

Matlock, Jack. *Autopsy of an Empire: The American Ambassador's Account of the Collapse of the Soviet Union*. New York: Random House, 1995. Print.

Mearsheimer, John J. and Stephen M. Walt. *The Israel Lobby and U.S. Foreign Policy*. New York: Farrar, Strauss and Giroux, 2007. Print.

Medvedev, Roy. *Let History Judge: The Origins and Consequences of Stalinism*. New York: Knopf, 1971. Print.

Moore, Jr., Barrington. *Terror and Progress – U.S.S.R.* Cambridge, MA: Harvard UP, 1954. Print.

Moroz, Valentyn. "A Report from the Beria Reservation." *Ferment in the Ukraine*. Ed. Michael Browne. New York: Praeger, 1971: 119–153. Print.

Motyl, Alexander J. *Sovietology, Rationality, Nationality: Coming to Grips with Nationalism in the USSR*. New York: Columbia UP, 1990. Print.

Motyl, Alexander J. "Inventing Invention: The Limits of National Identity Formation." *Intellectuals and the Articulation of the Nation*. Eds. Ronald Grigor Suny and Michael D. Kennedy. Ann Arbor: U of Michigan P, 1999: 57–73. Print.

Osadchy, Mykhaylo. *Cataract*. New York: Harcourt Brace Jovanovich, 1976. Print.

Petropoulos, Jonathan and John K. Roth. *Gray Zones: Ambiguity and Compromise in the Holocaust and Its Aftermath*. New York: Berghahn, 2005. Print.

Popovych, Myroslav. "Volyn': nashe i vashe hore." *Krytyka* May 2003: 2–3. Print.

Remnick, David. *Lenin's Tomb: The Last Days of the Soviet Empire*. New York: Random House, 1993. Print.

Rosenbaum, Alan S., ed. *Is the Holocaust Unique? Perspectives on Comparative Genocide*. Boulder, CO: Westview, 2001. Print.

Rudy, Sayres S. "Pros and Cons: Americanism Against Islamism." 2005. TS.

Said, Edward. *Orientalism*. New York: Vintage, 1978. Print.

Scott, James C. *Weapons of the Weak: Everyday Forms of Peasant Resistance*. New Haven, CT: Yale UP, 1985. Print.

Sebald, W.G. *On the Natural History of Destruction*. New York: Random House, 2004. Print.

Shifrin, Avraham. *The First Guidebook of Prisons and Concentration Camps in the Soviet Union*. Toronto: Bantam, 1982. Print.

Slezkine, Yuri. *The Jewish Century*. Princeton, NJ: Princeton UP, 2004. Print.

Smith, Hedrick. *The Russians*. New York: Quadrangle, 1976. Print.

Snyder, Timothy. *The Reconstruction of Nations: Poland, Ukraine, Lithuania, Belarus, 1569–1999*. New Haven, CT: Yale UP, 2003. Print.

Snyder, Timothy. "Holocaust: The Ignored Reality." *New York Review of Books*, 16 July 2009. Web. 4 July 2009. <http://www.nybooks.com/articles/22875>.

Solzhenitsyn, Alexander. *The Gulag Archipelago*. New York: Harper & Row, 1973. Print.

von Salomon, Ernst. *Der Fragebogen*. Reinbek bei Hamburg: Rowohlt, 1997. Print.

Woychuk, Denis. "The KGB Bar—A Brief and Distorted History." Web. 22 March 2010. < http://kgbbar.com/bar/>.

Zertal, Idith. *Israel's Holocaust and the Politics of Nationhood*. Cambridge: Cambridge UP, 2005. Print.

# 7

# Building Bridges and Changing Landmarks
Theory and Concepts in the Study of Soviet Nationalities*

Remarkably, if perhaps unavoidably, there is a void where there should be none. As even a casual perusal of the respective literatures quickly ascertains, a huge chasm separates Soviet nationality studies from comparative ethnicity studies. Indeed, it is no exaggeration to say that there are virtually no points of contact between these kindred scholarly pursuits. Students of the Soviet nationality question appear to be as indifferent to the theoretical findings of comparativists as the latter are to the relevance to their studies of the Soviet multinational state. There are, to be sure, some notable exceptions to this generalization, yet they are so rare as, literally, to prove the rule.[1]

A condition such as this is anomalous, to say the least. One would expect Soviet nationality experts to draw extensively on the accumulated knowledge of their colleagues who study other countries and other continents; one would also expect comparativists to be interested in a huge country with a multitude of ethnic groups. Instead, we encounter a mystifying gap, one that contravenes our expectations as much as it violates the logical unity of two branches of one discipline.

---

\* First printed in: Alexander J. Motyl, ed., *Thinking Theoretically about Soviet Nationalities: History and Comparison in the Study of the USSR* (New York: Columbia University Press, 1992), pp. 255-270. Reprinted with permission of the original publisher.
1 The leading example of a scholar who is perfectly at home in both worlds is, of course, John A. Armstrong.

## I.

While it is the purpose of this volume to bridge this gap and to chart landmarks for future research, it is the task of this conclusion to sketch the reasons for the lack of communication between two intimately related scholarly enterprises. Explaining an absence is no easy task, and it may be best to approach the problem by considering its obverse. If we engage in a thought experiment and ask what the necessary and sufficient conditions of interaction have to be, we may be able to isolate just those factors the absence of which is a necessary condition. That their respective literatures be theoretical is sufficient. might account for the void that is my central concern.

I begin at the highest level of abstraction by disregarding the actual disciplines under discussion and considering only two ideal types, regional studies and comparative politics. Let us assume that these two disciplines are engaged in fruitful dialogue. How and why would such contact be able to come about? What are the necessary and sufficient conditions of such a dialogue? Without what can such interaction *not* occur? And with what must it occur? As I explain below, that the practitioners of both disciplines be aware of each other's existence is a necessary condition. That their respective literatures be theoretical is sufficient,

The first point—that intensive interaction cannot take place if regional area specialists and theorists do not know of each other's existence and scholarly pursuits—is so obvious as to be trivially true, yet, as will presently be clear, it goes a long way toward explaining the lack of cross-fertilization between Soviet nationality studies and comparative ethnicity studies. The second point is rather more subtle than the first. Once a condition of mutual awareness exists, then it suffices if both sets of literatures are theoretical, in fact or in aspiration, for them to build bridges and seek points of contact and inspiration. A closer look at theory, which Giovanni Sartori defines as a "body of systematically related generalizations of explanatory value,"[2] illustrates why this particular condition should qualify as sufficient. Theory, as comparatively inclined scholars know, is the point of comparison, and comparison, as theoretically inclined scholars know, is the lifeblood of theory. Those scholars who seek explanations can but compare so as to uncover cross-national similarities and differences that may be subsumed under generalizations.[3] In particular, theoretically inclined regional specialists will search for confirmation of their locally derived theories beyond · the borders of their region, just as comparativists will, sooner or later, test their generalizations in as wide a variety of regional settings as possible. Thus, if area studies and comparative politics share a dedication to theory, both will be on the look-out continually for relevant comparisons, for cases that validate or invalidate existing generalizations. With theory, therefore, dialogue must occur.

If we apply this analysis to the case under consideration — the relationship between Soviet nationality studies and comparative ethnicity studies — we can begin to isolate the factors responsible for their isolation from each other. Sad to say, both necessary and sufficient conditions have been missing, to a greater or lesser extent, from that relationship. First, and most painful, is the fact that, with some exceptions, the practitioners of both disciplines have not followed each other's writings with any degree of interest or consistency. Lack of such awareness compounds, but does not produce, the second problem — that of theoretical inclinations. Here the diagnosis is mixed. Clearly, comparativists attempt to be theoretical; just as clearly, Soviet nationality experts generally do not.[4] We can restate these conclusions in the form of three questions: Why have comparativists by and large

---

2    Giovanni Sartori, "Guidelines for Concept Analysis," in Sartori, ed., *Social Science Concepts* (Beverly Hills, CA: Sage, 1984), p. 84.
3    For extended discussion of this issue, see Philip Kitcher and Wesley C. Salmon, eds., *Scientific Explanation* (Minneapolis: University of Minnesota Press, 1989).
4    For a similar evaluation, see David Laitin, "The National Uprisings in the Soviet Union: A Review Article," *World Politics*, forthcoming.

ignored the Soviet experience in their studies? Why have Soviet nationality experts been so reluctant to expand their vision to regions and problems outside their immediate areas of interest? And, why have Soviet nationality experts avoided theory?

That comparativists should overlook the USSR when it offers so rich a source of comparative study—a country of fifteen republics, over one hundred nationalities, and a stated commitment to the resolution of the nationality question—cannot be explained in terms either of the country's inaccessibility or of the relative lack of sources, as the USSR is manifestly neither much less accessible nor much less studied than many of the third world countries that attract the attention of comparativists.[5] Neither will it do to suggest that there is too little ethnic "activity"—strikes, riots, movements. struggles, and the like—in the USSR to warrant outside attention.[6] Rather, inattention appears to derive from two sources, one characteristic of comparative ethnicity studies, the other of Soviet nationality studies.

By and large comparative theories have been premised on one initial condition that immediately excluded the USSR from theoretical consideration. Theories of ethnicity, be they organized around modernization, political conflict, culture, or the like. required that the politic arena be relatively open or, to put the matter somewhat differently, that the state not be totalitarian. Because the Soviet Union has historically been just that, the Soviet state was presumed to be capable of directing, controlling, and managing ethnic processes to such a degree that

---

5    The literature on Soviet nationalities is vast and rapidly growing. Among the best recent empirical studies are: Hélène Carrère d'Encausse, *Islam and the Russian Empire* (Berkeley: University of California Press, 1988); Romuald J. Misiunas and Rein Taagepera, *The Baltic States: Years of Dependence, 1940-1980* (Berkeley: University of California Press, 1983); Martha Brill Olcott, *The Kazakhs* (Stanford, CA: Hoover Institution Press, 1987); Ronald Grigor Suny, *The Making of the Georgian Nation* (Stanford, CA: Hoover Institution Press, 1988); Orest Subtelny, *Ukraine: A History* (Toronto: University of Toronto Press, 1988).

6    See Ludmilla Alexeyeva and Valery Chalidze, *Mass Rioting in the USSR* (Silver Spring, MD: Foundation for Soviet Studies, 1985).

they lost the relative "naturalness" and "spontaneity" that would have made them comparable with similar processes in noncommunist settings. Whether or not this view of the USSR was valid need not concern us here. What is important is that its plausibility, which was grounded in the intersubjective perception of the incomparably greater directive capacity of the Soviet communist state, has been undermined no less than the Soviet state's totalitarian controls have crumbled under Gorbachev's misrule. As the USSR continues on its transition to some variant of authoritarianism or democracy, or perhaps degenerates into chaos, the problem of initial conditions will resolve itself automatically and comparativists will invariably begin seeing the Soviet Union's relevance for their own studies.

The second source of inattention is located within Soviet nationality studies, more specifically, in its marginal status within Sovietology. For reasons that I have discussed elsewhere, Sovietology's fixation on Russia in general and Moscow in particular has transformed what should be the core of the study of the Union of Soviet Socialist *Republics* into a peripheral, almost irrelevant, pursuit.[7] Indeed, Soviet nationality studies has traditionally been so marginal a component of Sovietology that nationality experts were rarely considered bona fide Sovietologists, to the point of actually being severely disadvantaged in the competition for jobs and grants. No less distressing, in marginalizing Soviet nationality studies, Sovietology has effectively concealed it from the view of outside disciplines. Even if comparativists had seen the USSR as theoretically relevant, they would have been hard pressed to pierce the shroud of obscurity draped over Soviet nationality studies by Sovietology. Fortunately, if somewhat belatedly for a generation of excellent scholars forced to subsist on the margins of the profession, here, too, *perestroika* has effected a fundamental shift. Now that the

---

7   I develop this argument in Alexander J. Motyl, "'Sovietology in One Country' or Comparative Nationality Studies?" *Slavic Review* (Spring 1989), 48 (1):83-88.

nationality question has assumed center stage in the Soviet Union—indeed, Nagorno-Karabakh has almost become a household word, even in the West—Sovietology will have to end nationality studies' exile. And when it does, a vast and suddenly relevant literature will be exposed to the scrutiny of interested comparativists.

There is, then, cause for some optimism. If the Soviet Union continues to change, comparativists will be impelled to embark on a rapprochement with their Sovietological colleagues. As they do so, however, it will be increasingly incumbent on the latter to come at least halfway. Can Soviet nationality experts reciprocate? In answering this question, we would do well to consider why they were isolated from comparativists in the past and whether the conditions of their isolation have changed, as they have for comparativists, in the Gorbachev period.

## II.

Two factors account for the isolation of Soviet nationality studies from comparative ethnicity studies, and the first of these has already been noted above: marginality within the Sovietological profession. Just as marginality has kept Soviet nationality studies hidden from outside view, so, too, it has impelled nationality experts to concentrate their efforts on correcting this condition by, logically enough, seeking integration into their immediate intellectual environment, Sovietology. In this sense, marginality has distorted Soviet nationality studies' potentially multiple vocations by forcing it to pay exclusive attention to Sovietology and its agenda and to subordinate, if not indeed ignore, aspirations toward rapprochement with its theoretical cousin, comparative ethnicity studies. As I noted above, however, marginality now is or soon will be a thing of the past. Once Soviet nationality studies is fully accepted into the fold of Sovietology, once it becomes as important to Sovietology as the nationality question is to the Soviet Union, its major intellectual ambition will have been fulfilled and new frontiers—integration with comparative ethnicity studies—can then be pursued.

The second reason for the isolation of nationality studies from comparative ethnicity studies involves theory, or more precisely, the lack of it. That Soviet nationality studies is so profoundly atheoretical is curious inasmuch as it is comparative by its very nature—there are, after all fifteen republics—it should be naturally inclined toward theory-building, if only within the Soviet context. Yet, this inclination has been suppressed, and, once again, the reason must be sought, not in Soviet nationality studies, but in Sovietology. I submit that Soviet nationality experts have traditionally evinced little interest in theory because their colleagues in mainstream Sovietology, who set the tone for the discipline in general and its marginal subfields in particular, were—and still are—averse to pursuing an explicitly theoretical understanding of their subject matter. It is no less ironic that most Sovietologists would dispute this proposition than it is significant that genuinely theoretical scholars would acknowledge its validity.[8] A recent assessment by Frederic J. Fleron, Jr. and Erik P. Hoffmann is worth quoting at some length:

> Multidisciplinary area studies and policy-oriented research dominated Sovietology in the 1970s and the 1980s. As if in response to a central directive, Western academics mastered or dabbled in new fields of Soviet studies. Some produced comparative research on different stages of Soviet and Russian history or creative contextual analyses at the interstices of various disciplines. Others parlayed their geographical area expertise into political influence and pecuniary reward through government and business consulting. A few senior academic specialists eagerly pursued temporary government assignments and business opportunities, and many junior specialists involuntarily abandoned academe because of the vagaries of the job market. Fewer and fewer Sovietologists sought to "construct" social

---

8   See the argument made by Joseph LaPalombara, "Monoliths or Plural Systems Through Conceptual Lenses Darkly," *Studies in Comparative Communism* (Autumn 1975), 8(3), 305-332.

science theory (macro-, middle-, or micro-level), and their professional ties to core disciplines diminished.⁹

Readers who disagree with this assessment may want to consider Gabriel A. Almond's thoughtful defense of "model fitting in communism studies," which claims to illustrate the theoretical ambitions of Sovietology and related disciplines, but which actually supports Fleron and Hoffmann's contention.¹⁰ Ironically, Almond's discussion of the various "models" that have inspired Sovietology—ranging from totalitarianism to political culture to pluralism—persuasively, if unwittingly, shows that Sovietology's overriding concern with "fitting" Soviet reality to models is pretheoretical at best and antitheoretical at worst.

The problem, of course, is not with models, but with model fitting, which misconstrues the point of models. Models are explanatory devices that offer simplified pictures of how things work; models are means toward, and not the end of, understanding. They decidedly are not all-encompassing structures into the parameters of which reality can be squeezed. Sovietology's elusive quest for the one model that, magically, will finally make complete sense of all of Soviet reality is about as quixotic as the search for a unified theory of the social world.

No less important, model fitting is inherently inimical to conceptual rigor. As its primary focus is on forcing reality onto the Procrustean bed of a model, model fitting inevitably downplays, if not indeed ignores, the priority of concepts and their meanings. Model fitting has the relationship between reality and concepts backwards: it is not the former that should be made to fit the latter, but the latter that should be superimposed on, or tailored to, the former. Worse still,

---

9   Frederic J. Fleron, Jr. and Erik P. Hoffmann, "Sovietology and *perestroika*. Methodology, Madness, and Lessons from the Past," unpublished paper (July 1990), p. 3.
10  Gabriel A. Almond, *A Discipline Divided: Schools and Sects in Political Science* (Newbury Park, CA: Sage, 1990), pp. 66-116.

model fitting blithely ignores the ontological interrelatedness of concepts and the interdependence of meanings in general. By enthroning one model, model fitting suggests that reality can be apprehended in a fundamentally nonconceptual manner and that concepts can be ascribed meanings independently of other concepts and their meanings.[11]

Just as problematic is that model fitting facilitates the avoidance of comparison. Inasmuch as its goal is confined to subsuming reality under some one framework, model fitting denies the importance of comparative enquiry to understanding. To be sure, model fitting does not reject comparison out of hand. Its mission is so self-regarding, however, as actively to discourage it and, thus, to weaken the theoretical impulse.

Finally, model fitting explicitly contravenes the possibility of explanation. At best, models show *how* things work; explanation, in contrast, is concerned with *why* things work as they do. Only theory, therefore, can explain the regularities identified by models. By substituting models for theory, however, model fitting reverses the proper relationship between theory and models, thereby undermining the quest for explanation that models can so usefully facilitate. Close to four decades of model fitting—and still so little theory— strongly suggest that this proposition is true.

## III.

How are we to explain Sovietology's manifest incapacity to think theoretically about the Soviet Union and its component political parts? There are several answers to this question, some simple, others complex, and none flattering to the profession. First, Sovietologists have historically tended to be descriptive in their approach, a fact that has much to do with the professional inclinations of the founding fathers –practical

---

11  For a discussion of these issues, see Alexander J. Motyl, *Sovietology, Rational, Nationality: Coming to Grips with Nationalism in the USSR* (New York: Columbia University Press, 1990), pp. 46-50.

revolutionaries, emigre politicians, journalists, writers, intelligence officers, and diplomats.[12] It is at least arguable that this tradition, like all traditions, is hard to shake and that model fitting is the best one can hope for from so ideographic a profession. Second, these ideographic inclinations are continually reinforced by policy makers and the media, and insofar as Sovietologists often act as advisers to the government or as sources for the media, it makes sense for them to eschew the complexities of theory and to focus on "the facts."[13] Finally, unlike most other social scientists, historically Sovietologists really have faced substantial empirical obstacles to their work, a difficulty that favors fact-gathering strategies over explicitly theoretical ones.

Although these explanations have some validity, too much and too little has changed in recent years for them to suffice. After all, Sovietology is now the preserve of professional scholars; government and media pressures are arguably no greater now than thirty years ago; while academic exchanges, journalists, and political detente have opened the USSR to scholarly scrutiny in a manner unknown to the scholars of the Stalin era. Despite two changes and one constant, contemporary Sovietology still remains only minimally theoretical—and, as I have argued elsewhere, may have become even less so in the 1970s and 1980s.[14]

The inadequacy of these factors impels us to consider another, at first glance rather less obvious, explanatory variable: Sovietology's well-nigh fundamentalist rejection of the "totalitarian model." Why this disregard, which is perfectly legitimate, should be so impassioned is, at least at first glance, somewhat of a mystery, as there is nothing intrinsic to the concept of totalitarianism, *as a concept,* that should call forth the

---

12  See Walter Laqueur, *The Fate of the Revolution* (New York: Collier Books, 1987), pp. 1-32; Barry M. Katz, *Foreign Intelligence: Research and Analysis in the Office of Strategic Services, 1942-1945* (Cambridge, MA: Harvard University Press, 1989).
13  See Stephen F. Cohen, *Rethinking the Soviet Experience* (New York: Oxford University Press, 1985), pp. 3-37.
14  See Motyl, *Sovietology, Rationality, Nationality,* pp. 1-13.

extreme revulsion and ridicule it encounters in so much of the literature.[15] After all, all concepts are more or less useful and more or less "accurate," but none can, by its very nature as a concept, be considered repulsive. Concepts may represent repulsive or ludicrous "things," but it is the moral overtone of the thing and not its conceptual underpinnings that make it repulsive. Contemporary Sovietology's continuing incapacity to deal with totalitarianism in a matter-of-fact manner may therefore have to do more with Sovietology as a profession than with totalitarianism as a concept. Indeed, it is quite possible that ideological persuasions, generational dynamics, and professional hubris hold the key to Sovietology's embarrassingly exaggerated ill-will toward totalitarianism.

A prima facie case for the priority of these factors might go along the following lines. First, that totalitarianism is tarred as an inherently conservative cold war concept says more about its detractors' own political predilections than it does about the concept's actual content, if only because totalitarianism is central to the discourse of decidedly progressive dissidents and democrats—as well as officials, such as Gorbachev[16]—in the USSR and Eastern Europe. Second, that totalitarianism is largely rejected by scholars who came of age in the rebellious 1960s and is currently returning to favor among the generation of the1980s suggests that the developmental years of the former, during which they were reacting to *the* conceptual preferences of their teachers, contain the seeds of their continuing rejection of totalitarianism. Finally, whatever the utility of the concept, the intolerance with which discussions of it are greeted suggests that the potential return of totalitarian terminology represents a

---

15  For an excellent discussion of totalitarianism, see Giovanni Sartori, "Totalitarianism: An Exercise in Conceptual Analysis," unpublished paper (1991).
16  Jacques Rupnik, "Totalitarianism Revisited," in John Keane, ed., *Civil Society and the State* (London: Verso, 1988), pp. 263-290; *New York Times* (November 1, 1990).

fundamental threat to the self-perceptions of scholars whose careers have been built on the repudiation of the notion.

Whatever the reasons for these attitudes, the *intensity* of Sovietology's rejection of totalitarianism—and not, I stress, the rejection itself—has had decidedly deleterious consequences for the profession as a branch of *the* social sciences. Once again, a brief excursion into the nature of theory tells us why. Regardless of the level at which theories are positioned—grand, middle-range, or low—all theories represent coherent complexes of assumptions, concepts, hypotheses, and evidence that relate particular issues to general dynamics. Inevitably, then, every bonafide theoretical explanation of any aspect of a political system relates that particular aspect to the general system and the larger forces that mold it.[17] In this sense, the *analysis* of particulars must have systemic underpinnings—it must be inextricably bound to some countervailing *synthesis*—in order to qualify as a theory; otherwise, it is just analysis. There is, of course, nothing wrong with the rigorous examination of parts of the Soviet system that analysis, or its offshoot, model fitting, does so well, but it is not, alas, theory. That can be attained only if greater attention is paid to the USSR's explicitly systemic characteristics, which, scholars may decide, are or are not best termed totalitarian, post-totalitarian, authoritarian, sultanistic, monist, or something else. The choice is theirs. All that matters is that a choice, any choice, be made.

It should be clear now why the all-consuming rejection of totalitarianism has placed Sovietology into a theoretical bind. Due to the exaggerated passion of totalitarianism's critics, the totalitarian model and everything it represented—in particular, an interest in explicitly systemic syndromes and the state—have been lumped together and consigned to the status of nonissues. As systemic features were marginalized, if not indeed purged, they came to be replaced with what

---

17  On these aspects of theory, see Douglas A. Chalmers, "Interpretive Frameworks: A Structure of Theory in Political Science," unpublished paper (1987).

were considered the only issues worth pursuing: such particulars as interest groups, bureaucracies, elites, classes, and the like. As most Sovietologists have been unwilling to discuss the USSR systemically, they have ipso facto proven incapable of being truly theoretical, even when paying attention to concepts, refining their statistical techniques, and actively aspiring to theory. At best, most Sovietologists could only analyze politically relevant phenomena and engage in model fitting, but, without connecting the analyses to systemic considerations, they could not make the jump to theory itself. The fact that wide-ranging discussions of Sovietology's theoretical options were so prevalent in the late 1960s suggests that the impulse for abandoning model fitting was there.[18] Alas, the countervailing force—"totalitarianism bashing"—proved too strong for the profession to make the great leap forward the times demanded of it.

Can such a leap still take place? Once again, *perestroika* comes to Sovietology's rescue. The fact that the USSR is obviously changing from something to something else will inevitably induce Sovietologists to consider just what these two "somethings" are. And the face that Soviet scholars and officials, along with growing numbers of graduate students who are rediscovering Merle Fainsod, Leonard Schapiro, and other early Sovietologists,[19] are increasingly referring to the pre-*perestroika* Soviet Union as totalitarian should inject greater sobriety into Sovietology's treatment of the concept. If both trends hold up, analysis may well assume systemic overtones, Sovietology may well become theoretical, models may well replace model fitting, and Soviet nationality studies, which increasingly will move to the center of Sovietology, may well be in the position to become theoretical as well.

---

18 Outstanding examples of Sovietology's potential for theory are Frederic Fleron, Jr., ed., *Communist Studies and the Social Sciences: Essays on Methodology and Empirical Theory* (Chicago, IL: Rand McNally, 1969) and Roger E. Kanet, ed., *The Behavioral Revolution and Communist Studies* (New York: The Free Press, 1971).
19 Merle Fainsod's *How Russia Is Ruled* and Leonard Schapiro's *The Communist Party of the Soviet Union* are still classics.

## IV.

There are, thus, not inconsequential reasons for viewing the likelihood of a rapprochement between Soviet nationality studies and comparative ethnicity studies with some optimism — and all thanks to *perestroika*. Gorbachev may or may not succeed in restructuring the USSR, but his policies have already transformed Sovietology in general and Soviet nationality and comparative ethnicity studies in particular. *Perestroika* has exposed the inadequacy of Sovietology's unrestrained opposition to totalitarianism, it has ended the marginality of Soviet nationality studies, and it has exploded the exceptionalism attributed to the USSR by comparative ethnicity studies.

Sovietology can facilitate this rapprochement by reintroducing explicitly systemic concepts into the study of the Soviet Union. Such concepts are necessary not only for generating genuine theory, but also for coping with *perestroika's* enormous impact on the USSR in general and on the nationality question in particular. What will remain of the USSR and what will the system be like several years from now may be unanswerable questions, although "little" and "chaotic" might not be inappropriate answers.[20] Rather more certain is that the Sovietized nations, having irrevocably become bona fide historical and political subjects, will no longer be mere receptacles of language and carriers of ethnicity. After *perestroika*, study of the Sovietized nations will require going beyond such traditional concerns of Soviet nationality studies as social mobility, educational attainments, language, book publishing, and the like and embarking on investigations with a distinctly historical-political focus.

Six concepts suggest themselves as ideal vehicles for viewing the USSR in a manner that is potentially theoretical and explicitly political: empire, state, political economy, transition,

---

20  For an elaboration of this argument, see Alexander J. Motyl, "Totalitarian Collapse, Imperial Disintegration, and the Rise of the Soviet West," in Michael Mandelbaum, ed., *Rise of Nations in the Soviet Union* (New York: Council on Foreign Relations, 1991).

breakdown, and revolution. As I illustrate below, each of these concepts is tailor-made for integrating Soviet nationality studies into Sovietology, for generating theory, and for building theoretical bridges between Soviet nationality studies and comparative ethnicity studies as well as between Sovietology and comparative politics. None of these concepts should be conceived of as a model to which Soviet reality can be fitted once and for all. Concepts, after all, neither suggest how things work, nor explain why, and although they are necessary components of theories and models, concepts are neither theories nor models. All that concepts do is isolate phenomena by distinguishing something from that which that thing is not. Concepts, thus, can figure in both the *explanans* and the *explanandum,* but they are never either of the two.[21]

The term *empire* is not a pejorative designation for the Soviet Union, but the source of insight into its dynamics, the basis for comparing the USSR with similar such historical entities, and the key to merging the USSR's nationality dimension with its institutional structure along center-periphery lines. Empire, as Michael W. Doyle writes, "is a relationship, formal or informal, in which one state controls the effective political sovereignty of another political society."[22] By this standard, the USSR is an empire both with regard to its titular republics and to its former holdings in Eastern Europe. Not only does the concept of empire hold open the possibility of comparing the republics with the former people's democracies of Eastern Europe — a research project that is the order of the day in light of the fact that the collapse of communism in Eastern Europe and the progressive dissolution of the Soviet system are obviously related phenomena — but it also suggests that comparing the Soviet empire with those of the Romanovs, Hohenzollerns, Habsburgs, Ottomans, and others could produce theoretical insights into the emergence, maintenance, decline, and

---

21 See Sartori, "Guidelines for Concept Analysis."
22 Michael W. Doyle, *Empires* (Ithaca: Cornell University Press, 1986), p. 45.

collapse of empires in general and of continental empires in particular.[23] Finally, *empires* are explicitly political relationships of domination and, as such, they transform the ethnic subordinates inhabiting imperial peripheries from ethnolinguistic categories into participants in a profoundly political game.

The second such suggestive concept is the *state*. Whether or not political institutions were ever left out of political science to the degree that supporters of the statist perspective insist (a point Almond vigorously disputes) is immaterial.[24] Clearly, in comparison to the new institutionalists' current infatuation with the state, the earlier period was characterized by a relative underestimation of political institutions. Even so, that the state should have seemed to matter less is understandable in light of the kinds of systems that were being studied in the 1950s and 1960s. The countries of the developed West did appear to be pluralist (and appearances may, of course, have been misleading), while the newly independent third world polities were still too young to be noticeably state-dominated, and, quite reasonably, they were analyzed in terms of the frameworks that were used with respect to Western Europe and the United States.

In contrast, the Soviet Union has always been characterized by a state that was enormously strong by any definition. Indeed, post-Stalinist developments notwithstanding, the USSR retained a formidable state for much of the 1960s, 1970s, and 1980s. It may have attempted to do more than it could, it may have been inefficient, but, once again, by any definition of state "strength," the Soviet state was strong. This, of course, is precisely what Samuel P. Huntington observed in *Political*

---

[23] See, for example, Alexander J. Motyl, "From Imperial Decay to Imperial Collapse: The Fall of the Soviet Empire in Comparative Perspective," in Richard Rudolph, *ed., Great Power Ethnic Politics: The Habsburg Empire and the Soviet Union* (New York: St. Martin's Press, 1992).

[24] See Gabriel A. Almond, "The Return to the State," and the critique by Eric A. Nordlinger, Theodore J. Lowi, and Sergio Fabbrini, *American Political Science Review* (September 1988), 82(3):853-901.

*Order in Changing Societies,* and rightfully so.[25] The state, in other words, never left communist systems of its own will. There would be no need to "bring it back in," had not the state been expelled by a generation of Sovietologists who replaced the so-called "totalitarian model" with a view of the Soviet system as just an aggregate of diverse outputs and inputs.

Introducing the concept of the state to Soviet studies makes enormous sense, therefore, because it could help bring the USSR back into political science as well as enable comparativists to test the validity of statist perspectives in a vastly larger context. It is remarkable, for instance, that the most prominent recent example of the statist literature, Peter Evans's *Bringing the State Back In,* has nothing to say about communist systems.[26] Moreover, bringing the Soviet state back in has two immediately salutary consequences: first, it embeds the Soviet nations within the context of political organizations with effective monopolies of violence and extractive and administrative jurisdiction in some territory, and, second, it frees them from the hold of vague allocators of still vaguer values, such as "political systems." States can but ascribe political significance to all their subjects for the simple reason that states, as structures of domination, are so political.[27] In contrast, political systems are far too involved with the goods, services, and values that concern, not genuinely political actors involved in hierarchical relationships, but mere cultural and linguistic categories.

The third concept is that of *political economy.* Regardless of what political economy actually is, and Martin Staniland

---

25 Samuel P. Huntington, *Political Order in Changing Societies* (New Haven, CT: Yale University Press, 1968).
26 Peter B. Evans et al., eds., *Bringing the State Back In* (Cambridge: Cambridge University Press, 1985).
27 Clearly, my use of "political," as controversial a term as any in the social sciences, imbues it with a strong, though by no means overwhelming, coercive component. See Dick Howard, *Defining the Political* (Minneapolis: University of Minnesota Press, 1989); Giovanni Sartori, "The Essence of the Political in Carl Schmitt," *Journal of Theoretical Politics* (January 1989), 1(1):63-75.

suggests that it is very many, perhaps far too many, things,[28] the essence of the "approach" is to ask questions about the relationship between political power and economic forces: How do the two interact? How do the two constrain each other? How do they influence each other? At least one reason why political economy was somewhat late in coming to Western scholarship is that politics and markets long appeared to be, and to a large extent actually were, different spheres of activity. There was and is, on the other hand, no similarly "objective" reason for rejecting political economy approaches in the study of such formerly communist systems as the USSR.

It is surely a truism to suggest that the relationship between politics and economics is of fundamental importance to the functioning of communist systems; (It was Lenin, after all, who insisted that under communism politics is economics.) Communist states are or, more precisely, *were* intrusive entities that attempted to manage the economy actively or, minimally, to meddle continually in its affairs. Such quintessentially economic issues as prices, production, labor, trade, investment, and construction are therefore central to the structure and policies of communist states. In turn, the influence of the economy on the communist state is profound, because of the unusually tight "fit" between the two.

One consequence of this fit is that unsuccessful economic policies inevitably have massive repercussions on the legitimacy, effectiveness and stability of the state, as, say, in Poland in the 1970s–1980s. Another consequence is, as Wlodzimierz Brus argues, that the loosening of the state's grip on the economy may facilitate the generation of social forces that could challenge its dominant political role.[29] For our purposes, however, the most important consequence is that the

---

28  Martin Staniland, *What is Political Economy?* (New Haven, CT: Yale University Press, 1985).
29  See Wlodzimierz Brus, *The Economics and Politics of Socialism* (London: Routledge & Kegan Paul, 1973); "Political Pluralism and Markets in Communist Systems," in Susan Gross Solomon, ed., *Pluralism in the Soviet Union* (New York: St. Martin's Press, 1983), pp. 108-30.

political economy approach assigns political significance to the economic role of the Soviet republics.³⁰ Political economy transforms their largely administrative economic functions into a political variable that can but have some impact on the state and empire within which the Soviet nations are embedded. In a word, political economy bridges the gap between the central political authorities and the peripheral economic bureaucracies and, thus, forms a coherent whole of empire, state, economy, and nationality.

In contrast to the preceding three concepts, which drew attention to features of the system, the next three focus on systemic change. It is only recently that Sovietologists began exploring the comparative politics literature on *transitions* in Latin America and other parts of the world, even though their own current focus, *perestroika*, seems to be prime example of a transition.³¹ By the same token, the fact that comparativists were so late in appreciating the magnitude of the processes taking place in the USSR and Eastern Europe could but undermine the validity of their own observations. If, indeed, the Soviet Union is in the process of making a transition from one form of regime to another, then Soviet strategies for effecting such a typological shift are obviously of value to studying transitions in general and transitions to democracy in particular. The reverse is also true: authoritarian-to-democratic transitions, especially in such multinational settings as South Africa and Spain, are surely of relevance to understanding ongoing processes in the USSR. Moreover, they can illuminate what the Soviet leadership must, but perhaps due to structural or other constraints cannot, do to

---

30 See Donna Bahry, *Outside Moscow: Power, Politics, and Budgetary Policy in the Soviet Republics* (New York: Columbia University Press, 1987).
31 On transitions, see Guillermo O'Donnell et al., eds., *Transitions from Authoritarian Rule: Comparative Perspectives* (Baltimore, MD: Johns Hopkins University Press, 1986); Guillermo O'Donnell and Philippe C. Schmitter, *Transitions from Authoritarian Rule: Tentative Conclusions About Uncertain Democracies* (Baltimore, MD: Johns Hopkins University Press, 1986); Samuel P. Huntington, "Will More Countries Become Democratic?" *Political Science Quarterly* (1985), 99(2):193-218.

effect a genuine and durable transition to some approximation of democracy.

Less generous interpretations of current developments in the Soviet Union might center on such concepts as *breakdown* or *revolution*.[32] After all, *transition* implies that the USSR is proceeding toward some definable end; especially in light of the failed anti-Gorbachev coup of August 19, 1991, one could just as easily argue that *perestroika* has accomplished little more than effect a breakdown of the Brezhnevite system, thereby creating all the necessary and sufficient conditions for a revolution, one that is likely to entail the collapse of the totalitarian state, the fall of the empire, and the transformation of the republics into sovereign entities. Thus, optimists may speak of transition, pessimists of breakdown, doomsayers of revolution. Whatever one's choice of concept, however, the important point for our purposes is that each can accommodate the fact that the formerly Soviet nations have alighted the world-historical stage and become the central actors in the USSR's transformation. It is not just that the nationality response to Gorbachev's initiatives may or may not affect the transition and perhaps produce a breakdown or lead to a revolution, but that these changes, whatever their designation, necessarily involve the transformation of an empire and a multinational state and, as a result, inevitably have a significant nationality dimension.

## V.

Empire, state, political economy, transition, breakdown, and revolution — the list of systemic concepts can be easily extended. Naturally, there is no reason why students of the Sovietized nations should employ only these six concepts or only systemic concepts. Even the notion of political system, after all, is inherently systemic; it, too, can easily serve as a bridge to theory,

---

32   On breakdowns, see, among others, Juan J. Linz, *The Breakdown of Democratic Regimes: Crisis, Breakdown, and Reequilibration*, (Baltimore, MD: John Hopkins University Press, 1978). The best work on the concept of revolution is Mark N. Hagopian, *The Phenomenon of Revolution* (New York: Harper & Row, 1974).

but only if, I suspect, Sovietologists finally inject some bona fide political content into it. And insofar as thinking theoretically also requires thinking conceptually, all concepts—even nonsystemic ones—are useful, if perhaps unequally so.

For the period of Sovietology's own transition to theoretical awareness, however, systemic concepts with explicitly political connotations will be key. Only such concepts can enable Sovietology to incorporateSoviet nationality studies on a basis that is appropriate to the nations' new stature after *perestroika*, and only they can help Sovietology overcome the gap between the particular and the general. Best of all, only systemic concepts can provide Sovietology and Soviet nationality studies with the conceptual bridges and the theoretical landmarks necessary for thinking theoretically-and, thus, embarking on the long road to rapprochement with the social sciences in general and comparative ethnicity studies in particular.

# 8

# Negating the Negation
## Russia, Not-Russia, and the West[*]

There is a savage irony at the core of Sovietology. Whereas the study of Soviet history and politics should have concerned itself with everything Soviet, it traditionally focused almost exclusively only on what was Russian. By ignoring the non-Russians as something not Russian and, thus, by implication, inconsequential, "Sovietology in one country" contradicted its own premises and, thereby, turned in upon, indeed even negated, itself.[1] By setting the center over the periphery, by detaching the center from the periphery that defined the center as a center, Sovietology in effect emptied the center of its "centrality." In so doing, Sovietology transformed itself into an inauthentic form of Russian studies — inauthentic in the sense of ostensibly being concerned with the Soviet Union, while, in reality, actually pursuing the study of something with which Sovietology was ostensibly unconcerned.

The issue is not of exclusively intellectual interest. As its never-ending surprise at recent events in the USSR has shown, mainstream Sovietology was incapable of incorporating the "nationality question" into its research agenda. Sovietology's inability to foresee *perestroika* may be forgiven; it is, after all, in the nature of revolutions from above to be unexpected. What is less comprehensible, however, is that the teachings of mainstream Sovietology left its practitioners wholly unprepared for the explosion of nationality unrest that followed in the wake of *perestroika*. So unexpected a shock, so rude an awakening, demands a Kuhnian paradigm shift within Sovietology; it necessitates a

---

[*] First printed in: *Nationalities Papers*, vol. 22, no. 1 (Spring 1994), pp. 263-271. Reprinted with permission of the original publisher.
[1] See Alexander J. Motyl, "'Sovietology in One Country' or Comparative Nationality Studies?" *Slavic Review*, vol. 48, no. 1 (spring 1989), pp. 83-88.

veritable revolution in the manner in which normal Sovietology is practiced.[2] At a minimum, Sovietology — or, more accurately perhaps, post-Sovietology — will have to abandon its self-contradictory concern with incomplete halves and finally integrate the periphery into the center and transform the non-Russians into something more than a negation of that in which Sovietology is really interested.

## I.

How did Soviet studies come to be enmeshed in such a web of contradictory aspirations? How are we to explain its remarkable inability to see what it claimed to be looking at? How are we to understand the fact that the central presence in Sovietology was in fact an absence? I shall propose two sets of overlapping answers, the first intrinsic to Sovietology, the second characteristic of the larger culture within which American Sovietology is embedded.

Part of the answer to Sovietology's blindness to the non-Russians involves the profession's origins and development as well as the historical continuity between the Romanov empire and its successor, the Soviet Union. The tsarist empire was Russia, while the Soviet Union, whose borders were so similar to those of the tsarist state, was the handiwork of Russia and Russians. In both systems the non-Russians were indeed peripheral: they were located on the periphery, and they were marginal to the workings of the political system. Small wonder that the first students of the new Soviet state were former students of Russia who transposed their earlier categories onto the new reality.[3] Moreover, to equate the Soviet Union with Russia made special sense after Stalin and his successors proved determined to make that same equation.

---

2 Thomas S. Kuhn, *The Structure of Scientific Revolutions,* 2nd ed: (Chicago, IL: University of Chicago Press, 1970).

3 For a discussion of the origins of Sovietology, see Walter Laqueur, *The Fate of the Revolution.* (New York: Collier Books, 1987). See also Alexander Dallin, "Bias and Blunders in American Studies on the USSR," *Slavic Review,* vol. 32, no. 3 (September 1973), pp. 560-576; Stephen F. Cohen, *Rethinking the Soviet Experience.* (New York: Oxford University Press, 1985), pp. 3-37.

Nevertheless, the appeal to historical origins is only of limited relevance to explaining Sovietology's long-term blindness to the non-Russians. The genetic fallacy cautions us against explaining current conditions in terms of their origins, while the overwhelming reality of the USSR's multinationality, the conceptual incompleteness of a center without a periphery, and the curious fact of the non-Russians' being defined in terms of what they are not suggest that an excursion into Sovietology's historical development is ultimately of little help in explaining such empirical lacunae and logical lapses.

By the same token, it is of little interest to note that Sovietologists were not trained to study the non-Russians, that non-Russians speak difficult languages, and that travel restrictions prevented scholars from visiting regions in the non-Russian periphery. While all of these qualifications are valid, they are unpersuasive. First, the lack of training, while a reality, simply begs the question of "why?": that is, why did senior Sovietologists not train their juniors in so manifestly relevant a feature of the Soviet Union as the nationality question? Language training is also unconvincing. Here, again, the question of "why?" insinuates itself. Moreover, the objection may even be irrelevant inasmuch as a substantial contingent of all Sovietologists has always consisted of non-Russians speaking the very languages that were neglected by mainstream scholars. Travel restrictions are somewhat weightier a problem. Still, not only did such difficulties apply to all of the USSR; but they also are ultimately immaterial. Historians need not travel to a country in order to study its past; so, too, Sovietologists have rarely felt impelled to establish an intimate relationship with the country of their interest. In short, none of the above objections accounts for the fact that the non-Russians were so resoundingly absent from Soviet studies, that this absence undermined Sovietology's insistence that it was concerned with a presence, the center, and, finally, that the non-Russians simply were not.

History can do little to resolve such complex logical, indeed ontological, problems. The problem is not to isolate the obstacles to Sovietology's seeing the non-Russians, but to explain why

Sovietology, which insisted that its domain was the Soviet Union, simply could not see what it claimed to be looking at. To pose the problem in this manner is to recognize that the major obstacle to clear sight is conceptual. In other words, Sovietology did not "see" the non-Russians; indeed, by defining the non-Russians as a negation, Sovietology confirmed this proposition. After all, how can one see something that is not there? How can one see an absence? In contrast, how can one avoid seeing a presence, Russia and the Russians? How can one avoid seeing what is so obviously the center?

Sovietologists were hardly unique in their blindness. Their handicap was no different from that afflicting Mikhail Gorbachev and other members of his original entourage. Gorbachev's notorious inability to deal with the Sovietized nations cannot have been due to some putative lack of experience with non-Russians. After all, how could a man who lived all his life in one of the USSR's ethnically most heterogeneous regions not be aware of the nationality question? Nor do Gorbachev's public statements support the view that such blindness is due to his being a closet Russian imperialist or chauvinist.[4] Instead, the most persuasive explanation for Gorbachev's lack of sight is conceptual: Gorbachev literally did not see the non-Russians as being anything more than "non-issues." For him, as for countless Western Sovietologists, the non-Russians were appendages at best, irrelevancies at worst. The non-Russians did not matter; the non-Russians were not, and they did not deserve to be anything but not.

Another comparison suggests itself—with the condition of blacks and women in the United States. Surely, it would be absurd to suggest that they did not really exist several decades ago, or that they were irrelevant to the life of the United States. Nevertheless, despite the fact that the former were a visible presence in most American cities, while the latter comprised some half of the

---

4 On Gorbachev's views on the nationality question, see Alexander. J. Motyl, "The Sobering of Gorbachev: Nationality, Restructuring, and the West," in Seweryn Bialer, ed., *Politics, Society, and Nationality inside Gorbachev's Russia.* (Boulder, CO: Westview Press, 1989), pp. 149-173.

population, both groups were in fact excluded from the existing language, from the discourse of society. Significantly, both groups also possessed the same status vis-à-vis whites and males as did non-Russians vis-à-vis Russians. They were negations of that which was: black was contrary to white, female was opposed to male. As negations, not only were blacks and women threats, but they were also inferior: they were mere non-whites and non-males. They lacked an identity, they lacked history, they lacked speech. In a word, they were nonexistent.

To argue that Sovietology's blindness to the non-Russians was conceptually conditioned is to suggest that meaning precedes reference, that the definition of a term not only delineates the concept but also determines the empirical referent. According to this argument, empirical referents can be grasped only by means of concepts; indeed, empirical referents have no determinable independent existence of their own and are, as it were, brought to life by means of the conceptual apparatus — the discourse — that shapes our perceptions of what we claim to be reality. The concepts comprising a discourse determine not only what we do see but also what we do not see. They structure reality; they tell us what is and they tell us what is not.[5]

This mode of argumentation implies that post-modernism may have more to tell us about Sovietology's blind spots than traditional intellectual history.[6] In particular, the deconstructive approach suggests that we would do well to examine the manner in which Sovietological language reflects the connotational logic embedded in the broader cultural context, to explore how

---

5  For a discussion of these views, see: Paul A. Roth, *Meaning and Method in the Social Sciences*. (Ithaca, NY: Cornell University Press, 1987); Michael T. Gibbons, "Political Science, Disciplinary History, and Theoretical Pluralism: A Response to Almond and Eckstein," *PS: Political Science & Politics*, vol. 23, no. 1 (March 1990), pp. 44-46; Pauline Marie Rosenau, *Post-Modernism and the Social Sciences*. (Princeton, NJ: Princeton University Press, 1992).

6  Regarding deconstruction, see: Christopher Norris, *The Deconstructive Turn*. (London: Routledge, 1989); Jonathan Culler, *On Deconstruction*. (Ithaca, NY: Cornell University Press, 1982); Mark C. Taylor, ed., *Deconstruction in Context* (Chicago, IL: University of Chicago Press, 1986); Rosenau, *Post-Modernism and the Social Sciences*.

"Russia" and "not-Russia" function as signs, and to determine how Sovietology's use of these signs deconstructs to produce the incoherent discipline described above. Ironically, such an approach means engaging in a form of interpretation that is completely foreign to Sovietology. Paradoxically, however, approaching Sovietology from such alien and, possibly, alienating premises may be the best way of coming to grips with its alienation from the non-Russians.

## II.

The key to the analysis is Russia. Like all signs, so, too, the sign that is Russia functions on two levels, that of the signifier and that of the signified. The signifier is, of course, the term itself, the word, the collection of letters that spell Russia. The signified refers to the connotations that the signifier evokes upon being stated or seen. Russia, evidently, is a most impressive signifier. Pronounce the word softly and you hear a distant rustle, the rumble of thunder, wind, leaves, birch trees, an approaching storm. Say it loudly and you hear the authoritative command of a drill sergeant. The signifier contains within itself both sets of onomatopoeic sounds. Two syllables, connected by a sibilant sound and headed by an imposing trill, combine to create a signifier that is both mellow and harsh, distant and close, absent and present. The appearance of the word enhances this image. The convex upper part of the capital "R" is echoed in the "u" that follows; the two letters then merge and become "ss"; the "ia," in turn, brings to mind the "Ru" and thereby closes the circle. This elegant play of curves is occasionally interrupted by harsh verticals and diagonals, but never too often or too much. The visual image of Russia is a flowing one, like that of a mighty river, such as the Volga.

Contrast the verbal and visual impact of this signifier with that of the non-Russian republic *par excellence,* Ukraine. Spoken aloud, Ukraine conveys an image of a traffic sign or a declaratory address. The images are not only not romantic, but they are also confused, incoherent. Viewed as a set of letters, Ukraine appears as an awkward amalgam of a definite article and a proper noun.

Taken alone, Ukraine appears as a random collection of curves and lines. There does not appear to be any obvious progression, as in Russia, of ellipses and curves toward wholeness and unity.

Not surprisingly, the mental images conveyed to us by the signifier that is Russia are inextricably connected with the signified. What exactly is Russia? It is vast, yet closed; it is spontaneous, yet controlled; it is gloomy, yet airy; it is cultured, yet dirty; it is loving, yet distant. Russia is, in a word, a mother, but a mother who is capricious, ill-tempered, unreliable, and disheveled. She is a mother who is not a mother. Russia is a living contradiction; she is everything, and she is nothing; she is both absence and presence, good and evil, living and dead. Simply stated, Russia is a mystery. Signifier and signified form a beautiful unity. The sound and sight of the word convey the very image of harmonious disharmony that our culture associates with Russia.

As a mystery, Mother Russia exerts unending attraction. It invites and teases. Indeed, Mother Russia is a temptress. More than that, Mother Russia is Lolita: seemingly young and innocent, but actually mature and experienced. And, like Lolita, Russia seduces its admirers. It blinds them to everything but itself; it takes hold of their senses, their wits, and forces them to engage in the self-destructive pursuit of a mystery that cannot be grasped or fathomed.

Russia is, thus, the unity of contradictions. As such, Russia is everything; it is life. There is nothing outside of Russia; everything is inside Russia. Russia defines existence, it defines presence, and everything that is not Russia is not. It is not-Russia. It does not have a character or life of its own. At best, not-Russia is but a parasite on the maternal Russian body, which alone gives life and sustenance. At worst, not-Russia is Lolita's spurned lover.

Not-Russia is, of course, a negation of that which is; it is a negation of life, of existence, of history. Indeed, not-Russia is outside of history: as Friedrich Engels so quaintly put it, nations without history are the *Völkerabfälle*.⁷ Like the "bourgeois nationalists" whom Soviet propaganda used to consign to the "trash heap of history," so, too, not-Russia is excluded from the historical process.⁸ And how could it be otherwise? History is life, and not-Russia is the negation of life, that is, of history. Evidently, not-Russia should not be. History would not be worse off without not-Russia. Indeed, the existence of not-Russia—a paradox if there ever was one!—is immaterial to history, which, like Russia, flows past the ash heaps and trash cans littering its shores.

Who inhabits the perverse world of not-Russia? It is the non-Russians. Not only do the non-Russians have no positive features of their own—that is, they are only that which is not—but they are also a negation of the life that succors those who inhabit that wondrous realm, Russia. In contrast to the mellifluous sibilance of Russia and Russians, the term non-Russian includes within itself a prefix that explicitly negates such pleasantries. Moreover, to the degree that non-Russians attempt to assert a positive identity, they fail miserably and only produce terms that grate on the eye or on the ear or on both. Lithuanian, Ukrainian, Azerbaijani, Kyrgyz, Uzbek—they are visually awkward and for the most part unsonorous constructs. This contrast is especially apparent with regard to proper names. Boris Godunov, like the Contadora peace process or the Arias plan, is a sound that commands authority. Chingiz Aitmatov, like the Rapacki plan, evidently deserves to be forgotten. Just as clearly, a Vytautas Landsbergis can be no match for a Mikhail Gorbachev.

But non-Russians do not only disturb the musical symphony that is Russia with their cacophonous sounds. Worse still, in denying life, they embody evil. Non-Russians do not create: they negate, they destroy. In a word, they are savages, beasts, at best children. Irrational, petty, vengeful, deceitful, they destroy all that

---

7   For a detailed discussion of Engels's views, see Charles C. Herod, *The Nation in the History of Marxian Thought*. (The Hague: Martinus Nijhoff, 1976).
8   Typical of this genre is Yevhen Sheremet, *Ukrainians by Profession*. (Kiev: Ukraina Society, 1981).

is good and alive. Temper tantrums, squabbles, riots, and pogroms are the handiwork of the non-Russians. Innately inclined to hate and to kill indiscriminately, the non-Russians are even worse than Nazis. Inasmuch as the Germans, like the Russians, embody both good and evil, life and death, the Nazis were merely the perverted excrudescence of only one side of the German soul. The non-Russians, in contrast, have only a dark side. Seen from this perspective, it is evident that the Nazis must have collaborated with the non-Russians, and not the other way around.

So destructive a force must of course be curbed. Life itself demands that non-life, the anti-Christ, be either controlled or transformed into life. In practical terms, this proposition means that the non-Russians must be dominated by the Russians: after all, who better to keep the unruly mobs under control than those who the non-Russians are not? Democracy, freedom, self-rule are alien to the non-Russians; moreover, the non-Russians would merely pounce on these gifts of civilization — to pillage and burn in the manner that their natures demand. A more lasting solution to the problem of the non-Russians is to eliminate it altogether by transforming them into Russians. Once the non-Russians become Russians, their negation of life and goodness will immediately cease.

Russia versus not-Russia, Russians versus non-Russians: it is a struggle of life and death, good and evil, light and darkness. In this epic contest, the choice of sides is clear: Russia. And, yet, even Russia can be transcended. Even life itself can be perfected — by means of the West. After all, whereas Russia is a bundle of contradictions and a mystery, and the non-Russians are only the negative side of the whole that is Russia, the West is the positive side of that whole. To be sure, the West — how sleek, swift, and efficient both the sound and the sight of the signifier appear! — lacks some of the life that Russia embodies. The West is all technique, expertise, and modernity. It can be cold, callous, and calculating. But neither is it as messy, complicated, and contradictory as Russia. And, of course, in contrast to the non-Russians, who only destroy, the West has a passion for building. It does so to a fault, perhaps, but the result is a clean, efficient, functional life; a life that, in lacking any opposites, is perhaps boring, sterile, and too sanitized, but obviously preferable to the destruction that the non-Russians herald.

There is then some hope outside of Russia for the non-Russians. If they join the West and become Western, they can redeem themselves, atone for their sins, and rejoin humanity. The West, then, is salvation; it is paradise. And to become Western is to undergo a baptism, a cleansing, a transformation. Naturally, to become Western means to join the "city of God," which involves leaving the "city of man," which is Russia. Paradise implies a certain loss of humanity, but for the non-Russians even a loss impliesan advance over their utter lack of humanity.

Which non-Russians are closest to salvation via westernization? The Czechs, Slovenes, Hungarians, and Balts head the list. Poles and Croats are next, but their status is uncertain, as their "national character" is somewhat too reminiscent of that of the Russians, somehow too messy, too contradictory. Ukrainians, Slovaks, Serbs, and Belarusians are too primitive to aspire to be truly Western; instead, the status of "Little Russians" may be the most they can hope for. Naturally, Romanians, Bulgarians, Macedonians, Montenegrins, Albanians, Moldovans, Georgians, Armenians, Azerbaijanis, and Central Asians are too exotic, too swarthy, too prone to squabble; too inclined to sport thick black mustachios to be Western. No matter that the Czechs did not bother to resist the Nazis, that the Hungarians brutally exploited their national minorities, that the Balts were singularly unsuccessful as democrats in the inter-war period –they are and remain Western, or at least potentially so. No matter that the Balkan nations never started a world war, that the Armenians experienced genocide, that the Ukrainians were the victims of Hitler and Stalin, or that Uzbeks were colonized by the Russians—they are and remain mere non-Russians.

## III.

Can these lower-order non-Russians ever be saved? Is salvation a realistic aspiration?

In terms of the semiotic network described above, the answer must be a resounding "no." The negation of life cannot undergo an *Aufhebung* and become life; the negation of life cannot become the perfection of life. Russia and the West will always remain beyond the grasp of the quintessential not-Russia. Peoples who are fired by thousand-year-old passions cannot become Western; peoples who are beasts cannot become human. Chains and the knout are the only way to prevent such barbarians from wreaking havoc upon the world.

It is hard to imagine how such a cultural framework can ever permit non-Russians to assert their humanity. There seems to be no way for not-life to be life: the existing discourse appears to forbid such a miraculous transformation. And yet, the last sentence suggests how non-Russian salvation might take place. The key is language, more precisely, the conceptual apparatus and the system of meanings that structure what we see and how we see it. Quite simply, the discourse will have to change for the non-Russians to be something, and not merely not-something.

There are three ways for such a transformation of concepts to occur. First and most important, the non-Russians themselves will have to claim their place in the sun by banishing from their own conceptual frameworks. the notion of their being only negations. For better or for worse, such a self-assertion will require the assertion of national identity, the claim of national authenticity, and the rejection of the "other," indeed, the transformation of that which the non-Russians are not, into not that which they are. Non-Russians throughout the entire Soviet empire are following in the footsteps of colonial peoples in Africa, Asia, and Latin America, adopting the language of Frantz Fanon and Albert Memmi, and reclaiming their souls for themselves.[9] The West is wont to call such self-assertion nationalism, chauvinism, and xenophobia, implicitly suggesting that non-Russians can never rise higher than the negation of what is. For better or for worse, however, the non-Russians are ignoring the

---

9   Frantz Fanon, *The Wretched of the Earth* (New York: Grove Press, 1968); Albert Memmi, *The Colonizer and the Colonized*. (Boston, MA: Beacon Press, 1967).

West. Instead, they are asserting themselves and infusing their selves with positive identities. Not only are they claiming to be Lithuanians, Moldovans, Armenians, and Uzbeks, but they are also transcending Russia and the West with their own culturally authentic terms—East Central Europe, Central Asia, Turkestan. The debate surrounding the concept of *Mitteleuropa* is perhaps most indicative of this active searching for a new, positive identity, one that is what it is and not what it is not.

The second manner of changing prevailing concepts is confrontational, and this, too, the non-Russians are pursuing. The non-Russians are invading Western and Russian consciousness, disrupting complacent views of them as animals, non-humans, and Nazis. And the non-Russians are doing this in the most direct manner possible: by declaring independence, they are seizing history and claiming it for themselves. In making history they are remaking it and thereby asserting that they are a constructive and life-giving force, and not merely a negation of that which is. Until recently, the non-Russians, as negations of life, had been viewed as being ahistorical, perhaps even antihistorical. History flowed without them. The last five years, however, have witnessed the entry of the "trash peoples" onto the historical stage. Poles claimed their nation and culture and demolished a totalitarian state in the process. Czechs, Slovaks, Slovenes, Croats, Romanians, Bulgarians, Balts, Belarusians, Ukrainians, Moldovans, Armenians, Georgians, Azeris, Kazakhs, Uzbeks, Kyrgyz, and Tajiks have also taken history by the horns, tamed it, forced it to do their bidding, compelled it to listen to them. In having imposed themselves on the historical process, the non-Russians have transformed themselves into historical beings; they have not only imbued themselves with the humanity that is reserved for historical actors, but also compelled other historical actors—in particular, the West and Russia—to take heed of them, to note their presence, to adjust to a shifting reality, to transform the conceptual apparatus they use. It is due to the remarkable "awakening" of the non-Russians, of course, that Sovietology itself has been plunged into the depths of a genuine crisis, forced to grope in the dark and search for new ways of defining a reality that has suddenly and inexplicably slipped out of its hands. We may be certain that Sovietology's paradigmatic crisis will be resolved in due time, no doubt as a byproduct of a heavy admixture of non-Russian concepts, ideas, and values into the prevailing discourse of not-Russia.

The third source of the transformation of prevailing language is immanent to the language itself. As I have attempted to illustrate above, the cultural context in general and Sovietology in particular deconstruct upon closer examination. Riddled with contradictions, both discourses are ultimately untenable and will have to be replaced lest they collapse on their practitioners. It is impossible to study the former Soviet Union with a conceptual framework that ascribes life and goodness to Russia and the negation of both to not-Russia. It is not that treating non-Russians as non-humans is offensive. Rather, the problem with such an approach is that Russia can have no substance, no essence, if its contrast, not-Russia, is the negation of Russia. If not-Russia is nothing and Russia is everything, then Russia is in the final analysis nothing as well. Just as not-Russia represents a negation of that which is, so, too, that which is everything is a negation of that which is only something. To ascribe totality to Mother Russia by treating her as a Lolita is to lose sight both of the mother and of the temptress, to transform bounded things into an unbounded universe, to reject the part for the whole that cannot be a whole without the part.

## IV.

Ironically, Russia needs not-Russia not to be a mere negation. By the same token, not-Russia needs Russia to be something less than the totality of human experience. Both concepts must be transformed: the former reduced in status, the latter raised. In the process of this transformation, the irreconcilable difference between them will disappear. Russia will be what it is; Eastern Europe, Central Asia, or Ukraine will be what they are. History will not end, of course, but this untenable dichotomy will.

Interestingly, the supersession of the Russia/not-Russia dichotomy will also spell the end of the supremacy of the West, at least in the East European part of the world. The West offers salvation and perfectibility only to those who are in need of salvation and perfection. As matters now stand, the non-Russians are damned, while the Russians are too full of contradictions to be able to claim happiness. More important, the contradiction between Russia and not-Russia, their opposition to each other, permits the West to stand above them both, as arbiter and savior. Once the opposition falls away, once Russia is reduced to human dimensions and not-Russia is incorporated into humanity, the West will no longer be able to present itself as the solution to the conflict between Russian thesis and non-Russian antithesis. A synthesis will not be necessary, as the dialectic will cease to function. Mother Russia will still tend to her children; Lolita will still seduce her admirers. But at least they will no longer be one and the same person.

# 9

# Can Ukraine Have a History?*

Writing in 1995,[1] Mark von Hagen posed a provocative question: "Does Ukraine Have a History?" The present essay explores the logical consequences for and compatibility with existing non-Ukrainian historical narratives of independent Ukraine's emergent national narratives.[2] I construct a set of "ideal type" narratives—Soviet, Russian, Polish, Jewish, and Western—and investigate the degree to which they are or are not compatible with ideal-type Ukrainian national narratives. Most of the contemporary conflicts over history in Ukraine are the result of logical incompatibilities between national narratives, and a common narrative is possible only between logically compatible narratives. Ukraine can therefore have a history only in the context of logically compatible non-Ukrainian historical narratives.

## Historical Controversies in Ukraine

The last three years have witnessed four major historical controversies—two surrounding leaders of the organized Ukrainian nationalist movement, Roman Shukhevych and Stepan Bandera, one surrounding the Hetman Ivan Mazepa, and one involving the 1932–1933 Famine, known as the *Holodomor*. In each case, the Ukrainian state—or, more exactly, then-President Viktor Yushchenko—organized official commemorations. Although Yushchenko was widely identified with these issues, his commemorations actually drew from extensive historical research

---

* First printed in: *Problems of Post-Communism*, vol. 57, no. 3 (May/June 2010), pp. 55–61. Reprinted with permission of the original publisher.
1 Mark von Hagen, "Does Ukraine Have a History?" *Slavic Review*, vol. 54, no. 3 (Autumn 1995), pp. 658–673.
2 I thank Nadieszda Kizenko, Thomas Sherlock, and Bohdan Vitvitsky for their criticisms of and comments on earlier drafts of this essay.

and writing by Ukrainian scholars and publicists who attempted to incorporate these individuals or events into emergent Ukrainian national narratives. These attempts at incorporation invariably produced howls of protest by neighboring states and non-Ukrainian historians, who usually viewed them as nefarious, hyper-nationalist endeavors to promote a narrow Ukrainian nationalism and reject existing understandings of history. Russia and Russian historians responded violently to all four commemorations, as did pro-Soviet Ukrainians. Poland and Polish historians, as well as Israel and Israeli/Jewish historians, took umbrage with the treatment of Roman Shukhevych and Stepan Bandera, viewing their historical incorporation as an attempt to justify, whitewash, or ignore the Ukrainian nationalist movement's anti-Polish and anti-Jewish activities.

The fact that these incorporations—like similar incorporations of individuals and events in the Baltic states and other non-Russian republics—followed identical trajectories and provoked identical outcries suggests that the controversies were not the handiwork of the hyper-nationalist mastermind Yushchenko, but, rather, symptoms of deeper tendencies within the logics of the emergent historical narratives of these countries. The protests were not serendipitous responses to serendipitous events, but logically predetermined responses to logically predetermined events. A closer look at history and at national narratives will explain this point in greater detail.

## What Is History?

I adopt the view of history developed by Arthur C. Danto in *Narration and Knowledge*.[3] In this view, there is and can be no perfect and complete "ideal chronicle" (*pace* Leopold von Ranke's "wie es eigentlich gewesen sei"—"the way it actually was"), as a chronicle of every single historical fact would just amount to an infinite collection of facts. In reality, all historians always and

---

3   Arthur Danto, *Narration and Knowledge* (New York: Columbia University Press, 1985).

everywhere write imperfect and incomplete narratives that make sense for the historians writing from particular perspectives and vantage points reflective of their place in time. Every history is therefore partial and every history is therefore "slanted."

Although Danto's view of history may, at first glance, appear to coincide with possible post-modernist claims about indeterminacy, meaninglessness, subjectivism, and relativism, his claims are actually rooted in fairly traditional understandings of history. Facts exist in Danto's reading, and historians are able to determine what they are. Historians must therefore pay obeisance to chronological time, they must produce coherent narratives, and they must demonstrate that the facts they claim as facts are indeed facts—that is, supported by persuasive evidence. Histories can therefore be "objective" accounts of what happened, but they can never be full or final accounts produced from some transcendental point of view. Multiple histories of anything are as inevitable and unavoidable as multiple lines intersecting some one point. Thus, a feminist history can therefore be as good, or as bad, as an anti- or non-feminist history. A nationalist or national history can, by the same logic, be as good, or as bad, as an anti-nationalist or non-national history.

If this view of history is persuasive, then it follows that prevalent or dominant—or hegemonic—historical narratives are histories that correspond to, reflect, embody, or incorporate certain present-day concerns. Such narrative may or may not be better as coherently organized chronological arrangements of facts, but they appear to be better because we—or, more precisely, historians and reading publics—deem them better. *Ceteris paribus*, certain histories strike us as "better" than others, not because they offer intrinsically better narratives of facts as facts, but because they are more relevant to present-day concerns. Thus, a feminist history may strike us as a better reading of something than a non-feminist history, but—ceteris paribus—that is so, not so much because "the way it actually was" is demonstrably feminist, as because, inspired by feminism, we look for, and find, feminist facts in "the way it actually was,"

The inevitability of dominant narratives invariably transforms non-dominant narratives into challengers that rock the boat. New, non-dominant narratives will, from the viewpoint of existing dominant narratives, always appear as upstarts—as revisionists that threaten to upend the right and established way of seeing things. Feminist history was treated in just this manner until it finally became part of the mainstream. Similarly, every formerly colonized nation has had to assert itself historically in the face of the existing dominant narrative, which, unsurprisingly, has usually been formed by the former empire or elites, groups, or professions with established historical narratives.

## National Narratives: State, People, or Territory

There is no necessary reason to write "national narratives"—one can, after all, write the history of salt, sex, celebrities, unknown toilers, and so on—but for better or for worse many, if not most, histories are written in this manner. Thus, there are histories of France, Russia, England, Italy, Japan, Brazil, the United States, and every other country, and there are histories of bits and pieces of the general histories of France, Russia, England, Italy, Japan, Brazil, the United States, and every other country. Unsurprisingly, newly independent nations and states have a proclivity for these types of narratives, because independence both creates a particular perspective or vantage point for history writing and arguably demands that national narratives emerge to provide legitimacy for the new nations and states.

There are three imaginable types of such national narratives. Consider a newly independent state called Slobbovia. First, one can write a history of the Slobbovian *state*. That would entail tracing all the political formations that somehow contributed to the emergence and consolidation of the administrative and coercive apparatus known as the State of Slobbovia. Second, one can write a history of the Slobbovian *people*, or nation. That would entail tracing all the social, economic, political, and cultural developments that led to the emergence and consolidation of a self-conscious ethno-cultural community called the Slobbovians.

Third, one can write a history of the *territory* of Slobbovia. That would entail tracing all the relationships between and among all the people and peoples inhabiting the territory of Slobbovia. Obviously, historians may write narratives that try to combine all three strands. Just as obviously, the historians who write these narratives may or may not be native Slobbovians.

Which of these narratives is better or best? The answer is that, ceteris paribus, they are all equally good or all equally bad. If the historians do their homework, act with integrity, and arrange genuine facts in logically coherent chronological narratives, then each resulting narrative is valid. Obviously, if the historian's perspective is statehood, the history of the Slobbovian state is the way to go. If the historian is interested in the nation, then the history of the Slobbovian people is the optimal approach. And if the historian is interested in the territory, then the history of the Slobbovian territory and its peoples is preferable. Combining all three strands in one narrative is not necessarily better — or worse — than any of these three alternatives. A mega-narrative may look better because it is more comprehensive, but we know from Danto that comprehensiveness is arguably an elusive goal. Similarly, a mega-narrative could actually be incoherent and thereby violate one of the historian's key goals — to produce a coherent narrative.

Let us now engage in two intellectual experiments regarding the relationship between dominant narratives and emergent national narratives. As noted above, narratives will be equally good or equally bad precisely because I have appended the ceteris paribus clause to my argument. That is, I am excluding from consideration, by definition, any and all narratives that are purposely and consciously written to advance certain ideological, political, or other agendas. The historians in this intellectual experiment are honest historians interested only in presenting a chronologically coherent narrative of some state, nation, or territory. They have no axes to grind, but wish only to tell the story. If I can show that dominant and emergent historical narratives will, even under such ideal-type conditions, be compatible or incompatible, then the inclusion of politics and ideology will of course only deepen compatibilities or incompatibilities.

## Narratives about Ukraine

Although Ukrainian historians have produced histories since at least the nineteenth century—the works of Mykola Kostomarov, Mykhailo Drahomanov, Mykhailo Hrushevskyi, and Viacheslav Lypynskyi come to mind—they never had the status of dominant narratives, except perhaps among Ukrainian émigrés in Western Europe or North America. As a result, Ukraine became independent in 1991 within the historical and historiographic setting of already existing, and, for the most part, non-Ukrainian, narratives about its state, nation, and territory. These already existing narratives formed a set of dominant, if not indeed hegemonic, views about Ukraine—not because, to repeat, they were more correct or more persuasive intrinsically, but simply because they had existed and been institutionalized for several decades or, possibly, even centuries. The emergent Ukrainian national narratives thus challenged the primacy of the historical status quo represented by Soviet, Russian imperial, Russian national, Polish national, Jewish Zionist, Jewish Bundist, and Western narratives.

Logically, the emergent Ukrainian historical narratives had to correspond with the above three ideal types of national narratives emphasizing state, nation, or territory. Thus, a Ukrainian *state* narrative would necessarily begin Ukraine's history in Rus; carry it through the Cossack rebellions of, especially, Bohdan Khmelnytskyi and Ivan Mazepa, the failed attempt to build a state in 1917–1921, and the activities of the integral nationalists of the inter-war period and World War II, and conclude with the collapse of the Soviet Union and the role therein of Ukrainian dissidents. Honest historians concerned with the history of the Ukrainian state could not fail to include all these entities, individuals, and events in a state narrative. They might disagree on the relative importance of entities, individuals, and events, and they might evaluate them differently, but they could not fail to conclude that all these entities, individuals, and events must be included in a state narrative.

A Ukrainian *people* narrative would have the same historical sweep of the state narrative, while focusing on how state building, together with developments in the society, culture, and economy, led to the emergence of nationally conscious Ukrainians (in particular, self-styled nationalists) and, eventually, a distinctly Ukrainian nation. Here, too, honest historians could not ignore states, elites, state builders, and nationalists, even though they might disagree on how to evaluate them.

Finally, a Ukrainian *territory* narrative would tell the story of relations between and among peasants, landlords, merchants, Ukrainians, Russians, Poles, Jews, Ruthenians, Catholics, Orthodox, and so on. Honest historians could probably downplay Ukrainian state-building processes, but they could not ignore nation building and nationalism in general, social and economic relations, cultural tensions, and the like—between and among all these nations, peoples, classes, and groups.

A Soviet narrative, like its twin, a Russian imperial narrative, contradicts the state and nation versions of the Ukrainian national narrative and is compatible only with the territory version. Thus, according to the Soviet/Russian imperial version, especially if practiced by honest historians with no axes to grind, Rus is either non-Ukrainian, Russian, or at best multinational, the Cossacks (with the sole exception of Khmelnytskyi, who wisely opted for union with Russia) are either troublemakers or traitors, the Ukrainian nationalists of both the World War I and World War II periods are German puppets or fascists, and the collapse of the USSR is, in Vladimir Putin's words, "a great tragedy." On the other hand, both the Soviet and the Russian imperial narratives can easily accommodate Ukraine as a territory with many diverse peoples, especially if it can be shown that they yearn for Russian overlordship.

In contrast, any distinctly Russian national narrative—one that focuses on the Russian state as it currently exists or the Russian people or the territory of Russia—can easily coexist with any Ukrainian national narrative. There will, of course, be points of contention, because Russia's relations with Ukraine, in any of the three imaginable versions, involve conflict and bloodshed, but none of these contentious issues necessarily undermines the logically compatible historical narratives of the Russian and Ukrainian states, nations, or territories. The same logic applies to the relationship between any Polish historical narrative and any Ukrainian one. If the former is imperial, then incompatibilities are inevitable. If the former is national, points of disagreement will exist, but they will not necessarily mar the logical compatibility of the narratives.

In contrast to the logically harmonious relationship between Russian/Polish, and Ukrainian national narratives, the relationship between a Jewish national narrative and a Ukrainian national narrative is intrinsically conflictual if the former is "Zionist" and potentially compatible if the former is "Bundist". A Zionist narrative presents the history of Jews in Ukraine as a history of anti-Semitism and pogroms. From that point of view, every possible Ukrainian narrative is necessarily only a chapter in the history of violence perpetrated by Ukrainians against Jews and teleologically culminating in the Holocaust. In contrast, a Bundist narrative, emphasizing relations between Ukrainians and Jews in a territory called Ukraine can be compatible—but if and only if these relations are viewed in all their complexity and multi-dimensionality, and binaries (such as evil Ukrainians and good Jews or evil Jews and good Ukrainians) are eschewed.

Prevailing Western narratives can easily accommodate any Ukrainian narrative, at least in principle, as the overriding reality of Western narratives is that they resoundingly ignore Ukraine as a state, nation, or even territory. In this sense, although introducing Ukraine into Western narratives will obviously take time, because converting a nothing into a something is intrinsically difficult, there is no reason that Ukraine cannot coexist as state, nation, or territory with the national narratives of Germany, France, the United States, and other countries.

## Can Common Narratives Be Forged?

Obviously, common narratives—even assuming such a thing is possible in Arthur Danto's view of history—between some Ukrainian and some non-Ukrainian narratives can arise only if the narratives are compatible. As Table 1 suggests, such a project is possible in most cases. Whether it is also practically possible is another issue.

## Relations between Ukrainian and non-Ukrainian narratives.

| Ukrainian Narrative | Soviet/Imperial Narrative | Russian/Polish National Narrative | Jewish Zionist Narrative | Jewish Bundist Narrative | Western Narrative |
|---|---|---|---|---|---|
| Ukrainian State | Incompatible | Compatible | Incompatible | Compatible | Compatible |
| Ukrainian Nation | Incompatible | Compatible | Incompatible | Compatible | Compatible |
| Ukrainian Territory | Compatible | Compatible | Incompatible | Compatible | Compatible |

Soviet and Russian-imperial narratives can coexist with a Ukrainian-territory narrative. For better or for worse, however, Ukrainians committed to state- or nation-building projects generally find this solution unacceptable. In contrast, Ukrainian and Polish historians, like Ukrainian and Polish policy makers, have been able to forge something resembling a "common narrative" without too much difficulty. Sticking points remain — such as the anti-Polish activities of the Organization of Ukrainian Nationalists and the Ukrainian Insurgent Army before and during World War II — but they are flies in the ointment precisely because narrative compatibility exists across the board.

There is, according to this logic, no way for any Ukrainian narrative to be reconciled with a Zionist narrative. If Ukrainians are state and nation builders and can co-exist with other peoples in a territory, they cannot just be represented as vicious anti-Semites preparing for the Holocaust. And if Jews are only victims of age-old Ukrainian anti-Semitism, they cannot co-exist with Ukrainian attempts at building a state or nation or, for that matter, even exist. A Bundist narrative that views Jews and Ukrainians as neighbors — albeit frequently hostile neighbors — can coexist with any Ukrainian narrative. A story of good and bad Ukrainians interacting with good and bad Jews can be constructed as long as both sides are willing to admit to the possibility of good and evil in their national narratives.

Last but not least, there is no logical reason that Ukraine cannot be included in Western narratives. Inclusion will be difficult for the simple reason that Western historians and Western publics are astoundingly ignorant of Ukraine and, thus, for the most part unaware of the need of any common narrative.

Consider in this light the Great Famine of 1932–1933. Ukrainian state and nation narratives generally treat the *Holodomor* as a genocide — which makes perfect narrative sense in the story of Ukraine's emergence as a state and Ukrainians' emergence as a nation. The *Holodomor* as genocide, however, is necessarily incompatible with Soviet and Russian imperial narratives. The *Holodomor* can only be accommodated by these narratives if it is reduced to a *holod*, or famine, that affected all nations more or less equally. In contrast, the Great Famine can, as a Ukrainian genocide, fit perfectly with a Russian national narrative that posits its own famine-genocide, one directed at Russians by a Soviet or imperial regime. The *Holodomor* as genocide threatens Zionist narratives that insist on the uniqueness of the Holocaust and view any comparison as an attempt to relativize the Holocaust and thus to promote anti-Semitism. In contrast, the *Holodomor* as genocide can easily coexist with Bundist narratives, as long as they consider how Jews and Ukrainians interacted at the time of the Famine. Finally, there is no barrier, besides ignorance, to including the *Holodomor* as genocide in Western narratives.

## Can Ukraine Have a History?

Unsurprisingly, Ukrainians are writing their own historical narratives, precisely because the writing of emergent national narrative is typical of all peoples with just-established independent states — whether in the United States in the nineteenth century or in the former colonies of Latin America, Asia, or Africa. Similar narrative-writing trends exist in all the former Soviet republics and ex-Communist states of Eastern Europe. Although attempts to write, or rewrite, history are often viewed as attempts to justify nationalist excesses or Nazi collaboration, the reality is that they are, above all, just attempts to write national histories and produce national narratives. There is nothing intrinsically sinister in such an endeavor, even if such efforts do appear suspect from the viewpoint of already established dominant narratives. If Soviet, Russian imperial, Russian and Polish national, Zionist and Bundist, and Western narratives may exist, then so too may Ukrainian and Estonian and Kazakh and Georgian national narratives. For better or for worse, however, the rise of the latter will inevitably lead to friction with the former, even if all the narratives are produced by impeccably honest historians with absolutely no ideological or political axes to grind.

As I have argued, it is simply impossible to ignore Mazepa, Shukhevych, and Bandera in the writing of any kind of Ukrainian national narrative. Whatever their moral, political, or other failings, they played critically important—and arguably constructive—roles in the twin projects of Ukrainian state- and nation-building. Mazepa's role in a Ukrainian territorial history is positive or neutral with respect to Poles and negative or neutral with respect to Russians, while Shukhevych and Bandera's is unquestionably negative with respect to Russians, Poles, and Jews. To incorporate Bandera and Shukhevych in state- and nation-building histories is not to whitewash their behavior vis-à-vis Poles, Jews, and Russians. It is only to construct different historical narratives, the logic of which highlights state and nation and downplays inter-ethnic relations. Americans, for instance, cannot avoid treating Thomas Jefferson as a Founding Father of both state and nation, even though his place in a territorial narrative is surely marred by his ownership of slaves. Harry Truman helped make America a great power and a strong, self-confident nation, even though the destruction of Hiroshima and Nagasaki was an act of genocide against the Japanese civilian population.

State and nation narratives are no better and no worse than territorial ones; they are simply different. However, as repertoires in the construction of national narratives, they are certain to appear, and controversy is, thus, inevitable. Such friction cannot be overcome by admonitions to Ukrainians and non-Russians to produce historical narratives compatible with hegemonic worldviews. Incompatibilities can be overcome only in two ways that do not entail state intervention and coercion. First, common narratives can be constructed only based on the compatible versions illustrated in Table 1. No amount of good will can force two incompatible versions to coexist. Second, it is likely that in some time some versions will disappear or lose their hegemonic status. The more the Soviet experience recedes into history, the less persuasive Soviet narratives will appear. The longer the Russian Federation exists as a national state, the less attractive the Russian-imperial narrative will be. The longer Ukrainian-Jewish relations appear to be "normal," the more the Bundist version will appear more plausible than the Zionist version. The longer

Ukraine and other post-Soviet states exist as states, the more likely it becomes that Western narratives will begin to incorporate them. In turn, Ukrainian national narratives will develop—inevitably and unavoidably—as long as Ukraine exists as an independent state.

Can Ukraine therefore have a history? Yes, but only in the context of logically compatible non-Ukrainian historical narratives.

# 10

## Should Ukraine Forget Its History?*

On November 25, 2010, Israel's President Shimon Peres advised Ukrainians to "forget history." I look more closely at the notion of "forgetting history." I argue that, in order to forget history, one must first remember it. And in order to remember history, one must first have a history—a recorded narrative relating the nation's development over time. I argue that histories can never be full or final accounts produced from some transcendental vantage point. Multiple incomplete histories of anything are as inevitable and unavoidable as multiple lines intersecting some one point. Dominant historical narratives are therefore histories that correspond to, reflect, embody, or incorporate present-day norms, views, and concerns. The inevitability of dominant narratives therefore transforms non-dominant narratives into upstarts that threaten to upend the only correct way of seeing things. Although Ukrainian historians have produced histories since at least the nineteenth century, they never had the status of dominant narratives. As a result, Ukraine became independent in 1991 in a historical and historiographical setting of dominant non-Ukrainian narratives. The immediate task before historians of Ukraine, therefore, is to produce a Ukrainian national narrative or narratives—in the same manner that other voiceless groups, such as women and African Americans, produced women's history and black history despite the opposition of dominant ways of interpreting history. It is only after such a Ukrainian national narrative exists that Ukrainians will be able to transcend and "forget" it.

Back on November 25, 2010, while on a state visit to Kyiv, Israel's President Shimon Peres noted: "If Ukrainians were to ask

---

\*  The Wolodymyr Dylynskyj Memorial Lecture University of Toronto, May 6, 2011.

me for advice, I would say: forget history." I confess to having been, and still being, stunned, intrigued, and perplexed by Peres's comment—so much so that I would like today to look more closely at the notion of "forgetting history" and try to determine whether and under which conditions such a thing might be possible or desirable, in general and in the case of Ukraine in particular.

Let us start by engaging in two thought experiments. Let us imagine what a society that forgets all history would look like. Then, let us imagine the opposite—a society that remembers all history.

A society that forgets all history would be even more nightmarish than George Orwell's. Remember: Orwell's state *needed* history. It manipulated history, by continually rewriting it to meet the political needs of Big Brother. A society that forgets history would have to destroy every single book, journal, article, blog, recording, film, and artwork no later than one day after it appeared. In effect, such a society would live exclusively in the moment and be engaged in an unceasing attempt to obliterate everything that could serve as memory. And since anything can serve as memory, it would have to destroy everything—starting with all religions, all commemorations, and all distinctive buildings and ending with years, months, days, and, possibly, even numbers. The past and future tenses would also have to be banned, the former for obvious reasons, the latter for implying that the present is the past in relation to the future. Indeed, semantic change would have to go and the meaning of words would have to be fixed forever.

A society that remembers all history would be equally dystopian. This society would not only *preserve* every single text—whether written, painted, filmed, or recorded—but it would have to *record* every conversation, every whisper, and every thought. No less important, it would have to incorporate every single recorded text into a continually evolving grand historical narrative. A society such as this would actually resemble Orwell's—not because it wants to distort history, but because it needs both obsessively to rewrite history every hour of every day and ceaselessly to propagate a maximally comprehensive narrative served up in its most up-to-date version.

Let us ask a few more questions about these dreadful societies.

First, is either society possible in today's world? The answer, fortunately, is no. An utterly forgetful society would require such a massive concentration of totalitarian power as to make Orwell's state—or North Korea—seem liberal by comparison. I do not see how such a system could emerge at a time of mass communications, market economics, mass diversity, mass education, and the like. At first glance, an utterly remembering society seems more possible, inasmuch as the Internet is creating a permanent record of every electronic communication. On closer inspection, however, it is clear that, since the amounts of data such a society must collect would be infinitely large, a comprehensive and grand historical narrative could never be attained.

Second, can we—living human beings—actually follow Peres's advice and, in the absence of a mega-totalitarian state, forget history of our own volition? I do not see how. For one thing, we would have to forget how to remember—not to remember accurately, but just to remember. That seems logically impossible. For another, most people in most countries of the world today live in societies that involve some form of public contention—and every form of public contention always draws on memories, histories, and some record of some past. For a third, we live in an age in which all people everywhere have some kind of collective identity with some sense of what the group's boundaries are and of where it came from. For better or for worse, identity presupposes memory or history or some combination of the two.

Finally, even if some society decided to forget history, it could succeed only if every other society were to forget history. Since non-forgetters could manipulate forgetters, however, there would be little incentive for potential forgetters to follow in the footsteps of the first forgetter. In that sense, forgetfulness resembles disarmament. Who would do it first, knowing that historical disarmament would encourage others to retain their arsenals of history? And just as it is extremely difficult to get countries with huge nuclear stockpiles to disarm, so too it would be extremely difficult to get countries with huge stockpiles of memory—such as all of Ukraine's neighbors—to forget history.

There is another barrier to forgetfulness, one specific to Ukrainians and other post-colonial nations. In order to forget history, one must first remember it. And in order to remember history, one must first *have* a history—a recorded narrative relating the nation's development over time. Call that a *national history* or *narrative*. Like any historical narrative, a national narrative is perfectly compatible with all norms, ideologies, and values that do not explicitly deny the very possibility of national narratives. Liberals, conservatives, nationalists, feminists, socialists, fascists, Catholics, Protestants, Orthodox, Muslims, Buddhists, and Jews can all produce equally good national narratives if they do their homework, write with integrity, and arrange genuine facts in logically coherent chronological narratives.

There is no necessary reason to write national narratives—one can, after all, write the history of salt, sex, celebrities, codfish, textile workers, rock music, and so on—but for better or for worse many, if not most, histories are written in this manner. And, as we know from Frantz Fanon, newly independent nations and states have a proclivity for these types of narratives, as independence creates a particular vantage point for history writing, demands that national narratives emerge to provide legitimacy for the new nations and states, and enables formerly oppressed peoples or groups to find their voices and recover their memories.

There are three possible types of national narratives. Consider a newly independent state called Slobbovia. First, one can write a history of the Slobbovian state. That would entail tracing all the political formations that contributed to the emergence and consolidation of the administrative and coercive apparatus known as the State of Slobbovia. Second, one can write a history of the Slobbovian people, or nation. That would entail tracing all the social, economic, political, and cultural developments that led to the emergence and consolidation of a self-conscious ethno-cultural community called the Slobbovians.

Third, one can write a history of the territory of Slobbovia. That would entail tracing all the relationships between and among all the people and peoples inhabiting the territory of Slobbovia.

Which of these national narratives is better or best? The answer is that, other things being equal, they are all equally good or all equally bad as historical narratives. If the historians do their homework, write with integrity, and arrange genuine facts in logically coherent chronological narratives, then each resulting narrative is valid.

Fair enough, one might say, but is not the very notion of national narratives passé? Should not truly serious historians develop non-national or post-national narratives that boldly venture into borderlands and other marginal spaces outside *the* state and *the* nation? Is not that kind of history intrinsically *better* history? The answer is no. As we shall see, there are excellent theoretical reasons for writing national narratives.

I adopt the view of history developed by the philosopher Arthur Danto in *Narration and Knowledge*.[1] Danto engages in a thought experiment and asks whether an "ideal chronicle" consisting of every single historical fact would amount to a genuine history. His answer is that an infinitely large collection of facts would not and could not be a usable or even adequate historical narrative. Why not? For the simple, if somewhat counterintuitive, reason that complete comprehensiveness is antithetical to history. In reality, every history is and has to be partial, every history is and has to be "slanted," and every history is and has to be a story. And stories, as you know, are always stories, never of everything, but always of *something* with a beginning, middle, and end. As a result, all historians always and everywhere, intentionally and purposefully, write intrinsically imperfect and incomplete narratives that make perfect sense for the historians writing from particular vantage points reflective of their place in time. Every history is thus a never-ending work in

---

1  Arthur Danto, *Narration and Knowledge* (New York: Columbia University Press, 1985).

progress, because the vantage point of the historian can never be frozen in time.

Although Danto's view of history may appear to coincide with post-modernist claims about indeterminacy, meaninglessness, subjectivism, and relativism, it is actually rooted in fairly traditional understandings of history. Facts exist in Danto's reading, and historians are able to determine what they are. Historians must therefore pay obeisance to chronological time, they must produce coherent narratives, and they must demonstrate that the facts they claim as facts are indeed facts—that is, that they are statements about reality that, by virtue of their being supported by persuasive evidence, actually correspond to reality.

Histories can therefore be "objective" accounts of what happened, but they can never be full or final accounts produced from some transcendental vantage point. Multiple incomplete histories of anything are as inevitable and unavoidable as multiple lines intersecting some one point. A feminist history can therefore be as good or as bad, *as a historical narrative*, as an anti- or non-feminist history. A nationalist or national history can, by the same logic, be as good or as bad, *as a historical narrative*, as an anti-nationalist or non-national history.

It follows that dominant—or *hegemonic*—historical narratives need not actually be better as coherently organized chronological arrangements of facts. They only *appear* to be better because we—or, more precisely, historians and reading publics—deem them better. Other things being equal, certain histories strike us as better than others because they are more relevant to present-day concerns or more reflective of present-day views or norms. Thus, a feminist history may strike us as a better reading than a non-feminist history, but that is so, not because, to quote Leopold von Ranke, "*wie es eigentlich gewesen sei*" is demonstrably feminist, but because, inspired by feminism, we look for, and find, feminist facts in "as it really was." By the same token, the current infatuation with borderlands is right to treat borderlands as a legitimate way of engaging history, but it is wrong to suggest that borderland approaches are intrinsically superior to national narratives. They are not. They just happen to be different, but it is a difference that, today, strikes us as better—and that, tomorrow, when our vantage point changes, could just as easily strike us as worse.

The hegemony of dominant narratives transforms non-dominant narratives into unwelcome shifts that rock the boat. New, non-dominant narratives will, from the viewpoint of existing dominant narratives, always appear as upstarts that threaten to upend the only correct way of seeing things. Feminist history was treated in just this manner until women made it part of the mainstream. Similarly, the histories of all formerly colonized nations had to assert themselves in opposition to hegemonic narratives generated by the former empire or by elites, groups, or professions with established historical narratives.

Although Ukrainian historians have produced histories since at least the nineteenth century, they have never had the status of dominant narratives. As a result, Ukraine became independent in 1991 in a historical and historiographical setting of hegemonic non-Ukrainian narratives that had existed and acquired institutionalized status in the course of decades or centuries. Emergent Ukrainian—or Kazakh, Georgian, or Estonian—national narratives could but challenge the primacy of the historical status quo represented by existing dominant narratives.

Logically, emergent Ukrainian historical narratives had to correspond to the above three ideal types of national narratives. Thus, a Ukrainian *state* narrative would necessarily begin Ukraine's history in Rus'. It would carry it through the Cossack rebellions of Bohdan Khmelnytskyi and Ivan Mazepa, the failed attempt to build a state in 1917–1921, and the activity of the integral nationalists of the inter-war period and World War II. And it would conclude with the development of the Ukrainian SSR, the collapse of the Soviet Union, and the role therein of Ukrainian national Communists and dissidents. A Ukrainian *people* narrative would have the same historical sweep of the state narrative, while focusing on how state building, together with developments in the society, culture, and economy, led to the emergence of nationally conscious Ukrainians and, eventually, a distinctly Ukrainian nation. Finally, a Ukrainian *territory* narrative would tell the story of relations between and among peasants, landlords, merchants, workers, Ukrainians, Russians, Poles, Jews, Ruthenians, Catholics, Orthodox, and others in the territory of Ukraine.

It is simply impossible to ignore Roman Shukhevych and Stepan Bandera in the writing of a Ukrainian national narrative. Whatever their moral, political, or other failings, these individuals played critically important—and arguably constructive—roles in the twin projects of Ukrainian state- and nation-building. Americans, for instance, cannot avoid treating Thomas Jefferson as a Founding Father of both state and nation, even though his place in a territorial narrative is marred by his ownership of slaves. Harry Truman helped make America a great power and a strong, self-confident nation, even though the destruction of Hiroshima and Nagasaki was arguably an act of genocide. Paul Robeson was a great African American civil rights activist and nation-builder, even though he was also an apologist for Stalin.

I wish to emphasize that to incorporate the Ukrainian nationalist movement into a Ukrainian national narrative is not to whitewash it or to ignore the tragedy and violence done to Ukrainians and non-Ukrainians. It is simply to tell the story of the Ukrainian nationalist movement—not as a *footnote* in the story of Russia, the Soviet Union, Poland, or the Holocaust, not as a *disruption* of established historical narratives, and not as a savage *negation* of civilization—but as an ontologically legitimate story with a beginning, middle, and end embedded in a distinctly Ukrainian historical narrative. Historians who prefer to embed the Ukrainian nationalist movement in non-Ukrainian narratives are free to do so, but they have the intellectual obligation to recognize that their doing so endows them with no intellectual superiority. They also have the moral obligation to ask just why their conceptualizations, interpretations, and representations are identical to those of Soviet propagandists, Russian imperialists, and neo-Stalinists and share in their ideological and normative predilections.

How, then, can Ukraine develop a "normal" relationship to history—one that might satisfy President Peres, historians, and Ukraine? I suggest that Ukraine must still go through two stages.

First, and as I have been saying, Ukraine must construct some sort of national history or histories. Constructing a national history will not be easy, at least as long as the Putin and Yanukovych regimes are in power and as long as historians deny or try to transcend national narratives that do not yet exist. But the good news is that none of these obstacles is likely to be permanent.

I belong to those wild-eyed optimists who believe that Putin's Russia, a system that draws on neo-imperialism and neo-Stalinism for its legitimacy, and Yanukovych's Ukraine, which draws on a denial of Ukrainian history for its legitimacy, are unstable. When they find their rightful place on what the Soviets used to call the ash heap of history, two of the hegemonic anti- or non-Ukrainian narratives—call them Soviet and imperial Russian—will experience a mortal blow.

That leaves the historians who wish to propel Ukraine into a post-national age or deny it a national narrative. Their views may have seemed plausible during the heyday of globalization, when nations, states, and borders appeared to be disappearing faster than speeding bullets, but the recent global economic crises and the state-led responses to them have surely taught us that national identities and state boundaries are here to stay—at least for a few more years. I suggest that the demise of globalization fever and the reassertion of both nations and states will frame the academic agenda in such a way as to make post-national narratives look increasingly quaint in the years ahead.

No less important, the urge to propel Ukraine into a post-Ukrainian age or deny it a national narrative is logically unsustainable and normatively retrograde. It is logically unsustainable because, as I have argued, a post-Ukrainian narrative is possible if and only if a Ukrainian narrative already exists and can therefore be transcended. It is normatively reactionary because, in the absence of an already existing Ukrainian narrative, post-Ukrainian revisionism amounts to a

Great Leap Forward that denies the legitimacy of Ukraine's efforts to attain post-colonial status, to find its own voice, and to be free. Such a denial is tantamount to instructing African Americans and women that they have no right to engage in black history and women's history, that their right is conditional on representing Malcolm X only as a violent criminal and Betty Freidan only as a frustrated housewife, and that their rejection of these strictures disqualifies them from having a voice.

Naturally, "international scholars" will write what they want to—and, indeed, they should write what they want to. And if they engage in irresponsible allegations and crude violations of academic standards, they harm above all themselves. But that also means that historians in Ukraine and historians of Ukraine are perfectly free to anticipate the end of the Putin-Yanukovych regimes, to decline to succumb to globalization mania, and to dismiss premature historical revisionism as being on the wrong side of both logic and liberation.

That freedom also entails a serious responsibility: to pursue the serious business of writing Ukrainian national narratives honestly and with integrity—by eschewing heroization and myth-making, by rejecting blank spots, and by addressing head-on all difficult, painful, complex, and embarrassing issues. The best way to counter racist depictions of Ukrainians in many hegemonic narratives as pure negations—as only anti-Russians, only anti-Soviets, only anti-Semites, and thus as only anti-human, brutish *Untermenschen*—is not to glorify them as unremittingly positive heroes and *Übermenschen*, but to depict them as *Menschen*—as multidimensional human beings, capable of both good and evil, rationality and irrationality, and identical in these respects to all other human beings, including Russians, Poles, and Jews.

The second stage is this. It is only if and when such Ukrainian national narratives are constructed and consolidated that Ukrainians will be able to move on—not forget per se, but stop obsessing about the past. It is at that point that two important developments will become possible. Once Ukrainian national narratives become routinized and naturalized, they will lend themselves to commercialization, kitschification, lampooning, satirizing, and the like. We will know that moment has arrived when a Ukrainian version of Mel Brooks's *The Producers* will feature "Springtime for Lenin" in Donetsk and "Springtime for Bandera" in L'viv. Exceptionally serious Ukrainians will react with horror to the prospect of Hollywoodization, but such corrosive influences will transform sacred historical narratives into mundane and secular artifacts and thereby enable the vast majority of the population to deal with history in the manner that it deserves—as the past and not the present, and as a taken-for-granted component of one's national identity.

Taken-for-grantedness will also take history out of the realm of society or the state and place it in the realm in which it is most suitably obsessed about—the realm of professional historians who do not and cannot take history for granted. That, of course, is what President Peres really had in mind—that Ukrainians should let their historians, and only their historians, worry about history. Peres is wrong to think that can happen at this point in Ukraine's historical and historiographical development. But if and when Ukrainian national narratives are constructed and consolidated, his advice will be correct. At that point, Ukrainians will be able to develop a variety of stances toward their history—ranging from sacralization to taken-for-grantedness to desacralization—while their historians, both the honest and the dishonest ones, will be able to fight over details, trajectories, and the utility of national versus post-national narratives.

Then and only then will post-Ukrainian revisionism be logically sustainable and politically progressive and then and only then will calls to settle the borderlands of the historical imagination make sense and be possible.

In a word, Ukraine must first *catch up with* and *have* a history, before it can *forget* it.

# 11

## The Holodomor and History
### Bringing Ukrainians Back In*

Three or more years ago, I would not have been standing here. As most of you probably know, I have never devoted any significant amount of time in my scholarly career to studying the Holodomor. I've written a few brief articles and given a few talks, but I have never been a Holodomor specialist. It is only in the last two years that I've been able to aspire to that designation. And that is due solely to my having co-edited, together with Bohdan Klid of the Canadian Institute of Ukrainian Studies, *The Holodomor Reader*.[1] Bohdan is the specialist, but I was his apprentice and, as such, I was able to come to an infinitely deeper understanding of this genocide than I had possessed when he and I embarked on this project in the summer of 2010.

My deepest thanks to Bohdan as well as to Marko Stech, Frank Sysyn, and Myroslav Yurkevych of the Institute for making this book a reality and for enabling me to learn so much.

The idea for this book came to Bohdan and me, separately, sometime during the seventy-fifth anniversary of the Holodomor in 2008. Both of us were struck by the fact that, although the amount of material relating to the Holodomor was huge and steadily growing, there was no comprehensive sourcebook on the famine for English-language readers. As a result, finding basic information on the Holodomor required the kind of research that most nonspecialists have neither time nor energy to pursue.

I was one of those nonspecialists. As a political scientist who has spent inordinate amounts of time defining concepts, I had no

---

\* The Toronto Annual Ukrainian Famine Lecture, November 9, 2013.
1 Bohdan Klid and Alexander J. Motyl, eds., *The Holodomor Reader: A Sourcebook on the Famine of 1932–1933 in Ukraine* (Edmonton and Toronto: Canadian Institute of Ukrainian Studies, 2012).

doubt that the Holodomor possessed all the defining characteristics of genocide. But I confess to having lacked a full appreciation of the magnitude of the tragedy that befell Ukraine in 1932–33. That changed in the course of our research and translations. More important, I've learned a thing or two about Holodomor studies in the West.

Several things now strike me as obvious.

First, the debate about whether or not the Holodomor was or was not a genocide is over—at least in the West. Consider where the famine was in the popular consciousness of the 1950s. The answer is: nowhere. Survivors, refugees, and émigrés wrote about it extensively, but primarily in Ukrainian, and their audience consisted largely of themselves. Although some Western journalists had written about the famine in the 1930s, their focus soon shifted to other stories, while Western scholars ignored the famine almost entirely. Even in 1983, during the fiftieth anniversary of the Holodomor, the regnant view of one of the great crimes of the twentieth century maintained that it was a minor tragedy at best and a consequence of agricultural policy gone awry at worst.

Since then, the status of the famine as a nonevent or an émigré fantasy has changed by 180 degrees. No serious scholar or political figure now disputes that millions of Ukrainians starved to death in 1932–33. There is general agreement in the West that the famine was avoidable and almost universal condemnation of it as a crime. And, as *The Holodomor Reader* demonstrates, the empirical evidence for regarding the Holodomor as genocide is overwhelming. If one is neutral, one will be persuaded. If one is a diehard cynic, lacks the capacity for human empathy, or has a political agenda, no amount of evidence will do the trick.

There is, thus, no more need to demonstrate yet again that the Holodomor meets the requirements of any reasonable definition of genocide. There is no need to produce any more treatises using United Nations documents to show that the Holodomor was as much of a genocide as the Holocaust, the Armenian genocide, the Rwandan genocide, or the Cambodian genocide. The Holodomor was not just a tragedy. It was a slaughter, and every person of good conscience knows that. There is as little reason to worry about Holodomor deniers in the West as there is to worry about the Flat Earth Society. Their numbers will, inevitably, decline. In the meantime, they should be treated with tolerance and compassion and, ultimately, with indifference. After all, the battle has been won, and it is time to move on.

Second, the debate about the exact numbers of Ukrainians who perished in the Holodomor is best left to the experts. We can now state with reasonable certainty that the number is at least four million. It may be more. But whether or not that number is four or six or eight or ten no longer matters once we understand that the Holodomor was genocide and that that genocide cost some 25,000 Ukrainian lives per day at its height. The demographers are currently hard at work generating numbers and data sets. They have the skills to do so, and they also have the techniques for interpreting these numbers and producing reliable estimates.

Let me remind you that, back in the 1950s and 1960s, the battle of numbers seemed as hopeless as the battle of intentionality. And this was true despite the fact that many of the Western journalists who wrote about the famine in the 1930s spoke of six to eight to ten million victims. After World War II and the outbreak of the Cold War, however, the 1930s were forgotten. A Soviet history atlas compiled by the reputable historian Martin Gilbert in 1972, for instance, illustrates the "main area of the forced collectivization of over 5 million peasant holdings 1929–1938" and notes that "thousands of peasants were killed when they resisted (some by armed force)."[2] Revisionist historians placed the number at several hundred thousand. Soviet propagandists, of course, denied any significant population losses at all. Consider where we stand today. No one disputes the fact that millions died. No one disputes the fact that the "kill rate" — the rate at which people died per day — was astonishingly high. The battle of numbers has been won, and it is time to move on.

---

2   Martin Gilbert, *Soviet History Atlas* (London and Henley: Routledge & Kegan Paul, 1979), p. 34.

Third, it is time to shift the focus of Holodomor studies from the big-picture questions—Was it genocide? Did millions perish?—to the small-picture questions: Who were the people who died? How did they die? What lives did they lead? Who killed them? In other words, we must *humanize* the Holodomor. We must remind ourselves, and others, that this was not just a genocide that cost millions of lives, but that each and every Ukrainian who perished in the Holodomor was a human being worth remembering as a human being.

As Bohdan and I were compiling *The Holodomor Reader*, the materials that impressed me most were not the scholarly articles and the diplomatic documents, but the survivor testimonies and literary accounts. They impressed me precisely because they brought the horrors of the Holodomor to life. They placed faces on the dying and they attached names to the numbers. These materials transformed the Holodomor from an abstract event to a human catastrophe. They gave life to the dead. They enabled me to feel for them, to sympathize and even empathize, to imagine what it must have been like to be a Ukrainian peasant condemned to a slow and awful extinction in the spring of 1933.

Listen to the following lines from a poem by Wira Wowk:[3]

> the forlorn
> field cries
> famine
> the Golgotha
> of a home without a roof
> distant are the storks
> how many years of woe
> did the cuckoo announce?
> how many eclipses of the sun
> how many scarecrows amidst poppies?
> a stream of blood
> flows through the fields
> a bleached skull in the black earth
> ravens circle above corpses
> the shadows of children
> along the fence
> blinded by tears

---

3   Wira Wowk, "Ikonostas Ukrainy," in *Holodomor Reader*, p. 349.

> the dark church
> its zinc cupola nodding
> where are you mallows
> near the multicolored walls
> where is the spindle of the song
> where is the wreath of the dance?
> death dances on the grass stubble
> the zither's strings
> snapped from the lament
> of millions of innocents

This is the power of memoirs and of literature: to bring the past to life. And we need much more of both. We need to hear the peasants and workers and urban dwellers. We need to do everything we possibly can to give them a voice and, thus, a presence. It is only in this manner that we will fully commemorate their sacrifice and their death. Abstractions and numbers are incapable of reaching into these inner realms of human experience and, indeed, of the human condition.

Which brings me to my fourth point. I wish to make a radical suggestion, one that will shock some Ukrainians and many non-Ukrainians. I wish to suggest that Ukrainians are human beings and that their history should be treated as the history of human beings. In a word, we need to reinvent Ukrainian history as the history—not just of elites, not just of masses, not just of peasants, not just of a territory or a state—but of people.

Some Ukrainians are heroes, and a few are saints. Some are cowards, and a few are criminals. The vast majority are just regular folk—no different from Canadians, Americans, Russians, Jews, blacks, Indians, and all the others. All Ukrainians, whatever modifier we append to them, are exactly like all other people. They want to live, and they generally don't want to die. They fall in love, they have relationships, families, and children, and they pass away. They do smart things and they do stupid things. They do good things and they do bad things. No more and no less than all the other billions of people populating the world.

## I.

I have often wondered why I find the scholarship of the contemporary school of neo-Soviet historians unacceptable. It is not, as they like to believe, because they say controversial or critical things about Ukrainians or about Ukrainian nationalists. Nor is it because they are the first to concern themselves with moral issues related to culpability for terrorism, violence, and crimes against humanity. People of my generation were exploring the same issues they are just discovering back in the 1960s and 1970s. Just read any issue of Student, New Directions, Meta, or Dialoh from that time.

No, I find their work unacceptable because it is offensive. That is, *it offends me*. But not as a Ukrainian. I'm used to that and have a thick skin. Rather, it offends me as a human being. Like Soviet specialists on bourgeois nationalism of the past, the neo-Soviet historians offend because they reduce Ukrainians from complex persons to one-dimensional stereotypes with no conscience, no feelings, no brains, and no voice. It's as if these historians had never read *The Merchant of Venice*, where Shylock states:

> I am a Jew. Hath not a Jew eyes? Hath not a Jew hands, organs, dimensions, senses, affections, passions; fed with the same food, hurt with the same weapons, subject to the same diseases, heal'd by the same means, warm'd and cool'd by the same winter and summer, as a Christian is? If you prick us, do we not bleed? If you tickle us, do we not laugh? If you poison us, do we not die? And if you wrong us, do we not revenge? If we are like you in the rest, we will resemble you in that.

Remember: in demanding a pound of flesh, Shylock was acting brutally. Even so, we empathize with him, we even commiserate with him, precisely because we know that he was responding to the sustained humiliation of repeated wrongs. And although Shylock acted brutally, we know that he was not therefore a brute.

Our response to Shylock stands in sharp contrast to how neo-Soviet historians treat Ukrainians: as savages, as brutes, as animals that respond on impulse and lack the capacity for rational thought and human empathy. Savages, naturally, want only to be savages. Savages can have no legitimate interests, no legitimate grievances, no legitimate concerns. Regardless of context, regardless of circumstances, they want only to kill, to rape, to pillage.

Such a view is of course profoundly, and manifestly, racist, and we would not countenance this kind of stereotyping of anybody else — certainly not of blacks, women, and Jews. Just imagine if black insurrections, women's self-assertiveness, and Jews' anger at discrimination were explained only in terms of irrational propensities to destruction, hysteria, and greed. We would be outraged. And yet, it is perfectly acceptable to view Ukrainians in this manner. Please do not misunderstand me. I have no doubt that Ukrainians are capable of and have committed crimes. After all, Ukrainians are human. But I also have no doubt that Ukrainians are rational beings and not savages. After all, Ukrainians are human.

Where does the view of Ukrainians as irrational beings driven by primitive urges come from? I suspect that the answer has something to do with the way in which Ukrainians are represented in three key cultures and historiographies or, to use a fashionable word, discourses. Although no culture, discourse, or historiography is uniform, it is not too great an exaggeration to suggest that long-standing Polish, Jewish, and Russian representations of Ukrainians are strikingly similar. The Polish discourse tends to view Ukrainians as savage *haidamaky*. The Jewish discourse tends to view Ukrainians as bloodthirsty pogromchiks. The Russian, and Soviet Russian, discourse tends to view Ukrainians as treacherous barbarians. In each instance, Ukrainians represent the savage "Other" that must be tamed, and in contradiction to which the nation or people or community in question is defined.

Consider in this light how Frantz Fanon describes colonial views of natives in his classic 1961 anti-colonialist treatise, *The Wretched of the Earth*:

> The town belonging to the colonized people ... is a place of ill fame, peopled by men of evil repute. They are born there, it matters little where or how; they die there, it matters not where, nor how. It is a world without spaciousness; men live there on top of each other, and their huts are built

one on top of the other. The native town is a hungry town, starved of bread, of meat, of shoes, of coal, of light. The native town is a crouching village, a town on its knees, a town wallowing in the mire. It is a town of niggers and dirty Arabs. The look that the native turns on the settler's town is a look of lust, a look of envy; it expresses his dreams of possession—all manner of possession: to sit at the settler's table, to sleep in the settler's bed, with his wife if possible. The colonized man is an envious man. And this the settler knows very well; when their glances meet he ascertains bitterly, always on the defensive, "They want to take our place." It is true, for there is no native who does not dream at least once a day of setting himself up in the settler's place.[4]

All nations engage in this kind of "othering." Indeed, one might say that it lies at the core of national identity formation. What is distinctive about the Ukrainian case is that three important discourses all agree on the same image of the Ukrainian as a savage, that all three mutually reinforce one another and thereby make the stereotype seem perfectly natural and acceptable, and that the Ukrainian alternative to this othering is at best recent, and at worst feeble.

That is not surprising. Ukrainian nation building began much later than Polish, Jewish, and Russian nation building. Moreover, unlike Poles and Russians, Ukrainians lacked a state and a political elite. And unlike Jews, Ukrainians lacked a literate urban class. Small wonder that all three discourses have been able to acquire a hegemonic status in so many of the cultural assumptions that guide historians, journalists, artists, and policy makers in their thinking about Ukraine and Ukrainians. The neo-Soviet historians—whether in Canada, Germany, or Dmitri Tabachnik's Ministry of Education—are, in this sense, no different than the Soviet historians and propagandists who depicted good Ukrainians as passive Little Russians and self-assertive Ukrainians as murderers.

Especially striking about neo-Soviet depictions of Ukrainians is their complete lack of empathy. This is hardly surprising in light of the deep-seated Orientalism of such depictions. When I view Ukrainian history—or, for that matter, African American or

---

4   Frantz Fanon, *The Wretched of the Earth* (New York: Grove Press, 1977), p. 39.

Jewish history—I am gripped with a profound and almost inexpressible sadness. I see fundamentally good people being confronted with impossible circumstances and impossible choices that have no good outcomes. The neo-Soviets and Soviets appear to view Ukrainian history as the story, not of powerless humans, but of powerful brutes.

Listen to Fanon again:

> When the settler seeks to describe the native fully in exact terms he constantly refers to the bestiary.... Those hordes of vital statistics, those hysterical masses, those faces bereft of all humanity, those distended bodies which are like nothing on earth, that mob without beginning or end, those children who seem to belong to nobody, that laziness stretched out in the sun, that vegetable rhythm of life—all this forms part of the colonial vocabulary.[5]

Naturally, reality is a tad more complicated than the Orientalist imagination would have it. Ukrainians are not interested, and have not been interested, only in killing Poles, Jews, and Russians. Like other peoples, Ukrainians do want to be masters of their own fates. They want to enjoy freedom. They want to make mistakes. They want to speak. And not just when they are spoken to or spoken about. They want to be human.

They also want to know who killed them and why. They want to bear witness. They want to remember.

## II.

I have had the good fortune this last year of occupying myself with my parents' memoirs. It was a good fortune that was premised on bad fortune. My father died in 2007 and my mother died in 2011. My father had written over 150 pages of memoirs in the course of the 1980s and 1990s, while my mother wrote some 15 pages in 1983. I took it upon myself to commemorate their lives by editing their memoirs, adding footnotes and photographs, and

---

5   Ibid., pp. 42-43.

publishing them in — where else? — Kinko's.⁶ What began as a seemingly simple project turned into a massive undertaking. My father's memoirs had to be edited extensively and the repetitions removed. Both sets of footnotes turned into research expeditions about their families and friends. I now know more about my relatives, and my parents' lives, than I ever did before. And, naturally, I am profoundly saddened by the realization that I could have learned so much more if I had only had more conversations with them.

The project has been immensely rewarding. Finally, after so many years, I think I understand my parents. Sad to say, I never fully appreciated that my father had spent several weeks in a Nazi prisoner of war camp in the fall of 1941. That, for a fleeting moment in 1944, he considered joining the nationalist underground but then, for reasons even he couldn't explain, decided to flee west. That he continually faced existential and moral choices with no easy answers. That he was persuaded by a friend that he was Ukrainian, and not Rusyn, while bicycling from a small town to their village — a distance of some 7 kilometers that can probably be traversed in 15 minutes. I know I've acquired a better understanding of myself. And I know I've acquired a better understanding of Ukrainian history and, dare I say it, of life.

Take my mother's home town of Peremyshlyany. Back in the interwar period, it had a population of about 5,000, with Poles and Jews comprising about 90% and Ukrainians the rest. All three communities had a highly exclusionary sense of identity and they all lived side by side, didn't like one another too much, but more or less got along. Since then, the town has been "erased," to use Omer Bartov's term,⁷ several times over. The pre-war Jews and their memories are gone. The pre-war Poles and their memories are gone. The pre-war Ukrainians and their memories are gone. And, now, the post-war Ukrainians, with their Sovietized

---

6   The two Kinko's versions eventually appeared as a book: Maria V. Motyl' and Oleksa Motyl', *Mizh Amerykoiu ta Halychynoiu: Spohady Marii ta Oleksy Motyliv* (Lviv: Manuskrypt-Lviv, 2019).

7   Omer Bartov, *Erased: Vanishing Traces of Jewish Galicia in Present-Day Ukraine* (Princeton, NJ: Princeton University Press, 2007).

memories, are also going—either to the West or, prematurely, to the graveyard.

The town generated many remarkable individuals. One is my uncle, Bohdan Hevko. He'd spent some five years in Polish prisons in the 1930s, underwent extensive beatings and torture, was arrested by the Soviets on June 22, 1941, and then killed during the "night of long knives," on June 30, along with thousands of other western Ukrainian political prisoners. The locals found him at the bottom of a pit, his hands tied behind his back with his underpants and his tongue torn out.

Another is my mother's best friend, Fania Lacher, a Jewish girl who survived the Holocaust by finding refuge in a Ukrainian Catholic monastery, converted to Catholicism, became a nun, Sister Maria, and turned into a leading figure in the underground church in Soviet times. The love of her life was a young Ukrainian nationalist, Volodymyr Zaplatynskyi, who helped hide her and her parents from the Nazis and took his life during a firefight with the Soviets in 1944.

Still another is Father Omelian Kovch, the parish priest who persuaded the local Gymnazium to let my mother finish her studies tuition-free and who, for his efforts to save Jews, was arrested by the Nazis and killed in the Majdanek concentration camp. The street my mother lived on is named after Kovch, who was beatified by Pope John Paul II in 2001.

And, finally, there was Adam Rothfeld, son of the head of Peremyshlyany's Judenrat and future Polish minister of foreign affairs, who survived the Holocaust in a nearby Ukrainian Catholic monastery.

My mother's short memoir has hardly resurrected these brave individuals from forgetfulness. But her memories give life to them in ways that more dispassionate studies cannot. Her memories remind us that these people were not just numbers, but human beings who lived exceedingly complex—that is to say, human—lives.

I am proud to have added two voices, by two average Ukrainians, to the written record of twentieth-century Ukrainian history. We need thousands more such voices. Some living

Ukrainians survived the Holodomor. Many of them left their testimonies: some have been published, many no doubt remain hidden in attics and basements. It is now the task of the descendants of Holodomor survivors to bring their parents or grandparents or great grandparents back to life. Many living Ukrainians experienced the horrors of World War II and of totalitarianism, whether of the Nazi or Communist variants. They too should be writing down everything they possibly can. The works need not be polished prose. Rough drafts will more than suffice to remind future generations of who they were and what they experienced. The all-important thing is to leave behind written, or even oral, accounts. There must be a record. There must be Ukrainian voices. If there are not, there can be no Ukrainian history.

## III.

I fully understand that national histories are considered passe in this day and age, but that particular academic fashion need not worry us. Whether the history of Ukraine is national, transnational, global, multiethnic, or something else, the fact is that the stories of Ukrainians form an important part of it—but, naturally, only if they exist on paper, whether real or virtual.

Let me give you an example of what I mean. I recently read the 1943 diary of one Samuel Golfard, a Polish Jew who fled Radom after the Nazis and Soviets divided Poland in September of 1939 and eventually wound up in Peremyshlyany, where he was killed.[8] As you would expect, his is a passionate, angry, and altogether persuasive voice. Several other Jewish voices appear in the volume. As a result, we feel for the Jews, we sympathize with their predicament, and we empathize with them. Peremyshlyany also had Polish and Ukrainian communities, but their voices are barely audible. Instead, in discussing the Holocaust in Peremyshlyany, the editor of the volume provides us with a

---

8   Wendy Lower, ed., *The Diary of Samuel Golfard and the Holocaust in Galicia* (Lanham, MD: AltaMira Press, 2011).

potted history of the town and its inhabitants and, wittingly or not, reduces both Poles and Ukrainians to bit players in a drama that countenances only three roles for Gentiles: those of perpetrator, victim, or bystander.

Naturally, some Poles and Ukrainians were perpetrators and some were victims. But the vast majority were not bystanders. They did not just *stand by* for three years and watch as the Holocaust unfolded. Indeed, they did not stand by at all: they ran, they hid, they hurried, they worked, they whispered, they cried. They lived—or tried to live as best they could—while the world around them was falling apart. The image of bystander is thus completely inaccurate. Poles and Ukrainians actually had lives, just as Samuel Golfard had a life. But you'd never know it, precisely because their voices are absent from the picture. If the Poles and Ukrainians could talk, we would learn just what they did or did not do during those terrible years. Instead, the editor treats them as "others" without a voice and with preconceived roles to play.

It is imperative, therefore, that *Ukrainians be brought back into history*—and especially their own history. Of course, Poles, Russians, Jews, Hungarians, Germans, Rusyns, and many others must have voices in the history of Ukraine. But those voices— especially if suffused with questionable assumptions about the humanity of Ukrainians—should not drown out the barely audible and all too few voices of Ukrainians.

All too often in the past, Ukrainians have been reduced to extras in the already existing scripts developed by their neighbors. As we struggle to produce histories of Ukraine that incorporate all the people who inhabited that land, we should not forget that Ukrainians also inhabited Ukraine and that they were not just the bad guys and heavies.

We can contribute to the humanization of Ukrainians and, thus, of Ukrainian history by remembering that the Holodomor was not an *abstraction* that affected some *imagined category* called a nation or a peasantry. Millions of human beings were exterminated. And the people who puffed up, grew listless, and died of hunger, the people who behaved as scavengers, as good

Samaritans, as ruthless cowards, and as cannibals did so, not because they were savages, but because they were forced into circumstances that deprived them of their humanity.

We should not compound that injustice by denying the victims and survivors of the Holodomor a voice. We should, instead, insist that they have a voice and that that voice matter to all honest historians.

Only when what Wira Wowk called the "lament of millions of innocents" is heard will those millions finally be free. Only then will their "distended bodies," as Fanon put it, assume human form again.

Thank you for your attention.

# 12

# The Paradoxes of Paul Robert Magocsi
# The Case for Rusyns and the Logical Necessity of Ukrainians*

Political scientists love puzzles, or paradoxes, so let me focus on one concerning Paul Robert Magocsi. Simply put, how is it possible for a Rusyn nation-builder to have contributed to the historiography of Ukraine to such a significant degree that one might suspect that Magocsi is really a Ukrainian nation-builder? Like all political-science puzzles, this one dissolves upon closer inspection. As I shall argue below, Magocsi resembles a Ukrainian nation-builder — or perhaps even *is* a Ukrainian nation-builder *malgré soi* — precisely because he is a Rusyn nation-builder.

Although Magocsi is a complex thinker with a rich, fascinating, and evolving bibliographic record, I will present only a "snap shot" of his thought and focus on two sources to make my case — the *Encyclopedia of Rusyn History and Culture* and the magisterial *History of Ukraine* (referred to hereafter as, respectively, the *Encyclopedia* and the *History*). The former work will be especially useful because, as an encyclopedia, it represents something in the nature of a programmatic compendium of inter-textually related views on an exhaustive range of semantically related topics.

## Magocsi's Concepts

Let us begin this exploration at the beginning — with a closer look at Magocsi's central concepts: nation, nationality, and ethnic group. According to the *History* (Magocsi, 352):

---

* First printed in: *Nationalities Papers*, vol 39, no. 1 (January 2011), pp. 105-109. Reprinted with permission of the original publisher.

- "Nation ... is used to refer to the legal citizens of a given state."
- "The term nationality ... is used to refer to a group of people who may have one of more of the following observable characteristics in common: a distinct territory (possibly but not necessarily statehood), language, historical tradition, religion, social attitudes, and ethnographic features. Taken together, these characteristics distinguish members of one nationality from their neighbors."
- "It should also be noted that ethnic or ethnographic groups ... also may have all or many of these same characteristics in common. What, then, distinguishes a nationality from an ethnic group? The primary distinguishing feature is not the presence or absence of all or some of the characteristics listed above, but rather an awareness among members of a given group of people that they have such common characteristics and that it is these characteristics which distinguish them from neighboring peoples or nationalities."
- "In other words, a nationality must have (1) certain objective elements, such as those listed above, in common; and (2) certain subjective elements – a self-perception as belonging and the will to belong to a distinct group."

Note some important features of these definitions. First, in contrast to most traditional nationalists who enthrone the nation, Magocsi does not. For Magocsi, a nation is nothing more than the people who happen to have a certain legal status called citizenship within a political entity called the state. There is nothing ethnic or ethnographic or even national about a nation. Indeed, by making a nation's possession of statehood one of the "observable characteristics" of a nationality—and, presumably, of an ethnic group—Magocsi effectively subordinates the nation, the state, and the nation-state to the nationality.

Second, like most traditional nationalists, Magocsi accepts, and indeed underscores, the importance of the distinction between objective and subjective characteristics. Different ethnic groups are different because they have different "observable characteristics" and therefore "look" different. But different nationalities are different both because they look different and because they *know* they look different. Looking different is thus a necessary condition of a nationality; knowing that one looks different is the sufficient condition. In other words, a nationality cannot exist unless it looks different; a nationality exists and thereby transcends the status of an ethnic group once it knows it looks different.

Observable characteristics feature prominently in this scheme, but they are secondary to subjective knowing — partly because the latter is the sufficient condition that transforms an ethnic group into a nationality, and partly because most of the observable characteristics Magocsi lists are rather less obviously observable than he suggests. Except for islands, it is not quite clear just where a "distinct territory" begins and ends. Unless codified and classified as a distinct set of speech rules, language also has fuzzy boundaries. Historical tradition, as historians would surely agree, is at least partly a function of historical writing and historiographic perceptions. Religion looks monolithic until one actually examines popular beliefs. Social attitudes, as any pollster can attest, are remarkably fluid. And ethnographic features do not appear as a brute fact of nature, but are open to interpretation. In contrast, the claim — "We are a nationality" — is a pretty clear and indisputable Cartesian statement with genuine ontological substance. One might disagree with the proposition being expressed by the claim, but one cannot — at least in a world where things are presumed to exist — dispute the claim's having been made.

My point is that, in Magocsi's scheme of things, "self-perception" and "will" are central. This view places him, as I have already hinted at above, among traditional nationalists, who also believed that their nationality actually existed in some observable sense — hence their interest in collecting ethnographic materials about the *narod* or *Volk* — but that it was, to use the common parlance, "asleep" and thus in need of "awakening." Waking the people from their slumber is the task of nationalists and nation-builders — the intellectuals, poets, writers, artists, politicians, and others who already possess that self-perception and will and can, therefore, engage in the natural task of transforming their self-knowledge into popular self-knowledge.

Nationalists and nation-builders believe that ethnic groups in Magocsi's sense precede them and make their activity both sensible and necessary. Like all political activists who make appeals to and claims about putative popular constituencies, nationalists and nation-builders assume that they are *responding* and not *imposing*. Responding presupposes a certain democratic sensibility; that is, a willingness to heed the needs of the people one represents. Such a democratic sensibility is at the very core of every self-styled nationalist or nation-building project even when, as is often the case, nationalists and nation-builders presume to know better than the people on whose behalf they claim to speak. In that sense, of course, nationalists and nation-builders are like all democratic leaders who also claim to know just what the true interests of the people are.

The actual beliefs and activity of nationalists and nation-builders contradict two widespread notions in the literature on nations (or, to use Magocsi's terminology, nationalities) and nationalism. The first notion, as succinctly expressed by Ernest Gellner (174), is that "nationalism ... creates nations." Gellner may or may not be right, but no self-respecting nation-builder would, or could, agree. The second notion, as represented by theories that emphasize social construction, endows nationalists with the ability to make nations/nationalities out of any collection of people. Here, too, nationalists and nation-builders—including Magocsi—would strongly disagree. Nationalities can emerge only from observably preexisting ethnic groups. Where Gellner and the social constructivists agree with nationalists and nation-builders is on the centrality to the nation building project of nationalists and nation-builders.

## Carpatho-Rusyns and the Necessity of Ukrainians

Magocsi is a Rusyn nation-builder. He has written extensively about Carpatho-Rusyns, and he has also actively participated in the Carpatho-Rusyn national revival of the last three to four decades. It is at just this same time, however, that Magocsi has also produced a large body of authoritative publications on Ukraine and Ukrainians and thereby helped to establish both groups as conceptually and politically real entities in North America and Europe. As I suggested above, Magocsi's Rusyn nation-building activities do not contradict his Ukrainian scholarship. Quite the contrary, Magocsi has effectively become a Ukrainian nation-builder (*malgré soi*, if you will), precisely because he needs a distinct Ukraine in order to make the case for a Rusyn nationality.

Recall that, according to Magocsi, there are two central features of all nationalities—the observable characteristics and the self-perception. Seen in this light, Carpatho-Rusyns are no longer just an ethnic group, but not quite yet a nationality. The *Encyclopedia* emphasizes the point, especially in the entries on Ethnography and History (Magocsi and Pop, 107-112, 177-188), that the History explicitly states: viz., that Carpatho-Rusyns have their own "distinct territory (possibly but not necessarily statehood), language, historical tradition, religion, social attitudes, and ethnographic features" (Magocsi, 352). The Carpathian Mountains, although not quite an island, are critical to this claim since their crests can be conceptualized as creating a distinct geographic space that, by virtue of being a borderland or boundary throughout history, could serve as the cradle for a particular people with particular objective characteristics. Not surprisingly, central to Magocsi's claims about Rusyn distinctiveness are two sub-claims: first, that the "early origins of the Carpatho-Rusyns ... were not, as is often asserted, exclusively associated with Kievan Rus'"; and, second, that "Carpathian Rus' has historically been within political and cultural spheres that are firmly part of central Europe" (Magocsi and Pop, 179).

At the same time, although distinctly observable Carpatho-Rusyn characteristics do exist in Magocsi's scheme—especially among the Dolyniane, or Lowlanders, inhabiting for the most part Ukraine's Transcarpathian oblast—it is obviously not the case that there exists an equally solid "awareness among members of a given group of people that they have such common characteristics and that it is these characteristics which distinguish them from neighboring peoples or nationalities" (Magocsi, 352). After all, even the putative core of the Carpatho-Rusyn ethnic group, the Dolyniane, is named after their place of residence. As a result, Rusyns as an ethnic group have been mobilized, and still are being mobilized, by nationalists and nation-builders with different national agendas. Historically, Rusynophiles, Russophiles, and Ukrainophiles have competed for the loyalties of Rusyns, with each set of nation-builders claiming that the ethnic characteristics they observe should translate into awareness of belonging to, respectively, a Carpatho-Rusyn nationality, a Russian nationality, or a Ukrainian nationality. At present, the primary competition is, as Magocsi recognizes, between the Rusynophiles and the Ukrainophiles.

The existence of three nation-building projects among Rusyns is hardly surprising, and it mirrors the existence at various points in time of similarly varied nation-building projects among the Ukrainians and all other ethnic groups. But it does raise questions about the validity of Magocsi's distinctions between nationality and ethnic group. His scheme implies that observable characteristics amount to an observable "proto-nationality" that, although asleep, can be best awakened by nation-builders committed to just those observable characteristics and the proto-nationality they underpin. That three or more sets of very different nation-builders can make plausible claims about representing the same ethnic group obviously suggests that observable characteristics are, as I have already noted, rather more fungible than meets the eye. At the same time, it is important to remember that Magocsi is decidedly not a Gellnerian or a social constructionist who believes that nationalists can make nations out of anybody. The ideological struggle over Rusyn nationality is waged among three elites, two of whom represent neighboring nationalities with significant similarities with Rusyns. The contestants are not, after all, Rusynophiles, Francophiles, and Sinophiles, as a strictly social constructionist interpretation would have to countenance.

For Magocsi, in any case, the fact that Rusyns do have a distinct set of observable characteristics and that Ukrainophiles can make plausible claims about representing the Rusyn ethnic group and transforming it into a Ukrainian nationality leads to two conclusions. First, the Rusynophile orientation must be defended and promoted — and Magocsi's writings about Carpatho-Rusyns and his extensive community activities on behalf of Carpatho-Rusyns do just that. Second, and paradoxically, the Ukrainian *alternative* to Rusyns must also be defended and promoted. Magocsi the Carpatho-Rusyn nation-builder needs Ukraine and Ukrainians for his case for Carpatho-Rusyn distinctiveness to be persuasive.

It is not that Ukraine represents some evil "other" for Magocsi. His thought is too sensitive and his political convictions are too liberal for so crude a view. Instead, Ukrainians *must exist* as a nationality with distinctly observable characteristics and a distinct self-perception of their own. The case for a distinct Carpatho-Rusyn nationality presupposes the ability to distinguish Rusyns from non-Rusyns, both in terms of observable characteristics and self-perception. Given the overwhelming ethnographic and demographic presence of Ukrainians and the strength of the Ukrainophile orientation, it is imperative that Rusyns be established as *not*-Ukrainians. In turn, that means establishing Ukrainians as *not*-Rusyns and as *not*-Russians.

Logically, Ukrainians *must* be different from both. They must be different from Rusyns, because that difference is the very *raison d'etre* of Carpatho-Rusyn nationality. And Ukrainians must be different from Russians, both because that difference is the *raison d'etre* of Ukrainian nationality and because, while resisting the hegemonic nation-building efforts of nationalists claiming to represent 45 million people with doubts about their observable characteristics and self-perception is conceivable, resisting the hegemonic nation-building efforts of nationalists claiming to represent 150 million Russians (and 45 million Little Russians) with few doubts about their observable characteristics and self-perception may be impossible.

Russians are the "absent presence" in Magocsi's thought. He generally does not discuss them in relation to Carpatho-Rusyns, but the importance of Russians to Ukrainian self-perceptions as a nationality means that — again *pace* the more radical claims of social constructivism—there is no way that a Carpatho-Rusyn nation-builder can ignore Russians or want Russian nation-building efforts to prevail among Ukrainians. While many Ukrainian nationalists and nation-builders might dispute the desirability of establishing Ukrainians as not-Rusyns and Rusyns as not-Ukrainians, all would surely welcome Magocsi's explicit claim that Ukrainians are not-Russians and his implicit claim that they must remain not-Russians.

In sum, Ukrainians logically *must* exist for Magocsi. They are, as it were, a necessary condition of his Carpatho-Rusyn nation-building efforts. To make the case for a distinct Ukrainian nationality and a distinct Ukraine—both with "a distinct territory (possibly but not necessarily statehood), language, historical tradition, religion, social attitudes, and ethnographic features" (Magocsi, 352)—is to make the case for a distinct Carpatho-Rusyn nationality and a distinct Carpathian Rus' homeland.

In this sense, as in so many others, Magocsi is acting in accordance with traditional nationalist beliefs—and I am tempted to say that Magocsi is very much the kind of liberal nationalist prevalent in an empire he has studied very closely, Austria-Hungary. The logic of his thought and activity is also identical to that of Ukrainian nation-builders who have needed, and continue to need, a distinctly Russian Russia in order to make the case for a distinctly Ukrainian Ukraine. The paradoxes of Paul Robert Magocsi therefore dissolve, only to reveal what may be a true paradox—that all nation-builders are always builders of at least two nations, their own and the other's.

## References

Gellner, Ernest. *Thought and Change*. Chicago, IL: University of Chicago Press, 1964. Print.

Magocsi, Paul Robert, and Ivan Pop, eds. *Encyclopedia of Rusyn History and Culture*. 2nd rev. ed. Toronto: University of Toronto Press, 2005. Print.

Magocsi, Paul Robert. *A History of Ukraine*. Seattle: University of Washington Press, 1996. Print.

# 13

# The Ukrainian Nationalist Movement and the Jews
## Theoretical Reflections on Nationalism, Fascism, Rationality, Primordialism, and History*

This paper has been prompted by the ongoing *Historikerstreit*[1] over the Ukrainian nationalist movement and the fact that one of its leaders, Stepan Bandera, was declared a Hero of Ukraine in early 2010 by former President Viktor Yushchenko.[2] Although an honest and open debate is surely welcome, especially on topics that were neglected by Soviet historiography and distorted by Soviet propaganda, the questionable manner in which this *Historikerstreit* is being conducted is not. In this chapter I therefore focus on concepts, theory, methodology, and the assumptions that underpin them. In particular, after examining the conceptual relationship between nationalism and fascism, this paper argues that the Ukrainian nationalist movement was a typical national-liberation movement whose primary goal was political—to achieve independent statehood for the Ukrainian nation—and not ideological; the movement's political strategy vis-à-vis potential allies fully reflected this priority; Jews and the Jewish question were a secondary, or perhaps even tertiary, consideration within this

---

\* First printed in: *POLIN: Studies in Polish Jewry*, vol. 26 (2014), pp. 275-295. Reprinted with the permission of the original publisher.
1 The Historikerstreit, or historians' debate, took place in Germany in the late 1980s, and concerned Germany's responsibility for the Holocaust and the comparability of German crimes against humanity with Soviet crimes against humanity.
2 See the "Bandera-OUN debate" in *The Ukraine List* (UKL), no. 441, compiled by Dominique Arel, 16 Feb., 2010: <http://www.ukrainianstudies.uottawa.ca/pdf/UKL441.pdf>.

strategy and the movement's anti-Jewish attitudes were primarily tactical and situational; the enmity of the movement was primarily directed at Poles and Ukrainian "turncoats," precisely because the Ukrainian nationalist movement was a national-liberation movement; although scholars eschew primordialism in explaining inter-ethnic violence, it is the dominant mode of explanation with respect to Ukrainians and Jews; and although the practice of history should preclude the open promotion of ideology and morality, the latter dominate in both radical critiques and radical apologias of Ukrainian nationalism.³

## Nationalism and Fascism: Conceptual Distinctions

I start with three simple, and obvious, conceptual propositions: first, in order to be meaningful, concepts in general, and nationalism and fascism in particular, cannot by definition encompass everything; second, nationalism is not fascism and fascism is not nationalism; and third, establishing the relationship, if any, between any two concepts—and in our case between nationalism and fascism—requires isolating their central defining characteristics and determining whether those characteristics are or are not identical.

With respect to the first proposition, it is a commonplace of conceptual analysis that concepts must, in order to be meaningful, have limited meanings and specific referents. If concepts are "stretched" to encompass everything, they become meaningless and thus useless.⁴ If nationalism is defined as encompassing all forms of "national identity"—indeed, according to popular

---

3   Eric Hobsbawm states "that no serious historian of nations and nationalism can be a committed political nationalist." Hobsbawm is right, but he does not appear to realize that his comments, if applied consistently, would also preclude unreconstructed communists (such as himself) from writing about the working class. See his *Nations and Nationalism since 1780: Programme, Myth, Reality* (Cambridge, 1990), p. 12.
4   On concept stretching, see G. Sartori, "Guidelines for Concept Analysis," in id. (ed.), *Social Science Concepts: A Systematic Analysis* (Beverly Hills, Calif., 1984), pp. 15-85; id., "Concept Misformation in Comparative Politics," *American Political Science Review*, 64 (1970), pp. 1033-53; id., "Comparing and Miscomparing," *Journal of Theoretical Politics*, 3 (1991), pp. 243-57.

parlance, nationalism supposedly includes feelings, attitudes, dispositions, and behaviors involving national identity, chauvinism, racism, and the like—and fascism is defined as encompassing all forms of non-democratic feelings, attitudes, dispositions, and behaviors, then it follows that everyone possessing some form of national identity is a nationalist and everyone who has doubts about democracy is a fascist. In that case, everyone on earth is a nationalist or fascist, and nationalism and fascism become tantamount to life.[5]

With respect to the second proposition, it is a commonplace of conceptual analysis that different concepts must, at least a priori, be assumed to have different meanings and different referents. A conceptual analysis may reveal that they are in fact synonyms, but the starting point must be that different things must be defined differently. They may overlap; they may be connected, but they cannot a priori be assumed to be the same. We cannot, therefore, resolve the problem of the relationship between nationalism and fascism by implicitly defining them identically—which is to say, by *assuming* that they are the same. Unsurprisingly, if we do engage in this conceptual sleight of hand, we shall quickly "prove" that nationalism and fascism are identical and that all nationalists are fascists and that all fascists are nationalist.

With respect to the third proposition, it is a commonplace of conceptual analysis that concepts have both "defining" and "associated" characteristics. Defining characteristics comprise the core of a definition and, thus, represent what a concept *is*. Associated characteristics are incidental to the definition and may or may not appear as circumstances dictate. It follows that two

---

[5] Just such a fate has, unfortunately, befallen the concept of anti-semitism, which appears to encompass a vast variety of feelings, attitudes, dispositions, and behaviors—ranging from the ravings of Adolf Hitler to the mutterings of some disgruntled *babushka* to the academic writings of University of Chicago and M.I.T. professors—that in some way concern, or are construed as concerning, all Jews, some Jews, or anybody or anything that happens to be, coincidentally, Jewish. Such a "concept of everything," whose intensions and extensions encompass just about everybody, is meaningless and useless—a twofold tragedy inasmuch as "genuine" anti-semitism does indeed exist. Needless to say, concept stretching cannot possibly help the struggle against anti-semitism.

concepts may not be assumed to be identical, even, or especially, if their empirical referents "look alike." Real nationalists may "look like" real fascists—or, for that matter, like real communists or real guerrillas or real Americans—but "looking alike" is completely irrelevant to the question of whether nationalism and fascism, or nationalism and communism, or nationalism and Americanism, are definitionally alike. It follows that mimicking a nationalist or a fascist does not make one a nationalist or a fascist. By the same token, cooperating, collaborating, or consorting with nationalists or fascists is not tantamount to being a nationalist or a fascist or to nationalism or fascism.

What then are nationalism and fascism? And what is the relationship between them?

Nationalism can be understood either as an ideology or as a movement. If understood as an ideology, nationalism is a set of ideas that argues that, and explains why, a nation should have its own independent state. If understood as a movement, nationalism is a set of organizations or individuals that pursue independent statehood for a nation. Nationalism, in short, is about "national liberation," which is its central defining characteristic.[6] It follows that there can be no nationalist nation-states or systems of rule, although there can obviously be chauvinist, racist, or (to use a confusing popular synonym for chauvinist and racist) "hyper-nationalist" nation-states or systems of rule.

Fascism can be understood either as an ideology, a system of rule, or a movement. If understood as an ideology, fascism is a set of ideas that explain why a specifically fascist system of rule is optimal for society. If understood as a system of rule, fascism is a peculiar set of expressly authoritarian political institutions that organize a state and its relations with society.[7] If understood as a

---

6   For an elaboration of this argument, see A. J. Motyl, *Revolutions, Nations, Empires: Conceptual Limits and Theoretical Possibilities* (New York, 1999), pp. 80-81.

7   For excellent discussions of fascism, see A. Lyttelton, "What Was Fascism?" *New York Review of Books*, 51/16 (21 Oct., 2004); A. C. Pinto, "Back to European Fascism," *Contemporary European History*, 15/1 (2006), pp. 103-15. For definitions of fascism, see J. J. Linz, "Some Notes Toward a Comparative Study of Fascism in Sociological Historical Perspective," in W. Laqueur (ed.), *Fascism:*

movement, fascism is a set of organizations or individuals that pursue fascism as an ideology or as a system of rule.

Must nationalism have fascist components? The answer is no. The striving for national independence is perfectly compatible with every philosophy, political ideology, culture, and economic theory—except, perhaps, with those that explicitly deny the existence of the nation or the state. Unsurprisingly, nationalist ideologies and movements have spanned the political spectrum, being found among democrats, liberals, authoritarians, militarists, fascists, Communists, capitalists, Catholics, Islamists, Protestants, and Jews. Prior to the First World War, nationalists tended to be socialists, inter-war nationalist movements tended to be influenced by the prevailing fascist ethos, while post-war national liberation struggles tended to be influenced by the prevailing communist ethos — which is simply to say that nationalism is malleable and can adapt itself to a variety of political ideologies, even, as in the nineteenth century, to liberalism.[8]

Must fascism have nationalist components? The answer is no. Fascism, whether ideology, movement, or system of rule, presupposes an independent state and then proposes to reorganize it along specifically fascist lines. Statehood is thus a necessary condition of fascism: genuinely fascist ideologies, movements, and systems of rule can exist if and only if an independent state is already in existence. That state need not be a nation-state, which is the goal of nationalism: in that sense, the putative connection between nationalism and fascism is not even mediated by the nation-state, but rather by the state. But that, in turn, means that

---

*A Reader's Guide* (Berkeley, 1976), pp. 12-13; R. O. Paxton, *The Anatomy of Fascism* (London, 2004), 218; M. Mann, *Fascists* (Cambridge, 2004), p. 13; S. G. Payne, *A History of Fascism, 1914-1945* (Madison, Press, 1995), p. 14; R. Scruton, *A Dictionary of Political Thought* (New York, 1982), p. 169. I have elsewhere discussed fascism in great length and defined it as "a non-democratic, non-socialist political system with a domineering party, a supreme leader, a hyper-masculine leader cult, a hyper-nationalist, statist ideology, and an enthusiastically supportive population." See A. J. Motyl, "Russia's Systemic Transformations since Perestroika: From Totalitarianism to Authoritarianism to Democracy — to Fascism?" *The Harriman Review*, 2010 Mar., 5.

8  One can even argue, as John Rawls did, that liberalism necessarily entails national liberation. See J. Rawls, *The Law of the Peoples* (Cambridge, Mass., 1999).

fascism is exactly like liberalism, democracy, authoritarianism, and communism in taking independent statehood as a given and recommending just how it and its relations with society should be structured.

The relationship between nationalism, statehood, and fascism can be illustrated in the following manner, where the arrow designates a goal and the colon a precondition.

nationalism→statehood: fascism→authoritarianism

The relationship between nationalism, statehood, and liberalism can be illustrated in the exact same manner:

nationalism→statehood: liberalism→democracy

Note that it would be just incorrect to conclude from these two illustrations that fascism and liberalism are identical as to conclude that nationalism and fascism or nationalism and liberalism are identical. Only conceptual sleight of hand or conceptual sloppiness could produce either conclusion, or both. On the other hand, it would be quite correct to conclude that nationalism can just as easily have liberal and democratic aspirations as it can have fascist and authoritarian aspirations.

One final point requires conceptual treatment. If nationalism and fascism are as different as I have suggested, then why do nationalists so often appear to "look like" fascists and why do fascists so often appear to "look like" nationalists? After all, when nationalists and fascists are politically active, they look like political activists—resembling terrorists at one time, union organizers at another time, and communist intellectuals at a third. Indeed, nationalists and fascists also look like human beings, as they do all the things regular human beings do. Why then do we "see" more similarities between nationalists and fascists? I submit that the empirical similarity rests on the conceptual confusions discussed above. We "see" more similarities, not because they are actually empirically present, but because our—incorrect—conceptual predispositions lead us to focus on just those similarities, between just those two categories of political activists, and not on other, even more marked, ones. Once a conceptually coherent conceptual apparatus is employed, empirical similarities appear as just what they are—either as incidental "overlappings" or as associated characteristics, and not as defining characteristics.

## Ukrainian Nationalism as a Typically Nationalist Movement

Claims that the Ukrainian nationalist movement—defined here as incorporating the Ukrainian Military Organization (Ukrayins'ka viis'kova orhanizatsiya; UVO), the Organization of Ukrainian Nationalists (Orhanizatsiya ukrayins'kykh natsionalistiv; OUN), and the Ukrainian Insurgent Army (Ukrayins'ka povstans'ka armiya; UPA)—was "typically fascist" are, thus, completely off the mark. This is not to say that the Ukrainian nationalist movement was free of fascist elements or that it was liberal, democratic, and without sin. To suggest that this movement was not "typically fascist" is, above all, to state that it possessed at its definitional core, not the defining characteristics of fascism, but the defining characteristics of nationalism.

My claim that the Ukrainian nationalist movement was a typical national-liberation movement rests on three arguments.

First, the one point every single organization and individual in this movement agreed on—from the movement's inception in the early 1920s to its demise in Ukraine in the mid-1950s to its survival in émigré form in subsequent decades—was national liberation and independent statehood. This is clear from official documents, letters, memoirs, interviews, eyewitness accounts, and secondary sources. I submit that this fact—the overwhelming centrality of national independence—necessarily makes the Ukrainian nationalist movement, first and foremost, nationalist.

Second, that movement's relationship to political ideologies changed continually, proceeding from an apolitical militarism to authoritarianism to fascism to democracy to social democracy. Thus, whereas nationalism was a constant, the political ideology was a variable. The UVO was a collection of patriotically inclined ex-soldiers with little sense of political ideology. The OUN began as a radical youth movement, then morphed into a quasi-authoritarian movement, adopted fascist elements by the late 1930s and early 1940s, abandoned them by 1943-1944, and began acquiring progressively more democratic and social-democratic characteristics in the mid- to late-1940s and 1950s. The picture looks even more complex if we consider that the OUN, throughout the 1930s, was divided into the émigré and homeland factions, with the former being more concerned with ideology and the latter more with action. As we would expect, post-Second World War émigré nationalists were divided into liberal, moderate, and authoritarian wings.

The accompanying figure illustrates this ideological change. The heights, depths, and slopes are meant to be only suggestive, and not indicative of actual heights, depths, and slopes. But the main point of the figure should be clear: that the nationalists' political leanings were arranged along an authoritarian vector, first deviating toward fascism and then deviating toward democracy. That is exactly what we would expect from a typically nationalist movement that had to survive in the underground by adopting authoritarian methods of struggle.

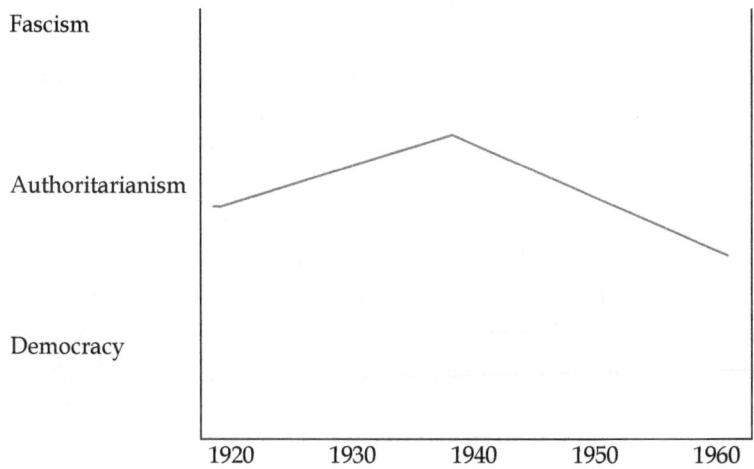

Political leanings of the Ukrainian nationalist movement in Ukraine

It is of course perfectly possible that the Ukrainian nationalist movement would have moved toward full fascism if it had been permitted to establish an independent state in 1941. It is also perfectly conceivable that the seemingly inexorable upward trajectory in the figure would have stopped well short of fascism. There is no way of knowing empirically, because the nationalists were arrested and their short-lived effort at state building was ended. Only a counterfactual experiment resting on already implicit theoretical views could suggest an outcome. Thus, if one already believes that the nationalists were fascists to the core, then fascism is the only imaginable outcome. If, alternatively, one believes that the nationalists were nationalists to the core, then any number of political outcomes, ranging from fascism to liberalism to communism, is conceivable. I suggest that the actual shift in political leanings, as documented by the OUN's Extraordinary Congress in 1943 and a variety of ideological writings, especially by the theorists Petro Poltava and Osyp Hornovy, suggests that political flexibility was at the "core" of Ukrainian nationalism. A "fascist to the core" would have remained a fascist to the core, regardless of circumstances.

Third, many of the fascist components of the Ukrainian nationalist movement can be accounted for by the very structure of illegal underground activity. The Ukrainian nationalist movement was a national-liberation movement similar in structure, ideology, ethos, and means to other twentieth-century national-liberation movements, as in Croatia, Vietnam, Algeria, Ireland, Spain, Israel, and Palestine. All such movements are hierarchical and conspiratorial; all emphasize the primacy of the political in general and the independent state in particular; all are hostile to real and perceived enemies, whether other movements, other nations, or potential turncoats within their own nations; and all employ violence and oftentimes terrorism.

These similarities are not accidental, as pursuing the goal of an independent nation-state in a world of powerful and hostile nation-states is rightfully perceived by existing states as profoundly subversive; movements are thereby forced to adapt accordingly. Although all nationalists develop elaborate ideological rationales for violence, it is important to emphasize that they do so in contexts of state violence—directed at them, of course, but also at all enemies of the state. Nationalists, we should remember, did not invent war, genocide, massacres, or ethnic cleansing. States did, many centuries before nationalists even emerged on the historical stage.

Fourth, the fascist components of the Ukrainian nationalist movement may also be explained by its existence within a "tough," anti-democratic neighborhood. Inter-war Europe in general and inter-war Eastern Europe in particular had very few exemplars of effective liberal democracy. Authoritarianism was the rule, and it would have been well-nigh impossible for an underground nationalist movement to have adopted liberal democratic goals in such circumstances. Moreover, authoritarianism and fascism seemed to "work," regenerating and revitalizing struggling societies—so much so, for instance, that even the uncompromising

Ukrainian communist, Mykola Khvylovy, expressed admiration for the "temperament of fascism."[9]

None of these points gets the Ukrainian nationalists off the hook. There is no doubt that they moved in the direction of fascism and, by the early 1940s, many of them had fully bought into its tenets. That said, they did so precisely because they were nationalists, first and last. Violence, authoritarianism, and conspiracy provided the means of national liberation, while fascism provided a vision of the future Ukrainian nationalist state. While violence, authoritarianism, and conspiracy are intrinsic to underground radical movements — one simply cannot imagine the Ukrainian nationalists without them — fascism was conditionally attractive. If it seemed to suggest the way to go, nationalists embraced it. If it proved not to be the way to go — as the German crackdown on the nationalists in mid-1941 seemed to demonstrate — then alternatives had to be found and, more important, were found. And they could be found precisely because fascism was not an intrinsic component of the Ukrainian nationalist movement or, for that matter, of any genuine nationalist movement.

Seen in this light, the appropriate comparison is not between the Ukrainian nationalists and, say, the Italian fascists, but between the Ukrainian nationalists and the Algerian nationalists in the National Liberation Front, the Palestinian nationalists in the PLO, the Jewish nationalists in the Irgun or the "Stern Gang," or the Irish nationalists in the Irish Republican Army. All five movements were unconditionally, and unchangeably, committed to national liberation and independent statehood. All had hierarchical structures, glorified violence and vitality, and acknowledged supreme leaders. All committed acts of violence against their perceived national enemies. All committed terrorism. All had authoritarian structures. And, despite having fascist elements, all were — typically nationalist. Roman Shukhevych and Stepan Bandera are rather more like Ahmed Ben Bella, Yasser Arafat,

---

9   Mykola Khvyl'ovy, *Sanatoriina zona* (Kharkiv: Folio, 2008), p. 374.

Menachem Begin, Avraham Stern, and Billy McKee, than like Benito Mussolini, Francisco Franco, and Adolf Hitler.

## The OUN's Political Strategy

It follows that, for all such movements as well as for the Ukrainian nationalist movement, the political is primary; indeed, the political is the goal that can justify all means. The Ukrainian nationalist movement's relationship with Jews must therefore be understood through the prism of the movement's (and especially the OUN's) political priorities in general and the overriding priority of independent statehood in particular. This is not to say that the OUN was free of anti-semitism, a point I discuss below. It *is* to say that the OUN's attitudes toward Jews (and all other nations) were a function of its larger strategic calculations regarding the attainment of an independent Ukrainian state and the threat to the survival of the Ukrainian nation presented by Stalinism's assault on the Ukrainian peasantry, intelligentsia, and church and interwar Polish policies toward Ukrainians.

I shall employ several very simple game-theoretic models to plot the choices and strategies facing the OUN and Germany on the eve of the war. The games assume that both sides are rational, i.e. that they want to maximize their ability to achieve their goals. The goal of Germany is "to defeat the USSR"; the goal of the OUN is "to attain an independent state." The choices facing both sides are to "cooperate" or to "fight". Although I fully understand that neither side was a unitary actor making clear-cut choices (especially after Colonel Ievhen Konovalets's assassination in 1938 by a Soviet agent and the split within the OUN) and am in no way endorsing game theory or rational choice (quite the contrary, I am a critic of both), a rationalist approach can reveal the underlying strategic *logic* of an interaction and is, thus, worthy of consideration, even by historians with an aversion to such ahistorical devices. The actual calculations are rather less important than their point—that Ukrainian nationalists, like all political actors, were not just dumb brutes responding to eliminationist urge. In all the games below, the first number designates the "payoff" of a certain choice for the OUN, the second the "payoff" for Germany. All the "payoffs" are my estimates of the relative benefits that would have accrued to both sides as a result of certain actions.

I chose the payoff scores for Game 1 with the following rationale. The OUN benefits enormously (6) from co-operating with a cooperative Germany, as Germany's attack on the USSR advances Ukrainian statehood. Germany benefits modestly, because the OUN does not have much of a fighting force. The OUN loses enormously (-6) if Germany fights it; the OUN gains nothing (0) if it fights while Germany co-operates. Germany, meanwhile, loses a bit (-1) if it fights the OUN.

There is no dominant strategy (one that offers a higher payoff regardless of how the other side moves) for either side, and co-operate/co-operate (6, 1) is the equilibrium outcome.

In Game 2, the OUN expects Germany to be defeated by the Soviet Union.

|  | Germany | |
|---|---|---|
| **OUN** | co-operate | fight |
| co-operate | 6, 1 | -6, 0 |
| fight | 0, -1 | -6, -1 |

**GAME 1**

There is no dominant strategy (one that offers a higher payoff regardless of how the other side moves) for either side, and co-operate/co-operate (6, 1) is the equilibrium outcome.

In Game 2, the OUN expects Germany to be defeated by the Soviet Union.

|  | Germany (expected to lose) | |
|---|---|---|
| **OUN** | co-operate | fight |
| co-operate | 6, 1 | -3, 0 |
| fight | -3, -1 | -6, -1 |

GAME 2

The payoffs for Germany stay the same as in Game 1. However, for the OUN co-operate/co-operate is best (6), as it is premised on Germany's weakening the Soviet Union and possibly enabling the OUN to establish a state. Fight/fight is worst for the OUN (-6), as it distracts Germany from fighting the Soviet Union and depletes the OUN's strength. Cooperate/fight results in (-3) for the OUN, as Germany is distracted from the Soviet Union, while the OUN's strength is relatively conserved. Fight/cooperate is equally disadvantageous for the OUN.

For the OUN, co-operation is the dominant strategy, as it always promises higher payoffs than fighting.

In Game 3, the OUN expects Germany to defeat the Soviet Union.

|  | Germany (expected to win) | |
|---|---|---|
| **OUN** | co-operate | fight |
| co-operate | 6, 1 | -6, 0 |
| fight | -6, -1 | -3, -1 |

GAME 3

Again, co-operate/co-operate is optimal (6) for the OUN. Co-operate/fight is highly disadvantageous (-6) for the OUN, because a hostile Germany that defeats the USSR will crush the OUN. Fight/co-operate is also disadvantageous (-6) for the OUN, as fighting a victorious, even if friendly Germany, is suicidal.

Fight/fight is moderately less disadvantageous (-3) for the OUN, possibly enabling it to salvage some of its goal. There is no dominant strategy for either player.

Note that in all three games, co-operate/co-operate makes most sense for both players, promising a big payoff for the OUN and a small one for Germany.

Consider, in contrast, Game 4, between the "West" and the OUN, where the West's primary goal is "stability" and the OUN's remains attaining an independent state.

|  | West | |
|---|---|---|
| OUN | co-operate | fight |
| co-operate | -1, -1 | -1, 0 |
| fight | 0, -1 | -1, -1 |

**GAME 4**

The West either gains nothing (0) from fighting a cooperative OUN, while losing marginally (-1) from cooperating with a revisionist movement or fighting a hostile OUN. By the same token, the OUN loses marginally (-1) from cooperating with states committed to maintaining stability or from fighting them, and it gains nothing (0) from fighting them if the West cooperates.

In sum, there is no payoff from Game 4 for the OUN — in contrast to a potential 6-point payoff from Games 1, 2, and 3.

Note that these four games provide a persuasive rationale for the OUN's strategy toward Germany and the West during and after the Second World War. The OUN's strategic preference was co-operate-co-operate (6) with Germany, regardless of whether Germany was expected to defeat or be defeated by the Soviet Union. When Germany turned against the OUN in mid-1941 (when it was still expected to defeat the Soviet Union), the OUN's optimal course (-3) was to fight — which it did. When Germany was expected to lose, and began retreating, the optimal course for both was co-operate-co-operate (6,1) — which they did. In turn, when the

OUN began interpreting the West's preferences vis-à-vis the Soviet Union as resembling Game 1, the OUN shifted its strategic alliance to the United States and the United Kingdom.

Using these insights, let us imagine a counterfactual — that not Nazi Germany, but a democratic Germany, had prepared for and unleashed a massive war against the Soviet Union in 1941. My analysis suggests that the Ukrainian nationalists would have acted no differently than in reality and would have sought and established a strategic alliance with a democratic Germany precisely because such an alliance would have made enormous strategic sense. In turn, the "West" in general and the United States in particular would have regarded the "Free Ukrainians" as a vital strategic asset, lauded them for their democratic aspirations, overlooked or contextualized their authoritarianism and situational anti-Jewishness, and praised them for their ability to organize, kill collaborators, and engage in terrorism. If victorious, the "West" would have granted the Free Ukrainians their own state, and whatever human rights violations they may have engaged in would have been explained away as part of the "business" of war. Finally, today's scholars would be studying a "typically nationalist movement" that helped win the war and, alas, committed "some" atrocities along the way.

## Jews and the OUN's Political Priorities

If we conceive of Nazi Germany's attitude toward Jews as being tantamount, in Daniel Jonah Goldhagen's phrase, to "eliminationist anti-semitism"[10] — that is, a deeply rooted belief that Jews are intrinsically evil and must therefore be exterminated — then the attitude of most Ukrainian nationalists and the OUN may be termed a "situational anti-Jewishness." By this I mean that, for most Ukrainian nationalists, Jews were a "problem" — either because they were implicated, or believed to be implicated, in communism and the Soviet leadership or because they were opposed, or were

---

10   D. J. Goldhagen, *Hitler's Willing Executioners: Ordinary Germans and the Holocaust* (New York, 1997).

believed to be opposed, to an independent Ukrainian state. Situational anti-Jewishness and eliminationist anti-semitism could and often did, as in a Venn diagram, overlap, but they were not identical. Eliminationist anti-semitism was an all-or-nothing proposition that was both immutable and immune to circumstances. In contrast, situational anti-Jewishness could ebb and flow with the circumstances. When Jews were no longer perceived as a "problem" in the manner defined above, situational anti-Jewishness could even morph into situational "pro-Jewishness."

It is significant that the OUN's political programs from the period 1939-1941 define Jews in just this manner—as a problem. After all, it was at just this time that both factions of the OUN were actively cooperating with the German military and counter-intelligence. There would have been no sanctions attached to officially propounding eliminationist anti-semitism; indeed, there might have been ample rewards from Berlin. Instead, the tone of OUN documents is nothing like the tone of Nazi ideology, and the space devoted to the "Jewish question" is strikingly small. Indeed, the resolutions of the Second Great Congress, held in Kraków in April 1941, specifically *cautioned* Ukrainians against anti-Jewish activity—a bizarre statement for allegedly eliminationist anti-semites to make just two months before Germany's attack on the Soviet Union.[11]

Two specific behavioral patterns are especially worthy of attention for what they say about OUN perceptions of Jews. First, of the sixty-three actual or attempted assassinations carried out by Ukrainian nationalists in eastern Poland in the interwar period, only one was directed at a Jew. The ethnic breakdown of the others

---

11 "The Jews in the USSR are the most faithful prop of the ruling Bolshevik regime and the vanguard of Muscovite imperialism in Ukraine. The Muscovite-Bolshevik government uses the anti-Jewish sentiments of the Ukrainian masses to divert their attention from the true cause of their misfortune and to direct them at a time of upheaval at pogroms against Jews. The Organization of Ukrainian Nationalists combats the Jews as a prop of the Muscovite-Bolshevik regime, while simultaneously making the masses conscious of the fact that Moscow is the principal enemy." See *OUN v svitli postanov Velykykh Zboriv, Konferentsii ta inshykh dokumentiv z borot'by 1929-1955 r.* (Munich, 1955), p. 36.

is as follows: thirty-six Ukrainians, twenty-five Poles, and one Russian.[12] Of this number, two communists—one Ukrainian and one Russian—were killed. That is to say, the primary enemies were "turncoat" Ukrainians and Poles; Russians, communists, and Jews—despite their putative centrality to the Ukrainian nationalist agenda—were actually incidental to nationalist political violence. The then-popular nationalist song—"Death, death to the *lyakhy* [Poles]; death to the Muscovite-Jewish commune"—conveys this point quite well. Poles are singled out; communism—and not Russians and Jews per se—then follows.

Second, it is only if one assumes that Ukrainian nationalists were motivated by situational anti-Jewishness that the defection of some two thousand Ukrainian policemen in late 1942 and their subsequent entry into the UPA makes sense. Eliminationist antisemites would have stayed in the Polizei, which would have offered them far better opportunities to pursue their agenda than retreat into the underground. By the same token, eliminationist anti-semites would not have joined the Waffen SS or, like Roman Shukhevych, have left the Nachtigall Battalion just as the destruction of Jews was assuming momentum.

Game 5 illustrates these points. It assumes that both Germany and the OUN are motivated exclusively by eliminationist anti-semitism. Both sides benefit (6,2) from co-operation, though the OUN benefits much more as its capacity to pursue eliminationist anti-semitism on its own is significantly smaller than Germany's. The OUN's payoff falls to (3) if it co-operates while Germany fights and gets (0) payoff. The OUN's payoff is (0) if it fights a co-operative Germany, which still manages to attain some eliminationist goals (1) by co-operating. Neither side benefits from fighting (0,0).

Note that both sides have a dominant strategy, one that promises a better payoff regardless of how the other side plays—and that is to co-operate. Thus, co-operate-co-operate (6,3) is the strategy that eliminationist anti-Semites would have always pursued. And yet, both Germany and the OUN violated the very

---

12  A. J. Motyl, "Ukrainian Nationalist Political Violence in Inter-War Poland," *East European Quarterly*, 1985 Mar., p. 50.

logic of maximizing putative eliminationist anti-semitism by engaging in all three other behaviors, thereby suggesting that the initial assumption of eliminationist anti-semitism as being the sole goal is incorrect.

|  | Germany | |
|---|---|---|
| OUN | co-operate | fight |
| co-operate | 6, 2 | 3, 0 |
| fight | 0, 1 | 0, 0 |

**GAME 5**

Note also that the minuscule payoffs for Germany suggest that the OUN was at best incidental to Berlin's pursuit of eliminationist goals. Although some Ukrainian nationalists, like some Ukrainians, may have contributed to the Holocaust, their contributions, although morally heinous, were practically insignificant. The Holocaust in Ukraine could not have taken place without Nazi Germany's ideological agenda and coercive apparatus and without Nazi Germany's war against the Soviet Union. If the Ukrainian nationalist movement had not existed or had not contributed to anti-Jewish activities, the Holocaust would, I suggest, still have taken place in just the manner that it did. Indeed, Hitler's war against the Soviet Union would have followed the exact same course. In a word, the Ukrainian nationalists, despite their own illusions of grandeur, were bit players in the war and, by extension, in the Holocaust.

## The Ukrainian Nationalists and Their Enemies

None of the above is meant to suggest that Ukrainian nationalists held benign attitudes towards Jews.[13] They did not—and there is

---

13　V. Vyatrovych, "Stavlennia OUN do ievreiv: formuvannia pozytsii na tli katastrofy," <www.ukrcenter.com/library/read.asp?id=7404&page=1>.

ample evidence to suggest that this is the case.[14] But it is also important to recognize that the OUN's primary enemies were Poles and Ukrainian "turncoats," and not the Jews. While Jews may have been perceived as being responsible, together with the Russians, for communism and Soviet power, the reality of the national-liberation struggle in Galicia confronted Ukrainian nationalists with ubiquitous everyday examples of Polish opposition to, and turncoat Ukrainian subversion of, Ukrainian nationalism's goals. Poles were the primary obstacle — both theoretically, because it was their state that had to be dismantled for an independent Ukraine to exist; and practically, because they held, or hoped during the war to reacquire, the levers of power in Galicia and Volhynia. Not surprisingly perhaps, nationalist enmity toward Poles, together with a strategic calculation by both sides that strategically important territory had to be seized before the Germans retreated and the Soviets approached, led to the bloodbaths in Volhynia in mid-1943.

Whether termed ethnic cleansing or inter-ethnic strife, the ethnic violence in Volhynia bears comparison, not with the state-directed destruction of ethnic groups by Nazi Germany, Ustaša Croatia, or Vichy France, but with the ethnic violence of Algerians against *pieds-noir* French, of Irish nationalists against the British, of Palestinian nationalists against Israelis, and of Jewish nationalists against Palestinians. In all these instances, nationalists attacked and killed members of nations that held political power or controlled contested territory. Their methods may be despicable — although they are not necessarily more despicable than the horrors of state-generated wars — but they are not just the actions of dumb brutes with no sense of strategic rationality.

Turncoat Ukrainians were the second obstacle for the Ukrainian nationalists, as they threatened to destroy the much

---

14 Even if authentic, Iaroslav Stetsko's autobiographical sketch is not, I suggest, of much use here, primarily because a document produced in Nazi Germany *after* interrogation and *before* arrest may not be assumed to represent the truthful views of its author. See K. C. Berkhoff and M. Carynnyk, "The Organization of Ukrainian Nationalists and Its Attitude toward Germans and Jews: Iaroslav Stets'ko's 1941 Zhyttiepys," *Harvard Ukrainian Studies*, 23/3-4 (1999), pp. 149-84.

desired national unity from within, thereby being the primary targets of both interwar and wartime assassinations. Here, too, the Ukrainians were acting no differently than Algerian, Irish, Palestinian, Jewish, and many other nationalists, who are always on the lookout for traitors and periodically cleanse their ranks of suspect elements. The opprobrium with which Americans still hold Benedict Arnold indicates just how strong such sentiments can be.

There are no comparably motivated anti-Jewish killings. The pogroms that erupted in many Galician towns in mid-1941 were not the result of strategic calculations driven by eliminationist anti-Semitic impulses. Instead, situational anti-Jewishness and the breakdown of law and order combined with the traumatic discovery of ten to fifteen thousand massacred Ukrainian political prisoners to produce a wave of "spontaneous" anti-Jewish violence.[15] To be sure, eliminationist Ukrainian anti-Semites and situational Ukrainian anti-Jews must have been implicated, and many of them were no doubt members or sympathizers of the OUN. But, importantly, once the wave passed, the OUN's strategic priorities reasserted themselves and the nationalists reverted to their situational anti-Jewishness. Accordingly, an "Instruction of the Security Service" issued just before the war foresaw the "neutralization" of Russians, Jews, and Poles "both individually and as national groups," inasmuch as the OUN's goal was to "crush in the bud every attempt by foreign elements in Ukraine to assert themselves in any organized fashion."[16] These are obviously not the sentiments of liberals. But they *are* the sentiments of national-liberation movements that oppose all enemies of their nation and fear *organization* more than anything else.

It is perhaps unsurprising that, by 1943-1945, situational anti-Jewishness was able, by virtue of the changing circumstances of the struggle and the war, to mutate into something approximating tolerance. Indeed, the fact that the nationalist underground eventually adopted a relatively benign attitude even toward Poles,

---

15  D. V. Vyedyenyeyev and H. S. Bystrukhin, *Mech i tryzub: rozvidka i kontrrozvidka rukhu ukrains'kykh natsionalistiv ta UPA* (1920-1945) (Kyiv: Heneza, 2006), p. 327.
16  Ibid., p. 155.

reaching a quasi-alliance with some underground Polish groups, suggests that attitudes toward Poles were not tantamount to eliminationist chauvinism but to "situational anti-Polishness".

## Explaining Interethnic Violence

I have used Goldhagen's term, "eliminationist anti-semitism," even though I strongly believe that it is completely inadequate for making sense of Nazi behavior.[17] Although it is perfectly possible that eliminationist anti-semitic attitudes may exist, Goldhagen endows the term with primordial, transcendent, and thus ahistorical qualities. Many of his critics have pointed this out, and there is no need to rehash their arguments.[18] Suffice to say that primordialism is almost universally rejected as an adequate explanation of ethnic violence.

Instead, students of ethnic violence find explanations not in "ancient hatreds", but in theories that emphasize structures, emotions, rationality, or organization.[19] Structural approaches focus on the "objective" relations between and among ethnic groups, emphasizing disparities, or contradictions, in power, wealth, status, and so on. Emotional approaches move from relations between and among groups to the feelings — frustration, anger, aggression, fear, and so on — within individuals and collectivities and to how those feelings may lead to certain forms of behavior. Rational approaches emphasize utility, profit, advantage, and other such calculations in the behavior of groups and individuals. Last, organizational approaches focus on movements and activists and their ability to mobilize resources, act as ethnic entrepreneurs, and pursue specific goals. Which of these approaches are better and which are worse is hard to say, as all of

---

17  See Motyl, *Revolutions, Nations, Empires*, pp. 88-9.
18  For one of the latest, devastating, criticisms of Goldhagen, see T. Snyder, "What We Need to Know about the Holocaust," *New York Review of Books*, 57/14, 30 Sept. 2010, p. 78.
19  Roger Petersen employs these approaches in his excellent studies, *Resistance and Rebellion: Lessons from Eastern Europe* (Cambridge, 2001) and *Understanding Ethnic Violence: Fear, Hatred, Resentment in Twentieth Century Eastern Europe* (Cambridge, 2002).

them can claim successes and failures. The important point for our purposes is that all these theories eschew primordialism and the simplistic and simpleminded division of ethnic groups into bad and good.

Ironically, although primordialism has no traction among serious students of interethnic violence, critics of Ukrainian nationalism generally adopt just this kind of explanatory framework. Ukrainians in general and Ukrainian nationalists in particular are simply assumed, first, to be vicious anti-semites, second, to be vicious anti-semites unalterably, unconditionally, and inevitably, and third to act on their anti-semitism always and everywhere. (The quotidian manifestation of this belief finds expression in the comment that "your people killed my people.") From this point of view, vicious anti-semitism defines all of Ukrainian history and all Ukrainian behavior vis-à-vis Jews, Ukrainian history is a history of primordial anti-semitism, and every Ukrainian in this narrative is, and can only be, a villain or a potential villain.[20]

This narrative logic is fully evident in discussions of the "*zhydokomuna* myth" and the "Ukrainians-as-anti-semites" stereotype. I submit that the *zhydokomuna* myth is not a myth, but a *stereotype*. A myth is something that, like unicorns or Aeneas' sojourn in Hades, has absolutely no basis in reality: we know for a fact that unicorns, Aeneas, and Hades do not exist. A stereotype, in contrast, is a logical mistake, but, ironically, one that is not irrational. It is simply not true that there were no Jewish communists or that Jews played no role in the establishment of Soviet power in Ukraine, as a *zhydokomuna* myth would have to

---

20 The larger issue is of course the transformation of anti-semitism in general into a mystical trait that, like Hegel's spirit, can appear, reappear, and disappear at will, "infecting" anybody or everybody, regardless of specific circumstances, attitudes, and behaviors. But that is exactly what one would expect from a concept that has been stretched to such a degree that it can be made to appear ubiquitous. The resultant primordial ascription of anti-semitism to, say, individuals of Ukrainian ancestry logically results in the claim that "your people killed my people." In primordial schemes, everyone is innocent, or everyone is guilty, by ascription.

insist.[21] Instead, what we have is a typical case of stereotyping, in which more or less accurate observation statements are transformed, by virtue of logical mistakes, into incorrect generalizations.

Stereotypes can take one of two logical forms, the first deductive, the second inductive. On the one hand, deductive stereotypes begin from the proposition that "All A are B" and then mistakenly conclude that it must follow that "All B are A." Thus, the statement, "All communists are Jews," even if true, does not imply that "all Jews are communists." "All CEOs are men," even if true, does not imply that "all men are power-holders." "All concentration camp heads are Austrians," even if true, does not imply that "all Austrians are anti-semites." "All anti-semites are Ukrainians," even if true, does not imply that "all Ukrainians are anti-semites." "All Nazis are Germans," even if true, does not imply that "all Germans are Nazis."

On the other hand, inductive stereotypes begin with the proposition that "Some A are B" and then mistakenly conclude that "All A are B." Thus, the statement, "Some Jews are communists," even if true, does not imply that "all Jews are communists." "Some men are CEOs," even if true, does not imply that "all men are power-holders." "Some Austrians are concentration camp heads," even if true, does not imply that "all Austrians are anti-semites." "Some Ukrainians are anti-semites," even if true, does not imply that "all Ukrainians are anti-semites." "Some Germans are Nazis," even if true, does not imply that "all Germans are Nazis."

Although both forms of stereotyping are obvious logical mistakes, they are not irrational. They serve as means of cognitive ordering and efficiency precisely because they are not unfounded empirically. As we often say, every stereotype has at least a "kernel" of truth. And the truth is that, while it is not the case that All A are B, it usually is the case that some A are B and that fact, for better or for worse, does help us navigate the complexities of

---

21  This is the line taken in, for example, Z. Gitelman, "The Jewish Presence in the NKVD and its Implications for Ethnic Relations"; Iu. Shapoval, "Jews in the Leadership Organs of the GPU/NKVD of the Ukrainian Soviet Socialist Republic during the 1920s and 1930s," papers delivered at the Ukrainian Jewish Encounter Initiative Meeting at Ditchley Park, 14-16 Dec. 2009.

reality. Sometimes we do so benignly. Dark clouds do not always signify rain, but if we assume they do and take an umbrella, we will never get wet—although we will always be encumbered with an umbrella. Sometimes we do so less benignly. Used car dealers may not all be dishonest, but if we assume they are and act accordingly, we will never get cheated—although we may also pass up genuine bargains. And sometimes we do so unjustly. Arabs may not all be terrorists, but if we assume that they are, we will never be attacked by Arab terrorists—although we will massively violate human rights in the process.

Seen in this light, anti-semitism, like every form of chauvinism or racism, may be understood as an attempt to reconcile incompatible stereotypes by means of an ascription of some form of evil to the target group. Thus, the two stereotypes—"all communists are Jews" and "all capitalists are Jews" (both mistakenly derived from the empirical observations, "communists are Jews" and "capitalists are Jews")—can be held simultaneously, as indeed they are by true anti-semites, if and only if Jews are defined as intrinsically evil. Anti-Ukrainian racism assumes that Ukrainians are intrinsically brutish and thus necessarily inclined to act as savages, especially when constraints on their behavior are lifted. In contrast to "crafty" Jews, "brutish" Ukrainians are incapable of holding logically incompatible positions. Instead, all they do is kill.[22]

Why then *must* the "*zhydokomuna* myth" be termed a myth in the radical critique of Ukrainian nationalism? Why can it not just be a stereotype? Belief in an obvious falsehood, a myth, logically goes hand in hand with a putatively primordial Ukrainian anti-semitism. In contrast, belief in a stereotype would suggest, first, that Ukrainians have the capacity to think (even if illogically) and, second, that there may be some truth to the stereotype. But that element of truth in turn means that the relationship of Jews to Ukrainians may also matter in explaining the Ukrainian

---

22 Unsurprisingly, their memoirs and eyewitness accounts cannot be trusted. Brutes and killers *must* be liars.

relationship to Jews—a possibility that primordialist approaches to Ukrainian-Jewish relations simply cannot countenance.

Significantly, while the association of Jews with communism must be an empirically preposterous claim and thus a myth, the association of Ukrainians with anti-semitism—which is no less of a stereotype than the *zhydokomuna* myth—must be accepted as empirically true. Indeed, the working assumption in most anti-nationalist narratives is that, as a Jewish friend once breezily informed me, "all Ukrainians are vicious anti-semites." Clearly, some kind of double standard is at work here. If *zhydokomuna* is a myth, then the Ukrainian as *der ewige Antisemit* must also be a myth. If *zhydokomuna* is a stereotype, then the Ukrainian as the eternal anti-semite must also be a stereotype. Instead, the primordial association of Ukrainians with anti-semitism has come to possess the status of an ontological, even if obviously racist, truth.

It may be time for scholars to abandon the extant stereotype of Ukrainians as unthinking, anti-semitic brutes—as the quintessential Orientalized Other—if only because primordialist assumptions about Ukrainians and their genetic proclivity to anti-semitism (which, according to popular versions, is "imbibed with their mothers' milk") explode all notions of any possible Ukrainian responsibility or guilt for real or imagined excesses against Jews. After all, sin requires some measure of free will. Since brutes lack the capacity to make choices, and especially moral choices, they can only be pitied, and certainly not condemned or encouraged to apologize or do penance.

## History, Ideology, and Morality

Although history, ideology, and morality all employ narratives based on a logically coherent ordering of chronologically arranged facts, they are not just variants of one another. In telling their stories, historians emphasize complexity, context, and change. They provide a maximally full picture of a variety of interconnected events, individuals, and groups. They situate that picture within some context or contexts. And they appreciate that the picture, the context, and the events, individuals, and groups are continually experiencing change. In contrast to historians, ideologists and moralists eschew complexity, context, and change. They tell simple stories that transcend time and space and brook no change. In that sense, ideology and morality are antithetical to history, while being perfectly compatible with, if not indeed identical to, each other.

Radical critics of the Ukrainian nationalist movement often fall into the ideological or moralistic camps.[23] Soviet historians and propagandists were overtly ideological; many of the current crop of radical critics are overtly moralistic.[24] Significantly, their narratives are mirror images of those produced by nationalist apologists[25]: the same individuals and the same events figure in both kinds of narratives, the only difference being that they are "bad" in the anti-nationalist narrative and "good" in the nationalist narrative.[26] As a result, just as apologists of the Ukrainian nationalist movement produce nationalist (and thus ideological and/or moralistic) narratives that have little in common with genuine history, so too radical critics of the Ukrainian nationalist movement produce anti-nationalist (and thus ideological and/or moralistic) narratives that have little in common with genuine history. Both write history without complexity, context, and change. That is, both nationalists and anti-nationalists write *history without history*—which is to say non-history or, perhaps, antihistory.

The following quotation by Keith Gessen, a journalist writing for *The New Yorker*, perfectly captures the spirit, and the letter, of the anti-nationalist, anti-historical narrative:

> Yushchenko walked into a firestorm. The O.U.N.-U.P.A. was courageous, stateless, persecuted — and also Fascistic and anti-semitic. It offered its

---

23 For a good example, see J.-P. Himka, "The Holodomor in the Ukrainian-Jewish Encounter Initiative," paper prepared for the Ukrainian Jewish Encounter Initiative Meeting at Ditchley Park, 14–16 Dec. 2009. <http://ualberta.academia.edu/JohnPaulHimka/Papers/492282/The_Holodomor_in_ the_Ukrainian-Jewish_Encounter_Initiative>.
24 A typical Soviet critique is K. Dmytruk, *Zhovto-Blakytni Bankroty* (Kyiv, 1982).
25 The classic nationalist apologist is P. Mirchuk, *Narys istorii Orhanizatsii Ukrains'kykh Natsionalistiv* (Munich, 1968).
26 See Oleksandr Zaitsev's excellent analysis, "Viina mitiv pro viinu v suchasnii Ukraini," *Krytyka*, 2010, nos.3-4, pp. 16-17.

services to the Nazis in the fight against "Jewish Bolshevism." Shukhevych, a brave soldier, entered Lviv in 1941 alongside the Wehrmacht. In the next couple of years, the Banderovites, as they were called, patrolled the villages and forests of western Ukraine. Their activities included the ethnic cleansing of the Polish population, so that Ukraine would be for Ukrainians, but, when they came across the few Jews in the area who had survived the work of the Einsatzgruppen and the deportations to the camps, they murdered them, too. This story, in its general outlines, had been known for a long time, but Yushchenko seemed genuinely to believe that it was all old Soviet propaganda.[27]

The problem with Gessen's narrative—and of other radical anti-nationalist narratives—is that it *really* is based on "old Soviet propaganda," presenting a chronologically ordered series of facts without any concern for complexity, context, or change. The nationalists, according to Gessen's account, were typically fascist and anti-Semitic and, as such, did and could only do those things that typical fascist anti-Semites must do: collaborate and kill Jews. The structure of this kind of narrative is, as I had suggested above, identical to that written by nationalist apologists. Both necessarily result in bad history.

In principle, the solution to bad history is simple: after all, *tertium datur*, but only if one looks for it and maintains a level head and even temper. One does not have to be a nationalist or an anti-nationalist scholar. One can write a good history of Ukrainian nationalism that appreciates complexity, context, and change and— *mirabile dictu!*—still be critical of Ukrainian nationalism. One can also write a good history of Ukrainian-Jewish relations that appreciates complexity, context, and change and—*mirabile dictu!*— still eschew primordialist stereotypes about evil/good Jews or good/evil Ukrainians.

Such an approach would avoid both nationalist and anti-nationalist depictions and, instead, present the Ukrainian nationalists neither as glorious heroes, who were really philo-semites in disguise, nor as savage brutes, who were really nothing but anti-semites with eliminationist agendas. Such an approach would provide some sense of the complexity of politics, society,

---

27  K. Gessen, "The Orange and the Blue," *The New Yorker*, March 1, 2010, p. 34.

culture, and economics in Ukraine in the interwar period and during the Second World War; it would provide a context for the developments taking place in Ukraine and within the nationalist movement; and it would accept the reality of change—of nationalists, fascists, Jews, Ukrainians, and everybody else. Such an approach could not ignore the myriad of political forces — Ukrainian, Polish, Jewish, communist, fascist, Soviet, and many others— that defined the reality of Ukraine in general and western Ukraine in particular during the 1920s, 1930s, and 1940s. Such an approach could ignore neither the devastation experienced by Ukraine during the First World War, the Famine of 1933, the Terror of the 1930s, and the Second World War, nor the role therein of Germans, Poles, Jews, Russians, and others, including Ukrainians. Finally, such an approach would avoid the primordialist temptation and acknowledge that no movement, no party, no people, no individual embodies timeless qualities.[28]

Such a genuinely historical approach is much more difficult and much more anxiety-producing than simplistic moralistic or ideological tales. An honest look at Ukrainian violence against Jews and Poles would not, in the spirit of the Soviet distinction between the good *narod* and the bad bourgeoisie, just put the blame on bad nationalists or primordial anti-semitism. It would, instead, examine the whole range of issues that theories of interethnic violence emphasize—everything from structures to emotions to rationality to organization. Such an examination would likely find that, in light of the complexity, context, and change in and of those relations, binary morality breaks down, grays dominate over blacks and whites, ideological interpretations of history make little sense, and there are few villains and ever fewer heroes on all sides.[29]

---

[28] Such an approach would also begin to address Timothy Snyder's concern: "We don't have a history of the Holocaust that is set in the Eastern European lands where the victims died, and that describes the interactions of the German invaders, the Jewish inhabitants, and the peoples among whom the Jews lived." Snyder, "What We Need to Know about the Holocaust," p. 76.

[29] The Ukrainian Jewish Encounter Initiative based in Toronto, Canada, appears to be going in this direction.

A good place to start is Henry Abramson's pithy summary of Ukrainian-Jewish relations:

> Students reflecting on the dual genocides that Ukraine endured during the twentieth century cannot avoid the cruel paradigm of Ukrainian-Jewish history, in which each group constructs competing and often mutually exclusive narratives of suffering at the hands of the other. Viewed from afar, the pendulum of abuse and violence seems clear: the Jewish *orendars* exploit the Ukrainian peasantry, who exact terrible revenge in 1648-49 and the *Kolivshchyna*; Jewish Russophiles undermine the fledgling Ukrainian state, which is then submerged in the bloody pogroms of 1919. Convinced that the Ukrainian national movement represents a distinct threat both physical and ideological, Jews join the Communist Party, and both engineer and enforce the policies that lead to the Holodomor; Ukrainians retaliate with widespread collaboration with the Nazis in the Holocaust.[30]

The fact of the matter is that both "the Ukrainians" and "the Jews" have been locked, historically, in a set of social, economic, political, and cultural relations that have generated exploitation and violence, on the one hand, and ethnic stereotyping by both sides on the other. There is no need to resort to primordialism, anti-semitism, and racism to explain this tragic relationship. A simple appreciation of the humanity of both Ukrainians and Jews and of their victimization — by "history," by "outside forces," and by each other — suffices to produce a more nuanced, and presumably more correct, understanding of their histories.

Unfortunately, anything like an evenhanded, genuinely historical examination is almost impossible under current conditions, which have been aggravated by the openly anti-Ukrainian policies of President Yanukovych's notorious minister of

---

30 H. Abramson, "Holodomor and Holocaust," *Holodomor Studies*, 2/1 (2010), pp. 131-132.Were this "paradigm" the conventional wisdom, at least among scholars if not among general publics, then Abramson's desire to refine, and perhaps even transcend, it would be fully understandable. Unfortunately, this kind of interactive historical narrative, in which Jewish and Ukrainian attitudes and behaviors are assumed to be causally interrelated, is anything but the conventional wisdom. Quite the contrary, the standard approach, as I have tried to suggest in this essay, is primordial, entailing the prescription of intrinsic attitudes that necessarily lead to certain behaviors, regardless of context and regardless of the actions, beliefs, and dispositions of others.

education and science, Dmytro Tabachnyk.[31] In the battle between apologists and radical critics, every plea for nuance will invariably be made to appear either as a betrayal or, much worse, an apologia for anti-semitism. And, of course, once that particular accusation rears its head, all debate comes to an end, in just the manner in which it is intended to come to an end.[32] In circumstances such these — so wearily reminiscent of the manner in which homosexuals were tarred before gay liberation — simplicity and simplemindedness will triumph. Those who aspire to understanding should refuse to debate the hotheads and quietly head for the hills — until the storm passes and reasoned discourse becomes possible.

---

31 Even the generally cool-headed Timothy Snyder could not resist titling his otherwise nuanced discussion of Bandera and the nationalists, "A Fascist Hero in Democratic Kiev." Binaries are always more attractive than conditional assertions (how many people would read an article entitled, "A Radical Nationalist Hero with Fascist Inclinations in Democratically Unconsolidated Kiev"?), especially as they transform appeals for nuance into seeming apologias of fascism. There's just no arguing with such titles. See: <http://blogs.nybooks.com/post/409476895/a-fascist-hero-in-democratic-Kiev>.

32 One such radical critic, for instance, has produced the equivalent of a "black list" consisting of scholars with different degrees of presumed guilt. See M. Carynnyk, "Antisemitic Discussions within the Organization of Ukrainian Nationalists, 1929–1943," paper prepared for the Ukrainian Jewish Encounter Initiative Meeting at Ditchley Park, 14-16 Dec. 2009.

# 14

# On Nationalism and Fascism[*]

Ukrainian "nationalism" has been in the news these last few years. As usually happens with words that have seeped into our daily vocabulary, nationalism in general and Ukrainian nationalism in particular have come to mean just about anything. Its detractors, many of whom believe that Adolf Hitler's National Socialism demonstrates that nationalism and fascism are inextricably connected, insist Ukrainian nationalism is a form of fascism. Its supporters, who often invoke Giuseppe Mazzini, say it's noble and empowering.

Compounding the problem, many of the historians who study Ukraine show little interest in conceptual clarity. How we define things matters enormously, because definitions enable us to group similar things together and explain them systematically. The alternative, a habit of sloppy scholars, is a seat-of-the-pants approach that permits flawed comparisons. So please bear with me, as we go through some conceptual exercises.

Let's start our enquiry by asking what fascism is not. Well, for starters, it's not any of the things that casual users of the term appear to mean when they apply it to people they dislike. Intolerance may be a bad thing, but it is not fascism. Violence may be abhorrent, but it too isn't fascism. Nor is conservatism, xenophobia, or racism. Richard Nixon may have been soft on all these features, but it would be absurd to suggest, as many on the left do, that he was a fascist. The term fascist is not and cannot and should not just be shorthand for stuff we don't care for, if only because everybody soon becomes a fascist.

---

[*] First printed in: Alexander J. Motyl, *Ukraine vs. Russia: Revolution, Democracy, and War* (Washington, DC: Westphalia Press, 2017), pp. 524-529. Reprinted with permission of the original publisher.

So how do we define fascism? Fascism, I suggest, is best conceived of as a type of regime, political system, or state on the same order as democracy, authoritarianism, dictatorship, oligarchy, totalitarianism, and the like. That is, fascism, like other types of regimes, political systems, or states, is fundamentally concerned with how regimes, political systems, or states are structured and organized. Fascism is thus "about" the political institutions of regimes, systems, and states.

Fascism may also be conceived of as an ideology or as a movement, group, or organization. Fascism as an ideology is a set of core beliefs that justify and promote fascism as a type of regime, political system, or state, while fascism as a movement, group, or organization is a human collective that shares a fascist ideology. A fascist individual would obviously be someone who believes in such an ideology.

Fascism as a type of regime, political system, or state; fascism as a set of beliefs about the correct organization of a regime, political system, or state; and fascism as a human collective with a fascist ideology all presuppose an existing state that should be transformed into one that corresponds to fascist ideals. Fascism and fascists aspire to change existing non-fascist regimes, political systems, or states into fascist regimes, political systems, or states. Fascism and fascists may aspire to do so legally, democratically, and constitutionally or they may aspire to do so illegally, undemocratically, and unconstitutionally, but their end goal is always anti-democratic.

The type of regime, political system, or state that fascism and fascists aspire to create is generally acknowledged to be a variant of authoritarianism or totalitarianism. Fascist regimes, political systems, or states are thus invariably anti-democratic, but, in contrast to run-of-the-mill authoritarian or totalitarian regimes, political systems, or states, fascist regimes, political systems, or states exalt "the leader." In turn, fascist leaders in fascist regimes, political systems, or states are, or attempt to be, charismatic, and they usually view themselves as spokesmen for "the nation," an entity that fascism treats as a monolith.

As the quintessential fascist, Benito Mussolini was the charismatic leader of a movement with a fascist ideology that proceeded to establish a fascist regime within an already existing Italian state. Adolf Hitler, if you consider Nazism to be an extreme variant of fascism, acted in the exact same manner as Mussolini, the only difference being that the former won power in an election while the latter seized it. Francisco Franco came to power by winning a civil war. Vladimir Putin, whose regime I've called quasi-fascist, came to power both legally and illegally. The way in which fascists seize power may therefore vary, but where they seize it (within an existing state) and what they then do (transform it into an authoritarian state with a charismatic leader) is pretty much constant.

To summarize: Fascism's two preconditions are an already existing state and an already existing non-fascist type of regime, political system, or state. Fascists do not build states de novo; nor do they build types of regimes, political systems, or states de novo. Unsurprisingly, it is in fact the case that fascism and fascists are always found in already existing states with already existing non-fascist types of regimes, political systems, or states.

## I.

In contrast to fascism, nationalism is not best conceived of as a type of regime, political system, or state (on the same order as fascism, democracy, authoritarianism, dictatorship, oligarchy, totalitarianism, and the like) for two very simple conceptual reasons. First, a nationalist regime, political system, or state would have to be a set of political institutions that are fundamentally different from those that characterize fascism, democracy, authoritarianism, dictatorship, oligarchy, or totalitarianism. But there is no such distinctly different nationalist regime, political system, or state with its own distinct political institutions. Instead, every supposedly nationalist regime, political system, or state is always just a variant of fascism, democracy, authoritarianism, dictatorship, oligarchy, or totalitarianism.

Second and unsurprisingly, it is in fact the case that every type of regime, political system, or state contains some national characteristic — be it the claim that "the nation" is a monolith or the claim that "the nation" is the basis of popular sovereignty or the claim that "the nation" must be embedded in proletarian internationalism. One should resist the temptation to conclude that every type of national regime, political system, or state is therefore "nationalist," since to argue in this manner is to confuse "nationalist" with "national" and thereby to reduce "nationalism" to everything and everybody that somehow entails "the national," thus producing a semantically bleached and utterly meaningless concept.

Now that we know what nationalism is not, what is it? Nationalism, I suggest, is best conceived of as an ideology or as a movement, group, or organization with a nationalist ideology. Nationalism as an ideology is a set of core beliefs that sometimes justify and promote national liberation and the creation of nation-states in general and always justify and promote national liberation and the creation of a nation-state for some particular nation. Nationalism, in this sense, is always particularistic and only sometimes universal. Nationalism as a movement, group, or organization is a human collective that shares a nationalist ideology. A nationalist individual would obviously be someone who believes in such an ideology. Nationalism is thus "about" the creation of states, and not about how the political institutions of regimes, systems, and states should be structured.

Seen in this light, the popular term "hyper-nationalism" is meaningless. If nationalism is an ideology, then hyper-nationalism would have to be a hyper-ideology. If nationalism is a movement, group, or organization, then hyper-nationalism would have to be a hyper-movement, hyper-group, or hyper-organization. Obviously, such conceptual obfuscation is not useful. What scholars really mean by hyper-nationalism is, quite simply, chauvinism. Appending the modifier "hyper" to the term "nationalism," however, is a convenient sleight of hand that creates a putative connection between nationalism and chauvinism when none such connection need exist, whether conceptually or empirically. After all, the ideological or organizational promotion of national liberation and nation-states is fundamentally different from the hatred of or superciliousness toward other nations—which is what we presumably mean by chauvinism. To define fascism as hypernationalism only compounds the problem, reducing fascism either to some sort of incomprehensible hyper-ideology or hyper-collective or, worse, to nothing but chauvinism.

In contrast to fascism as an ideology or as a movement, group, or organization, nationalism as an ideology or nationalism as a movement, group, or organization with a nationalist ideology does not presuppose an existing state that should be transformed into one corresponding to nationalist ideals. As a result, nationalism cannot and does not presuppose an existing type of regime, political, system, or state. Quite the contrary, nationalism presupposes the non-existence of an independent state and therefore concludes that the existence, or creation, of such a state is imperative. Like fascism and fascists or communism and communists or democracy and democrats, nationalism and nationalists may aspire to create such a state legally, democratically, and constitutionally or they may aspire to do so illegally, undemocratically, and unconstitutionally.

The type of state that nationalism and nationalists aspire to create can be authoritarian, democratic, liberal, totalitarian, and so on. Unlike fascist states, which are invariably anti-democratic, the states to which nationalists aspire are not invariably anti-democratic. Unsurprisingly, nationalisms and nationalists have ranged across all political ideologies, including fascism, and individual nationalists and nationalist movements, groups, or organizations have always displayed a remarkable political flexibility, being able to change their political ideology whenever and wherever the circumstances so demand. This is not, as is mistakenly assumed, opportunism. Nationalisms and nationalists can be so chameleonic precisely because their ideology is fundamentally indifferent to the type of regime, political system, or state that emerges within the newly created state.

The key distinction among nationalisms and nationalists concerns not the goal (they all agree that national liberation and a nation-state is their goal), but the means. Whereas legally, democratically, and constitutionally inclined nationalists will employ legal, democratic, and constitutional means, illegally, undemocratically, and unconstitutionally inclined nationalists will employ illegal, undemocratic, and unconstitutional means. That is to say, they will break laws, be conspiratorial, disciplined, and hierarchical, and use violence. This is why sloppy scholars believe that nationalists "look like" fascists. But if the willingness to break laws, be conspiratorial, disciplined, and hierarchical, and use violence makes one a fascist, then every revolutionary movement (from that of the Americans in 1776 to that of the Israelis in 1947), every criminal organization (from the mafia to Mexican drug traffickers), every secret police (from the KGB to the CIA), and every assassin (from Brutus to Lee Harvey Oswald) is fascist — a claim that is almost as useless, and absurd, as the reduction of nationalism to "the national." Clearly, "looking like" somebody or something is no basis for claiming that things "are like" somebody or something.

To summarize: Nationalism's only precondition, both conceptually and empirically, is the non-existence of a state. Unlike fascists, nationalists build states *de novo*. Unsurprisingly, it is empirically the case that nationalism and nationalists are always found in stateless territories.

## II.

These reflections suggest that the most useful way of conceptualizing the interwar Organization of Ukrainian Nationalists (OUN) is as a nationalist movement with a nationalist ideology along the lines described above. In turn, this means that the OUN is most usefully compared to other nationalist movements that aspired to national liberation and the creation of nation-states (such as the American revolutionaries of 1776, the Palestine Liberation Organization, the Algerian National Liberation Front, the Irish Republican Army, the interwar Croatian Ustasha, the Vietnamese National Liberation Front, the Chinese Communist Party, and the Haganah in the British Mandate of Palestine, to name just a few) and not to fascist regimes or to fascist movements (such as Italian fascism, Nazism, the Polish Falanga, the Romanian Iron Guard, the Hungarian Arrow Cross, and the like). This is not to say that individual members of the OUN or individual planks of the OUN's constantly changing ideology were not, or could not have been, fascist, but it is to say that to focus on these fragmentary fascist elements is, first, to mistake the part for the whole and therefore to misunderstand the OUN; second and much worse, to misunderstand both fascism and nationalism; and, third and worst of all, to engage in conceptual nonsense.

The Ukrainian nationalist movement's relationship to political ideologies changed continually, proceeding from an apolitical militarism to authoritarianism to proto-fascism to democracy to social democracy. Thus, whereas nationalism as national liberation was a constant, the political ideology was a variable. The OUN's predecessor in the 1920s, the Ukrainian Military Organization, was a collection of patriotically inclined ex-soldiers with little sense of political ideology. The OUN began as a radical youth movement, then morphed into a quasi-authoritarian movement, adopted fascist elements by the late 1930s and early 1940s, abandoned them by 1943–1944, and began acquiring progressively more democratic and social-democratic characteristics in the mid- to late–1940s and 1950s. The picture looks even more complex if we consider that the OUN, throughout the 1930s, was divided into the émigré and homeland factions, with the former being more concerned with ideology and the latter more with action. As we would expect, post–World War II émigré Ukrainian nationalists were divided into liberal, moderate, and authoritarian wings.

If you really want to understand what made such Ukrainian nationalists as Stepan Bandera and Roman Shukhevych tick—both were made Heroes of Ukraine by President Viktor Yushchenko and both were subsequently unmade as Heroes by President Viktor Yanukovych—don't compare them to Adolf Hitler, Benito Mussolini, or Francisco Franco, but to George Washington, Jefferson Davis, Giuseppe Mazzini, Giuseppe Garibaldi, Menachem Begin, Vladimir Jabotinsky, Theodor Herzl, Ahmed Ben Bella, Ho Chi Minh, Mao Zedong, Josip Broz Tito, Simón Bolívar, and Emiliano Zapata. Personally, if I were doing comparative biographies, I'd do one on Bandera and Begin as political leaders and another on Shukhevych and Tito as military leaders. And then I'd compare the Ukrainian nationalist theorist Dmytro Dontsov with the Zionist theorist Jabotinsky.

If you want to understand what kind of arguments Ukrainian nationalists, like all nationalists, make and how they justify their claims for national self-determination, go no further than the American Declaration of Independence, Theodor Herzl's *The Jewish State*, or the PLO's National Charter. You won't find anything in any of those three documents that any nationalist in any country at any time wouldn't have agreed to. Consider the opening passage of the Declaration:

> When in the Course of human events it becomes necessary for one people to dissolve the political bands which have connected them with another and to assume among the powers of the earth, the separate and equal station to which the Laws of Nature and of Nature's God entitle them, a decent respect to the opinions of mankind requires that they should declare the causes which impel them to the separation. We hold these truths to be self-evident, that all men are created equal, that they are endowed by their Creator with certain unalienable Rights, that among these are Life, Liberty and the pursuit of Happiness. — That to secure these rights, Governments are instituted among Men, deriving their just powers from the consent of the governed, — That whenever any Form of Government becomes destructive of these ends, it is the Right of the People to alter or to abolish it, and to institute new Government, laying its foundation on such principles and organizing its powers in such form, as to them shall seem most likely to effect their Safety and Happiness. … But when a long train of abuses and usurpations, pursuing invariably the same Object evinces a design to reduce them under absolute Despotism, it is their right, it is their duty, to throw off such Government, and to provide new Guards for their future security.

Begin, Bandera, and Mao might have used different language, but they could easily have subscribed to the core logic of Thomas Jefferson's argument. Unsurprisingly, all four were equally nationalist, even though the first two tended toward authoritarianism, the third was a totalitarian Communist, and the fourth was a slave-owning democrat.

To summarize: Fascism is always anti-democratic and it always emerges within an already existing non-fascist state.

Nationalism may or may not be anti-democratic and it always emerges within an already existing non-national state. Fascism aspires to change a state and make it fascist. Nationalism aspires to create a state. Like fascists and scores of other ideologically inspired individuals, nationalists can be violent. Like fascists and scores of other ideologically inspired individuals, nationalists can be chauvinists. But, like democrats, liberals, and other champions of human rights, nationalists can also be democratic and liberal champions of human rights. Unsurprisingly, Ukrainian nationalism, like Jewish nationalism (or Zionism), has contained all these elements at various times and in various places. The most striking thing about Ukrainian nationalism, therefore, is not that it is unique, but that it is so commonplace — no better and no worse than all other nationalisms: just as committed to liberation and just as likely to fall short of its ideals as to meet them.

It makes perfect sense for liberals and democrats always to oppose fascism. When it comes to nationalism, their attitude should be welcoming but cautious. Welcoming, because liberals and democrats should welcome every form of liberation: the political philosopher John Rawls even suggests in *The Law of Peoples* that liberalism demands recognizing the right of nations to self-determination and is, thus, intrinsically nationalist. Cautious, because nationalism, like all political projects, can be flawed. Like most things, come to think of it.

# 15

# Putin's Russia as a Fascist Political System*

There is a broad consensus among students of contemporary Russia that the political system constructed by Vladimir Putin is authoritarian and that he plays a dominant role in it. By building and expanding on these two features and by engaging in a deconstruction and reconstruction of the concept of fascism, I suggest that the Putin system may plausibly be termed fascist. To make that argument, I shall, in a move that many scholars will consider Quixotic, first attempt to salvage the concept of fascism from the conceptual confusion that surrounds it. Then, once a plausible definition of fascism is on hand, I shall argue that the Putin system meets fascism's definitional requirements and is, thus, fascist.

Throughout, I draw only on secondary sources, scholarly consensus, and logic. Indeed, my argument is primarily a syllogism whose premises rest on a plausible definition of the concept of fascism on the one hand and on the scholarly consensus regarding Putin's Russia on the other. If my definition of fascism and the consensus regarding Putin's Russia are accepted as valid, then it follows, logically, that Putin's Russia may legitimately be termed fascist or, at the very least, fascistoid. If my definition of fascism and the consensus regarding Putin's Russia are not accepted as valid, then it follows, logically, that Putin's Russia may not legitimately be termed fascist or fascistoid.

I argue that four features—full authoritarianism, mass support, a personality cult, and an active, personalistic leadership style (whether wise or vigorous)—are the key components of fascism as a system of rule.[1] In order to justify applying fascism to

---

\* First printed in: *Communist and Post-Communist Studies*, vol. 49, no. 1 (March 2016), pp. 25-36. Reprinted with permission of the originial publisher.
1 According to Payne (1995:12), a "fundamental characteristic" of fascism is "the insistence on what is now termed 'male chauvinism' and the tendency to

Putin's Russia, it will be necessary to engage in a conceptual deconstruction of the concept and a subsequent conceptual reconstruction. Developing a conceptual framework that identifies fascism's defining characteristics within a typology of political systems is perfectly doable, and the next sections will attempt to do just that. That said, it is important to appreciate that no definition and no conceptual framework is perfect (Gerring, 1999). Definitions and frameworks only help organize our thinking. Some do it better; some do it worse. Some are more useful; some are less. All are flawed. Definitional pluralism and a multitude of competing frameworks are therefore inevitable, and expecting unanimity, or even lasting consensus, is illusory.

Part of the problem is the unhelpful public discourse in North America, Europe, and the former Soviet Union, where fascist has come to denote anyone or anything one dislikes. In the United States, for instance, Donald Trump, who may be a populist and demagogue, but who surely wants to practice his populism and demagoguery within the institutional framework of American democracy, has recently been called a fascist by American commentators (Tucker, 2015). In Putin's Russia, much of the confusion traces back to the intentional semantic obfuscation of Soviet and Russian ideologists, who, as Mykola Riabchuk and Taras Kuzio show in this issue, used fascist as a synonym for anti-communist or anti-Russian. As a result, any perceived enemy of Putin's Russia is a fascist, with the bizarre Orwellian result that Ukrainian, Estonian, and other non-Russian democrats are termed fascist by the propaganda apparatus of what in fact is a fascist system. By the same token, Putin's Russia must be a paragon of democracy and any suggestion to the contrary is immediately met with invective and vituperation.

Given this controversy, one might be perfectly justified in suggesting that the term, fascism, has become so broad and controversial as to be meaningless—or, perhaps even worse,

---

exaggerate the masculine principle in all aspects of activity... Only fascists ... made a perpetual fetish of the 'virility' of their movement and its program and style ..."

useless — and that terming Putin's Russia fascist in no way clarifies matters. I suggest that the concept of fascism can be saved from the conceptual confusion surrounding it, but only after a serious deconstruction and reconstruction of the term is undertaken. Even then, it may still be impossible, given the conceptual chaos within fascism studies, to find more than extremely limited acceptance by its practitioners of any definition, framework, or typology. Although there is general agreement on the broad outlines of what constitutes an authoritarian and democratic system, there is no agreement whatsoever about what fascism is. As a result, no matter how serious and persuasive the deconstruction of the concept of fascism and the reconstruction of a plausible minimal definition thereof, the reception will be, at best, mixed, on the part of both Russia scholars and fascism scholars. Faced with this distressing prospect, one can either shrug and continue or shrug and discontinue. I have chosen the former route.

## Conceptual Confusion in Defining Fascism

This is not the place to discuss the extreme conceptual chaos[2] surrounding the term, *fascism*; suffice to say that it may be greater than that surrounding other "essentially contested concepts".[3] Consider the vast differences among the following definitions of fascism.

- Buchheim (1986:23): "The essence of fascism is rebellion against freedom."
- Corner (2002:351): "fascist dictatorship ensured, for the vast majority of people, that there were no choices to be made; that this is what constitutes the real totalitarian nature of fascism (and not the greater or lesser level of open and direct repression); and that it is this that makes Italian fascism directly comparable to its justly reviled partner and ally, German Nazism."

---

2   Excellent analyses of this chaos were provided in Payne (1980) and Griffin (1993).
3   The term is Gallie's (1956). See also Connolly (1983).

- Linz (1976:12-13): fascism is "a hypernationalist, often pan-nationalist, anti-parliamentary, anti-liberal, anti-communist, populist and therefore anti-proletarian, partly anti-capitalist and anti-bourgeois, anti-clerical, or at least, non-clerical movement, with the aim of national social integration through a single party and corporative representation not always equally emphasized; with a distinctive style and rhetoric, it relied on activist cadres ready for violent action combined with electoral participation to gain power with totalitarian goals by a combination of legal and violent tactics. The ideology and above all the rhetoric appeals for the incorporation of a national cultural tradition selectively in the new synthesis in response to new social classes, new social and economic problems, and with new organizational conceptions of mobilization and participation, differentiate them from conservative parties."
- Lyttleton (1973:12): "Fascism, reduced to its essentials, is the ideology of permanent conflict."
- Mann (2004:13): "fascism is the pursuit of a transcendent and cleansing nation-statism through paramilitarism."
- Payne (1995:14): "fascism may be defined as a form of revolutionary ultra-nationalism for national rebirth that is based on a primarily vitalist philosophy, is structured on extreme elitism, mass mobilization, and the Führerprinzip, positively values violence as end as well as means and tends to normalize war and/or the military virtues."
- Paxton (2004:218): "Fascism may be defined as a form of political behavior marked by obsessive preoccupation with community decline, humiliation, or victim-hood and by compensatory cults of unity, energy, and purity, in which a mass-based party of committed nationalist militants, working in uneasy but effective collaboration with traditional elite groups, abandons democratic liberties and pursues with redemptive violence and without ethical or legal restraints goals of internal cleansing and external expansion."

- Paxton (1998:17): "The fourth stage [of fascism is] the exercise of power."
- Riley (2005:288): "I treat Italian fascism and de Rivera's Spain as instances, respectively, of hegemonic authoritarianism and an economic corporate dictatorship."
- Scruton (1982:169): "Fascism is characterized by the following features (not all of which need to be present in any of its recognized instances): nationalism; hostility to democracy, to egalitarianism, and to the values of the liberal enlightenment; the cult of the leader, and admiration for his special qualities; a respect for collective organization, and a love of the symbols associated with it, such as uniforms, parades, and army discipline."

Confronted with such variety, a person might rationally conclude that fascism is meaningless or nonexistent. I attempt to minimize confusion by developing a definition of fascism in what I trust is a conceptually transparent and useful manner. I first delineate what fascism is not (or what it is less usefully conceived as) before suggesting what it is (or what it is more usefully conceived as). That is, I proceed by a process of elimination until, *faute de mieux*, only one definitional category remains. I propose a definition of fascism that identifies it, not as a type of group (movement, party, or organization), disposition (state of mind or set of attitudes), ideology (worldview or belief system), or politics (exercise of power or competition for scarce resources), but as a type of polity (political system, regime, or state). I submit that these five categories—which refer to agglomerations of individuals (groups), agglomerations of affects (dispositions), agglomerations of ideas (ideology), agglomerations of behaviors (politics), and agglomerations of institutions (polities)—comprise the universe of possible relevant categories of which fascism can be a type.

Obviously, "reality" is more complex, multifaceted, and messy than definitions. In "reality," fascism appears to be many things. In social science, however, we cannot formulate typologies or classifications—or answer the question of whether Putin's Russia is fascist, fully authoritarian, or something else—without clear, concise, and persuasive definitions that reduce complex phenomena to one key dimension, their "essence," or what they "really" are. Such simplifications usually strike historians as reductionist, and they are—for historians. Small wonder that many historians of fascism regard the search for a generic definition as pointless. For social scientists, clear definitions, as Sartori (1970) has emphasized, are indispensable to clear thinking about causes and effects.

Unsurprisingly, the definitions listed above fit under these five categories. Thus, Buchheim's (1986:23) notion of fascism as "rebellion" effectively reduces fascism to a rebellious disposition or politics. Linz specifically calls fascism a movement. Lyttleton calls it an ideology. Mann's notion of fascism as the "pursuit of a transcendent and cleansing nation-statism" is, like Buchheim's, dispositional and political. Payne sees fascism as an ideology (an ultra-nationalist, vitalist philosophy), while Paxton (2004): ("a form of political behavior marked by obsessive preoccupation") clearly places it in the realm of disposition and politics as well. Paxton (1998) and Riley see fascism as a form of rule or regime. Scruton ascribes elements of ideology, disposition, and politics to fascism.

Why is there such a broad variety of conceptualizations of fascism? Paxton (1998: 2-5, 8) provides five reasons for the lack of consensus:

> Five major difficulties stand in the way of any effort to define fascism. First, a problem of timing. The fascist phenomenon was poorly understood at the beginning in part because it was unexpected. ... A second difficulty in defining fascism is created by mimicry. In fascism's heyday, in the 1930s, many regimes that were not functionally fascist borrowed elements of fascist decor in order to lend themselves an aura of force, vitality, and mass mobilization. ... This leads to the third problem with defining fascism, posed by the dauntingly wide disparity among individual cases in space and in time. They differ in space because each national variant of fascism draws its legitimacy, as we shall see, not from some universal scripture but from what it considers the most authentic elements of its own community identity. ... A fourth and even more redoubtable difficulty stems from the ambiguous relationship between doctrine and action in fascism. ... [T]he words of fascist intellectuals—even if we accept for the moment that they constitute fundamental philosophical texts—correspond only distantly with what fascist movements do after they have power. Early fascist programs are poor guides to later fascist policy. ... The fifth and final difficulty with defining

fascism is caused by overuse: the word "fascist" has become the most banal of epithets. Everyone is someone's fascist.

Paxton's fourth reason — that scholars too often take fascists at their own word and accept their self-depictions as accurate reflections of the reality — is worth some attention. Mussolini's discussion (2004) of fascism is instructive: if we believe him, fascism amounts to everything. Fascists are obviously welcome to believe that, but there is no reason that we should follow in their footsteps. Fascists claim to have totalitarian states, but, despite their self-image, fascist states rarely, if ever, are totalitarian. Hitler Germany came closest, but even it fell short of Stalinist totalitarianism by retaining a market economy, religious autonomy, and significant amounts of rule of law for Aryans.

Consider in this light Eco's (1995) list of "Ur-Fascism's" characteristics. Like many other students of fascism, Eco emphasizes its supposed irrationality and love of action for action's sake. And yet, a closer look at Hitler Germany or Mussolini Italy shows quite clearly that, the poetic claims of fascist ideologists notwithstanding, both the German Nazis and the Italian Fascists pursued eminently rational policies of seizing and maintaining power. Nor did they engage in action just for the sake of action. Quite the contrary, their actions generally had some point or goal. By the same token, even though Mussolini insisted that the fascist state was totalitarian, it was anything but that. Indeed, as Bosworth (2006:563) notes, "On every occasion when the Fascist 'revolution' sought to manipulate and control Italians, Italians were hard at work manipulating and adapting Fascism. Like all modern and most ancient ideologies, Fascism talked as though it wanted to impose only one version of history on its people. In reality, however, Italians at the interstices where ideology and practice met clung stubbornly to many pasts and presents and vested their hopes in many futures."

Although we should approach fascist self-representations with caution, there is one claim that deserves to be taken seriously. Importantly, Mussolini, in his famous essay on fascism (Mussolini, 2004: 310), emphasizes that fascism is a state: "The keystone of

Fascist doctrine is the conception of the State, of its essence, of its tasks, of its ends." Mussolini's use of the word, keystone, is important. Although he begins by defining fascism as a "political conception," a "spiritualized conception," and "ethical conception," a "religious conception," and a "historical conception" in that essay (Mussolini: 305-306) — in short, as an all-encompassing way of life that includes groups, dispositions, ideology, and politics — Mussolini recognized that all these conceptions depended on the political core of a state for their coherence. As Bosworth (564) notes, "Mussolini told Franco in October 1936, what the Spaniard should aim at was a regime that was simultaneously 'authoritarian', 'social', and 'popular'. That amalgam, the Duce advised, was the basis of universal fascism."[4]

I suggest we take Mussolini's recognition of the centrality of the state seriously. All fascists want, above all, to capture the state and transform it into a peculiar kind of authoritarian entity. Groups, ideologies, dispositions, and politics are never ends in themselves. They are means to the end of seizing power and imposing fascist rule on some population. The key to understanding what fascism is may therefore be in understanding what fascist rule is.

Continuing with these insights, I argue in the next section that it is unhelpful to think of fascism as a type of group, disposition, politics, or ideology. I also argue that reducing fascism to nationalism is a serious blunder. If neither a group, nor a disposition, nor a politics, nor an ideology, fascism can only be a type of polity. If so — and after explaining why I prefer political system to regime or state — all that will remain to be done is to

---

[4] Interestingly, dictionary definitions of fascism also emphasize fascism's political quality as a form of rule. Thus, Oxford Dictionaries (2015) define fascism as, first, "an authoritarian and nationalistic right-wing system of government and social organization," and, second, as "(in general use) extreme right-wing, authoritarian, or intolerant views or practice." Merriam-Webster (2015) defines fascism as, first, "a way of organizing a society in which a government ruled by a dictator controls the lives of the people and in which people are not allowed to disagree with the government" and, second, "very harsh control or authority."

demonstrate that the defining characteristics of fascism as a political system are identical to those of late Putin's Russia.

## What is Fascism?

The case against fascism as a group (movement, party, or organization) rests on the claim that there is nothing intrinsically fascist about them *as such*. That qualifier, as such, is critically important. All groups, whether fascist or non-fascist, have leaders, all have followers, all have hierarchies, all have flags, parades, and marches, all are demagogic, and all draw on affect as much as, if not more than, on reason in their efforts at mobilizing constituencies. Many are also violent. Adolf Hitler's comments on organization and propaganda in *Mein Kampf* differ little from Vladimir Lenin's in *What Is to Be Done?*, and both could easily serve as handbooks for all manner of movements across the entire political spectrum. If we are to distinguish fascist movements, parties, and organizations from their non-fascist counterparts, we have to leave the realm of groups *per se* and explore their dispositions, ideologies, politics, or preferred polities. Naturally, to claim that fascism is not a type of group is not to state that fascist groups cannot empirically exist. They obviously can and do exist — not because of their intrinsically fascist "groupness," but because of their appropriation of fascist programs.

Fascism as a psychological disposition (state of mind or set of attitudes) appears at first glance to have some conceptual traction.[5] As Eco suggests, fascists are supposed to be excitable characters prone to various forms of "extremism," and extremism is a disposition *par excellence*. However, reducing fascism to a psychological condition — such as lethargy, extremism, or moderation — is unhelpful. After all, although some fascists may be psychologically excitable and attitudinally extremist, so are most dedicated political activists on the left, right, and center as well as all devotees of a radical politics. More important, as I already noted,

---

5  As Alfredo Rocco (2004: 313) said, "It is true that Fascism is, above all, action and sentiment ..."

we must distinguish between fascist self-representations and actual fascist behavior. Although they may claim to be irrational, excitable, and action-oriented, the fact is that most fascists at most times behave quite rationally, coolly, and calmly — as do, indeed, most serious political activists on the left, right, and center. If they did not, they would never have been able to seize power in the first place. By the same token, this is not to say that temperamental fascists cannot exist. They can and do, but not because temperament is an intrinsic feature of fascism.

Fascism as politics (exercise of power or competition for scarce resources) is open to the same criticism directed against fascism as group. If we conceptualize fascism as a radical, extremist, or right-wing politics (or as any other kind of politics), we would ultimately have to define these modifiers in terms of dispositions, ideologies, or polities. An excitable, vigorous, or tough politics would direct us to dispositions. An ideologically radical, extremist, or right-wing politics would direct us to ideology. A politics that aspired to build a radical, extremist, or right-wing polity would direct us to polities. In sum, fascism as politics only begs the question: what kind of politics? Once again, a caveat is in order. My claim is not that fascists cannot and do not practice politics; obviously, they do. Rather, my claim is that their politics is not intrinsically fascist.

The case against fascism as an ideology (worldview or belief system) rests on the empirical fact that no such thing as a coherent fascist ideology exists. There is no fascist Karl Marx or John Stuart Mill. There is no fascist equivalent of Marxism or liberalism. Instead, there are bits and pieces of oftentimes contradictory writings and bits and pieces of oftentimes contradictory beliefs produced by self-styled and non-self-styled fascists, but there is nothing comprehensive, systematic, and, most important perhaps, obligatory for all fascists. Mussolini's writings on fascism are a case in point (Mussolini, 2004). They are a jumble of claims about reality, life, politics, society, and the spirit that provide little practical guidance about how to behave and what to do in order to promote the fascist cause. Paxton (1998:4) puts it well: "Fascism is a political practice appropriate to the mass politics of the twentieth century. Moreover, it bears a different relationship to thought than do the nineteenth-century 'isms.' Unlike them, fascism does not rest on formal philosophical positions with claims to universal validity. There was no 'Fascist Manifesto,' no founding fascist thinker. Although one can deduce from fascist language implicit Social Darwinist assumptions about human nature, the need for community and authority in human society, and the destiny of nations in history, fascism does not base its claims to validity on their truth."[6]

Griffin (1993) attempts to salvage the fascism-as-ideology project by arguing that fascism is nationalism[7] or, as he puts it (1993:26), "Fascism is a genus of political ideology whose mythic core in its various permutations is a palingenetic form of populist ultra-nationalism." The primary flaw with Griffin's analysis is that nationalism — whether understood as the exaltation of one's nation or a desire for national liberation (Motyl, 1990) — is ubiquitous in today's world. Who, in the modern world, does not support national "palingenesis"[8] — or the rebirth, regeneration, or revival of one's nation? Modern political discourse, in both democracies and non-democracies, is suffused with claims about reviving and regenerating a nation's pride, glory, prosperity, stature, or status. Every nation, whether communist, liberal, or fascist, has a flag that it regards with pride, a tomb of the unknown soldier and a pantheon of heroes that it venerates, a national narrative that it reproduces in textbooks, and national holidays that it uses to stage parades. Every regime, political system, or state contains some national characteristic — be it the claim that "the nation" is a monolith or the claim that "the nation" is the basis of popular sovereignty or the claim that "the nation" must be embedded in proletarian internationalism. Nation exaltation has become so quotidian (or "banal," to use Billig's [1995] term) that nationalist has become a synonym for human being. But if everyone is a nationalist, then everyone must also be a proto-fascist. Moreover,

---

6   On the other hand, Roberts (2000) takes fascist ideology seriously.
7   Payne (1995) makes similar arguments.
8   According to Griffin (1993:32-33), "the term 'palingenesis' ... refers to the sense of a new start or of regeneration after a phase of crisis or decline ..."

since ultra-nationalism is, as an ultra-form of nationalism, immanent in nationalism,[9] and fascism is ultra-nationalism, fascism must be immanent in nationalism. The fascist bacillus is thus present in every form of national exaltation, no matter how innocent, liberal, tolerant, and progressive. Every society is thus proto-fascist, a claim that seems excessive, to say the least.

Although flawed, Griffin's conflation of nationalism and fascism does enable us to get a better conceptual handle on fascism. In contrast to nationalism, fascism's two preconditions are an already existing state and an already existing non-fascist type of regime or political system. Fascists do not build states *de novo*; nor do they build regimes or political systems *de novo*. Fascism and fascists are always found in already existing nation-states with already existing non-fascist types of regimes or political systems. Fascism and fascists do not exist simply in order to assert the ontological reality of fascism as groups, ideologies, dispositions, or politics. They come into being precisely because they aspire to change existing non-fascist regimes or political systems into their fascist counterparts.[10] As I argue in the next section, getting a handle on fascism therefore requires looking at fascism as a form of regime, political system, or state.

---

9  Griffin (1993:37-38) does not adequately distinguish between nationalism and ultra-nationalism. While he says that ultra-nationalism refers to "forms of nationalism which 'go beyond', and hence reject, anything compatible with liberal institutions or with the tradition of Enlightenment humanism which underpins them," he also speaks of "[n]ationalism (by which scholars clearly mean a profoundly illiberal form which corresponds to what we have called ultra-nationalism)." The first claim suggests ultra-nationalism is an ultra-form of nationalism; the second suggests they are identical. In fact, what scholars really mean by ultra-nationalism is, I suspect, chauvinism. If so, appending the modifier "ultra" to the term "nationalism" is a sleight of hand that creates a putative connection between nationalism and chauvinism when none such connection need exist, whether conceptually or empirically.

10  In contrast to fascism, which is invariably anti-democratic, the regimes to which nationalists aspire are not. Nationalisms and nationalists have ranged across all political ideologies— Rawls (2001) suggests that liberalism demands the recognition of the right of nations to self-determination and is, thus, an intrinsically nationalist project—because their ideology is fundamentally indifferent to the type of regime that characterizes the nation-state.

## Fascism as a Political System

If fascism as group, disposition, politics, or ideology does not persuade us, then we have one option only: viewing fascism as a type of polity (political system, regime, or state). My preference is for fascism as a type of political system. The concept of political system, as defined by Easton (1953), enables us to go beyond the political institutions that comprise regimes and states and incorporate relevant social actors implicated in the system's repression of its subject population. As a type of political system, fascism therefore concerns the relationships between and among the actors, rules, and institutions that constitute political systems.

In order to grasp what kind of system fascism is, we need a typological framework that encompasses the major types of political systems, differentiates between and among them along a set of identical criteria, and locates fascism within that typology. Table 1 provides a comparative overview of the defining characteristics of competitive authoritarian, fully authoritarian, democratic, and fascist political systems (I exclude totalitarian systems, not because they do not exist, but because they are irrelevant to this discussion). In contrast to Zimmerman, Levitsky and Way, and Gel'man, who essentially define authoritarianism as the absence of democratic institutions, I have chosen ten dimensions that, while fully consistent with their schemes, give authoritarianism some positive content. They include: political institutions, leader, worldview, popular attitude toward the regime, economy, opposition and civil rights, non-state institutions, coercive apparatus, propaganda apparatus, and violence. Many other features that are commonly assumed to mark fascist systems are not intrinsic to the concept. Some fascist systems are warlike; others are not. Some are racists and/or anti-Semitic; others are not. Some build concentration camps; others do not.

## Political Systems and Their Features

| Features | Democracy | Competitive (hybrid) authoritarianism | Full (consolidated) authoritarianism | Fascism |
|---|---|---|---|---|
| Political institutions | Multiple parties; genuine elections; autonomous parliament; independent judiciary | Dominant party; semi-rigged elections; subordinate parliament; semi-independent judiciary in non-political sphere | Dominant party; rigged elections; rubber-stamp parliament; semi-independent judiciary in non-political sphere | Dominant party; rigged elections; rubber-stamp parliament; semi-independent judiciary in non-political sphere |
| Leader | Elected official | Gray eminence or junta | Gray eminence or junta | *Personalistic dictator* |
| Worldview | Incoherent; State and nation admiration | Incoherent; State and nation exaltation | Incoherent; State and nation exaltation | Incoherent; State, nation, and *leader* exaltation |

| Popular attitude toward regime | Support | Acquiescence | Acquiescence | *Mass support* |
|---|---|---|---|---|
| Economy | Minimal state interference in market economy | State alliance with dominant forces in market economy | State alliance with dominant forces in market economy | State alliance with dominant forces in market economy |
| Opposition | Substantial | Intimidated | Wholly or mostly neutralized | Wholly or mostly neutralized |
| Civil rights | Respected | Greatly circumscribed | Routinely violated | Routinely violated |
| Coercive apparatus | Subordinate to government | Part of ruling elite | Part of ruling elite | Part of ruling elite |
| Propaganda apparatus | None or minimal | Significant, but limited | Significant, but limited | Significant, but limited |
| Violence and coercion | Sporadic violence and coercion | Targeted violence, widespread coercion | Targeted violence, widespread coercion | Targeted violence, widespread coercion |

Source: composed by the author

In fascist systems, as in fully authoritarian systems, the pro-regime party is dominant, electoral outcomes are preordained, parliaments are rubber-stamp institutions, and judiciaries do what the leader tells them in the political sphere. In contrast to authoritarian systems, which are ruled by gray eminences or juntas, and democratic systems, which are ruled by elected officials, fascists systems are ruled by personalistic dictators. Like competitive and fully authoritarian systems (and unlike totalitarian systems), fascist systems do not penetrate into a country's political, economic, social, and cultural life and do not propound all-embracing ideologies that answer all of life's questions. Instead, fascist systems attempt to dominate and control non-state institutions and espouse limited worldviews. Like authoritarian and, to a lesser degree, democratic systems, fascist systems exalt the state and the nation; unlike authoritarian and democratic systems, fascist systems also exalt the leader. Unlike competitive and fully authoritarian systems, fascist systems are genuinely popular. Like competitive and fully authoritarian systems, fascist systems also reject socialism and embrace capitalism: they tacitly acknowledge the autonomy of capitalists, even while circumscribing it by means of dirigisme, occupation of the strategic heights, or corporatism. Like competitive and fully authoritarian systems, fascist systems are highly centralized and hierarchical, giving pride of place within the authority structure to the army and secret police. Like fully authoritarian systems, fascist systems limit freedom of the press, freedom of speech, and freedom of assembly and their oppositions are either wholly or mostly neutralized. Like authoritarian systems, fascist systems have significant, but limited, propaganda apparatuses and engage in targeted violence against regime opponents and widespread coercion against the population in general.

Fascism is thus a sub-type of full authoritarianism, differing from it in three respects. Fascist dictators exercise a personalistic leadership style, whereas authoritarian dictators are gray eminences or juntas. What passes for an authoritarian worldview centers on the state and nation, while the fascist equivalent also celebrates the wise or vigorous personalistic leader. Finally, authoritarian populations acquiesce in authoritarian rule, whereas their fascist counterparts willingly submit to fascism in exchange for promises of a grand and glorious future. I therefore define fascism as *a popular fully authoritarian political system with a personalistic dictator and a cult of the leader*. In turn, a competitive authoritarian political system with a personalistic dictator and a cult of the leader may be termed fascistoid — that is, almost, but not quite fascist (Motyl, 2010). Importantly, this definition applies to classic fascist political systems such as Mussolini Italy, Hitler Germany, Franco Spain, and Ustasha Croatia — and suggests that Saddam Hussein's Iraq, the Ayatollah Khomeini's Iran, Muammar Qaddafi's Libya, Hafez-al Assad's Syria, Idi Amin's Uganda, Papa Doc Duvalier's Haiti, and Kemal Atatürk's Turkey may be classified as fascist. Obviously, to classify these systems as fascist is not to preclude the possibility of their having morphed into something else at various times. In contrast, Hugo Chavez's Venezuela, Józef Piłsudski's Poland, and Juan Peron's Argentina may not, as they were not fully authoritarian. Although my definition does not (and cannot) capture all the features of all these systems, it does capture their common "fascist" core and therefore enables us to classify and group them as well as compare and contrast them. If one wants to differentiate between and among sub-types of fascism, one can easily append any number of modifiers (partial vs. full, authoritarian vs. near-totalitarian, violent vs. coercive, etc.) to isolate the different species within the larger genus.[11]

This definition also enables us to make sense of fascism. A fascist group is thus a movement, party, or organization aspiring to construct a popular fully authoritarian political system with a personalistic dictator and a cult of the leader. Hitler's Nazis, Mussolini's Fascists, Ante Pavelić's Ustasha, and Ion Codreanu's Iron Guard clearly fit the bill. By the same token, a fascist is a person

---

11  If one imagines totalitarianism as being an extreme form of authoritarianism, then fascism may also be conceptualized as an "imperfect" sub-type of totalitarianism, inasmuch as it would have all of totalitarianism's characteristics except for one: full state control of the economy.

aspiring to construct a popular fully authoritarian political system with a personalistic dictator and a cult of the leader. By these standards, Trump is obviously no fascist. Fascist dispositions and politics are no different from those of other political activists, while their ideas about the world might be termed an ideology only if they were to constitute a coherent set of beliefs about constructing and sustaining a popular fully authoritarian political system with a personalistic dictator and a cult of the leader.

## Putin's Russia as a Fully (Consolidated) Authoritarian System

Given my definition of fascism as a popular fully authoritarian political system with a personalistic dictator and a cult of the leader, I shall now argue that Putin's Russia is just such a political system. As noted above, I rest my case solely on the consensus in the scholarly literature on Putin's Russia.

Zimmerman (2014: 7-8) captures the consensus within the field about the nature of Russia's current political system:

> There was no unanimity in the literature as to how to characterize Russia's political system in the mid-1990s—democracy (Myagkov), electoral democracy (McFaul), competitive authoritarianism (Levitsky and Way). Most Western specialists, however they classified Russia circa 1996, agreed with Levitsky and Way's statement a propos Russia at that juncture, "[t]he regime was quite open in the early and mid-1990s" with "highly competitive elections," a "legislature [that] wielded considerable power, and private mass media ... [that] regularly criticized Yeltsin and provided a platform for opposition."

Zimmerman (2014: 7-8) continues:

> At the same time, whether using McFaul, Levitsky and Way, or Freedom House as their basis for judgment about how to categorize post-Soviet Russian politics, few scholars would dispute the within-system changes in the Russian political system in the dozen years subsequent to the 1996 election. Over that time period, the trend was away from what had been—warts and all—a highly competitive system. Instead, in the period between the 1996 Yeltsin electoral victory and 2008 when Vladimir Putin selected Dmitry Medvedev as his replacement as president, presidential elections became decreasingly open, decreasingly competitive, and increasingly meaningless. ... There was hyperbole in Gerald Easter's characterization of

Russia by 2008 as having become "a normal police state." Grigory Golosov was not, however, out of line to term the 2008 selection of Dmitry Medvedev to serve as Vladimir Putin's replacement an "election-type event." This was much of the basis why, of the thirty-five states Levitsky and Way coded as competitive authoritarian in 1990–95, Russia and Belarus were the two that were coded as "full authoritarian" in 2008.

In sum, scholars generally agree that Putin's Russia is authoritarian, and I see no reason to dispute that assessment. Where scholars disagree is on whether Putin's Russia is competitive authoritarian or fully authoritarian. According to Levitsky and Lucan Way (n.d.: 4, 6), "Competitive authoritarian regimes are civilian regimes in which formal democratic institutions are widely viewed as the primary means of gaining power, but in which fraud, civil liberties violations, and abuse of state and media resources so skew the playing field that the regime cannot be labeled democratic. Such regimes are competitive, in that democratic institutions are not merely a façade: opposition parties use them to seriously contest for power; but they are authoritarian in that opposition forces are handicapped by a highly uneven—and sometimes dangerous—playing field. Competition is thus real but unfair." In turn, Levitsky and Way (n.d.: 4, 6) "characterize as closed authoritarian all regimes that are non-competitive, in that no viable channels exist through which opposition forces may contest legally for power. This category includes regimes in which democratic institutions do not even exist on paper.... Yet it also includes regimes in which formal democratic institutions exist on paper but are reduced to façade or 'window dressing' status in practice.' Levitsky and Way (n.d.: 4, 6) point out that "In these regimes, which are often characterized as 'pseudo-democratic' or 'electoral authoritarian,' elections are so marred by repression, restrictions on opposition candidates, and fraud that there is no uncertainty about their outcome. Though legally tolerated, much opposition activity is forced underground by repression, and leading regime critics are often imprisoned or exiled."

Zimmerman straddles the fence with respect to the question of whether Putin's Russia is a competitive or fully authoritarian system. According to him (Zimmerman, 2014: 11-12), the "2011-12 electoral cycle ... lacked the attributes of a fully authoritarian regime that had been evidenced in the 2008 election cycle, though it bore some resemblance to a modernized analogue to the Soviet system with its 'circular flow of power,' to wit, a one-person selectorate accompanied by some cheering from the sidelines by a small but growing group who felt entitled to express their views regardless of their actual impact on the outcome."

Levitsky and Way (2010: 186, 190, 200) also adopt a middle ground, stating that "Russia was a stable competitive authoritarian regime through 2008. ... Under Vladimir Putin (1999-2008), increased state and party capacity helped eliminate many potential sources of regime instability, and the regime – largely immune from outside pressure – consolidated. ... As we shall see, increased state and party capacity helps to explain Russia's transformation from a relatively fragile regime under Yeltsin to an increasingly stable and closed one under Putin. ... Putin succeeded in consolidating authoritarian rule mainly by eliminating key organizational sources of vulnerability. In a context of very low leverage and a weak opposition, he met virtually no resistance as he eliminated the last vestiges of democracy."[12]

Much of the ambiguity about the degree to which Russia has moved beyond competitive authoritarian and toward full authoritarian status is due to the fact that some of the criteria distinguishing competitive from full authoritarianisms are themselves ambiguous. Levitsky and Way (n.d., 2010) distinguish between the flawed democratic institutions that characterize competitive authoritarian regimes and those that are mere façades, which are found in fully authoritarian regimes. Conceptually, the distinction makes perfect sense, but it should be obvious that there is no clearly identifiable point, whether conceptually or empirically, at which a flawed institution becomes a mere façade. We can certainly identify the point at which a flawed institution ceases to

---

12 In contrast to Zimmerman (2014) and Levitsky and Way (n.d., 2010), who see Putin's Russia as moving from competitive authoritarianism toward, if not necessarily quite reaching, full authoritarianism, Gel'man (2015: 7) claims that Putin's regime deserved to be called a competitive authoritarian regime.

exist, but even a façade-like institution may serve some genuine institutional purpose. In the Soviet Union, for instance, the republics enjoyed no real sovereignty, despite being termed sovereign by the Soviet Constitution. Even so, the façade-like nature of their sovereignty did provide republican elites with some degree of autonomy from Moscow even in Stalinist times. Even façades are never only façades.

The ambiguity is also due to the fact that, while scholars agree that Putin has been actively eviscerating democratic institutions throughout his entire tenure in office, that evisceration became most pronounced after the 2011-2012 anti-regime protests in Russia and the Euromaidan revolution of 2013-2014 in Ukraine, reaching its apex during Russia's war with Ukraine and economic crisis in 2014-2105. Significantly, it is within this timeframe (2014-2015) that a variety of Russian analysts (Iampolski, 2015; Ikhlov, 2015; Shiropaev, 2014; Zubov, 2015; Inozemstev, 2015a, 2015b) have claimed that Putin's regime is fascist. Gerasimov (2015:67) openly states that Putin's Russia is "a classical fascist regime of a corporate state." Inozemtsev (2015a) agrees: "The state that is currently being formed in [Russia] in many respects accords with the scholarly definition of a 'fascist' [state]. Ikhlov (2015) finds that fascism is at the core of Putinism, which "reactivated the fascist tendency in full gear. At that time, there were no more anti-market or Soviet-cosmopolitan components in the state ideology. Thus, Brezhnevite 'left-wing fascism' became classic 'right-wing [fascism].' And it is all the more becoming the essence of Putinism." Finally, while emphasizing the uniqueness of Putin's political system, Zubov (2015) insists that it is comparable to a variety of authoritarian states, including those that were fascist:

> Contemporary Russia is highly reminiscent of Latin American dictatorships. Or of Thailand in the 1940s-1950s. But it is not at all reminiscent of anything in Russian history. Putin is constructing an unprecedented state. On the one hand, he evinces tendencies toward authoritarianism, with a controlled pluralistic economy: a seeming corporative economic system reminiscent of Italian fascism under Mussolini with its nationalism and alliance with the church. Although, I repeat, there is no complete similarity. In a word, what is currently transpiring in Russia is, I believe, quite unique. Although it has already been found in the history of other countries in the twentieth century.

> What is currently being built, simply put, is a corporative state of the fascist type wrapped up in Soviet ideology, the ideology of Stalinism.

These analysts obviously sense that the Putin regime has continued moving in a more than fully authoritarian direction within the last two years. We need not agree with them, of course—just as we need not agree with Putin's supporters, who might claim that the system is becoming ever more democratic—but their willingness to use a term, fascism, that has so many distinctly negative, and provocative, connotations within the Russian context is significant. These analysts clearly believe that something qualitatively different has transpired in Russia, as Putin has concentrated ever more power in his hands and eliminated remaining democratic residues from the system, and that a new vocabulary is necessary to capture this change. A sharp turn toward full authoritarianism in 2014-2105 should not surprise us. Internal threats, wars, and economic decline—and Russia experienced all three as a result of the Euromaidan revolution, its invasion of Ukraine in 2014, the subsequent Western sanctions, and the sharp drop in the price of oil and gas (Connolly, 2015; Deuber and Schwabe, 2015)—generally lead to a concentration of power in the hands of the executive, intolerance of dissent, and increased pro-government propaganda. Shiropaev (2014) emphasizes the Ukrainian angle: "The Kremlin sharply fascisized the country on the wave of its anti-Ukrainian policy. Many today call that a national transformation, a restoration, the rebirth of and return to Russianism. In fact, it is simply a galloping FASCIZATION. Russian fascism … has become a FACT." Iampolski (2105) focuses on the economic dimension: "In the current economic downturn, the appeal of quasi-fascist discourse was predictable.… Anything that could be seen as a sign of weakness or femininity is rejected; this includes liberalism and homosexuality. Typically, it is these same negative qualities that end up projected onto the 'enemy.' This, too, is a feature of projective identification. Thus Ukrainians are systematically accused of fascism, while Russian fascism is displaced by a false idealization of one's own image."

Shevtsova (2015) summarizes the overall trends within Russia since 2104 and is worth quoting as some length:

> The events of 2014 in neighboring Ukraine—the EuroMaidan protests and the fall of President Viktor Yanukovych—gave the Kremlin an opportunity to test its new doctrine. By annexing Crimea and backing pro-Russian separatists in eastern Ukraine, the Kremlin was able to justify its military-patriotic mobilization of society and its transformation of Russia into a "besieged fortress." This was a traditional survival maneuver, but with a new twist for a new century. The Kremlin's style of "hybrid warfare" used military force without admitting it, and "weaponized" other areas of life. Thus we now have customs wars, natural-gas wars, information wars, culture wars, and history wars. ... Public mobilization around the leader and the motherland rose to a new pitch, aided by the lack of traditional cultural or moral regulators ... capable of shielding an atomized society of disoriented, demoralized individuals from the schemes of an overweening state.

Shevtsova (2015) continues:

> Individuals are invited to compensate for their helplessness by looking for meaning in collective national "successes" that promise to bring them together and restore their pride. The annexation of Crimea has become such a "success," giving ordinary Russians a chance to forget their woes and feel a surge of vicarious optimism. ... The Kremlin's shift to a war footing will mean more than higher military spending and a resurgent military-industrial complex. Russian militarism is a unique form of the order-based—as opposed to the law-based—state. Although turning Russia into a Stalin-era armed camp is no longer possible, the Kremlin is militarizing certain walks of life and imitating militarization in other areas where it cannot achieve the genuine article.... The Kremlin has demonstrated its ability not only to use the traditional means of autocracy, but also to invent new means of prolonging its life. Among the traditional instruments of influencing the public is the elimination of any remaining channels of self-expression.

Finally, says Shevtsova (2015):

> Under Yeltsin and the earlier Putin, the regime tended to tolerate some protests and preferred "managed political pluralism." Today, the pocket parliament has passed a series of laws that liquidate basic constitutional freedoms and point the way to full-scale dictatorship. There are several dimensions to this subjugation of society. First, the Kremlin has robbed elections of their meaning by barring popular candidates whom the authorities do not control, and by falsifying results. With no access to television or major newspapers, genuine oppositionists can no longer compete. Second, the authorities have continued an unprecedented

> campaign of reprisals against civil society. The NGO and "anti-extremist" laws ... feature deliberately ambiguous wording that allows authorities to clamp down on any civil activity.

If we look more closely at Zimmerman's (2010: 4) emendation of Levitsky and Way's (n.d., 2010) criteria, it is clear that the current Russian system meets four of his five characteristics of full authoritarianism. Thus, "core democratic institutions" are "nonexistent or reduced to façade status." "Electoral uncertainty" is "low."[13] A "handful" actually select, while the "ejectorate" is "unlikely." "Regime goals" are "international and domestic security," and the regime "resists external influence." The only criterion of full authoritarian status that falls a bit short of the criteria concerns the "major opposition." In a competitive authoritarian system, the opposition "exists legally, but is significantly disadvantaged by incumbent abuse," while in a full authoritarian system, the "major opposition" is "banned or largely in exile or underground." Putin's Russia's opposition is at present still somewhere between the two, though moving in the direction of being banned, in exile, or underground.

Freedom House's (2015) Nations in Transit ratings refine these findings. They focus on somewhat different criteria (electoral process, civil society, independent media, national democratic governance, local democratic governance, judicial framework and independence, and corruption), but reach the same conclusion about the nature of Russia's current regime (termed a "consolidated authoritarian regime"), showing a marked deterioration in 2014 (Freedom House, 2015). Whereas the cumulative Democracy Score (with 1 as the best score and 7 as the worst) declined from 6.11 in

---

13 There is an unresolvable ambiguity in any assessment of Putin's Russia's electoral institutions. It is impossible to say just what national elections in Russia would be like if they were held today. How such a counterfactual question would be answered depends on one's assumptions about the system. If one believes it is now fully authoritarian, then one would expect elections to be fully rigged. If one believes it is still competitive authoritarian, then one would expect the elections to be merely slanted. A related test of one's underlying assumptions would be the question of Putin's eventual possible departure. If one cannot imagine his being voted out of office, then one obviously believes that elections are a sham.

2008, to 6.14 to 2009, to 6.18 in 2010 and 2011, to 6.21 in 2012, and to 6.29 in 2013, it experienced a huge 0.17 decline in 2014, falling to 6.46.

## Putin as a Personalistic Dictator

Central to Russia's move toward full authoritarianism is the person of Putin. Unfortunately, while conceptualizations of Russian authoritarianism generally emphasize the absence of democratic institutions, they do not devote sufficient attention to the nature of the authoritarian leader or leaders. More fundamentally, their understanding of authoritarianism is marked by little substantive content. Thus, authoritarian systems appear to be characterized by what they lack: democratic institutions. While true, authoritarianism is not just non-democracy or the absence of democracy. The overwhelming emphasis scholars place on elections distracts from an equally important feature: the relationship between and among the branches of government. In democracies, the executive, legislature, and judiciary exist, are meaningful and are balanced; in authoritarianisms, the executive dominates, sometimes to the point of transforming the others into façades. Following Aristotle, we expect an authoritarian system to exhibit a strong concentration of power in the hands of one individual or a few. The few who rule are juntas, cliques, and camarillas; the one who rules is a dictator, autocrat, monarch, leader, or emperor. Fully authoritarian systems ruled by juntas, cliques, and camarillas obviously differ from fully authoritarian systems ruled by individuals. In the former, some degree of consensus is necessary for decision-making to take place, and consensus presupposes some forms of compromise, horse-trading, and negotiating. In the latter, the ruler dictates and therefore imposes his will on the elites. The dictator may or may not be an autocrat—the only one who makes decisions—but he or she is always the *primus* without *pares*.

In turn, rule by one can be divided into two types: rule by a gray eminence or rule by a personality. A gray eminence is withdrawn, making decisions in the privacy of his or her cabinet. A personality plays a direct, hands-on, activist, ever-present role in policymaking. He is not some unapproachable philosopher king or an anonymous general in uniform. Quite the contrary, the personality is always and everywhere actively present, openly and publicly ruling the people by virtue of one of two assets—his wisdom or his vigor. Naturally, these comments apply to leaders in all types of political systems. Democracies tend to produce gray eminences bound by the rules of office. Competitive and fully authoritarian states connote images of dour old men such as Augusto Pinochet ruling a sullen population. Totalitarian states connote images of wise patriarchs. In contrast, fascist leaders are always personalistic, though there is no reason that wise or vigorous personalistic leaders cannot rule democratic, authoritarian, or totalitarian systems. Vigor was the trademark of Benito Mussolini, Juan Peron, Aleksandr Lukashenko, Hugo Chavez, John F. Kennedy, and George W. Bush. Wisdom was the trademark of Adolf Hitler, Joseph Stalin, Francisco Franco, Nursultan Nazarbayev, Józef Piłsudski, Dwight D. Eisenhower, Abraham Lincoln, and the Ayatollah Khomeini.

These two forms of leadership style—gray eminence vs personalistic rule—have their own advantages and disadvantages. The gray eminence's legitimacy and authority rest to a large degree on her ability to get the policies right. The advantage is that a smart autocrat with a sense of realism may be able to generate a "winning streak" that makes her look good. The danger is that, if policies fail or appear to fail, only the autocrat is to blame and elite and popular support may erode. The personality attempts to legitimize policy by means of an active outreach to the people and elites. The ability of the personality to produce and sustain the appropriate image, whether of the wise or vigorous ruler, is thus of extreme importance. The advantage of such an approach is that the personality can sustain legitimacy by means of the clever manipulation of image and representation by a vast propaganda apparatus. The danger is that images and representations can easily fall out of sync with actual lived facts. A wise leader may never commit blunders. A vigorous leader cannot grow old.

Russia's President Putin is a good example of a personalistic dictator with a vigorous leadership style. There is little disagreement among scholars that Putin plays an exceptional role in Russia's authoritarian system. Scholars capture Putin's central role by calling him an autocrat, dictator, tsar, and the like and terming Russia's political system "Putinist" (Applebaum, Spring 2008), a tyranny, or autocracy (Carafano et al., 2015). Trenin (2015), for instance, writes that "Russia's political system is clearly czarist, and Putin is the leader closest to a present-day absolute monarch." Lipman (2015) states that "His power is unchallenged and unchecked. Everyone recognizes his superior authority, and everyone pledges allegiance." Shelin (2015), meanwhile, argues that "the features of feudalism along with its monarchical spirit, the uncontrolled dominance by all manner of bosses, and the transformation of the rest of the people into a mass of humiliated simple folk have long since been visible.... But to say 'feudalism' is to say far from everything. The movement backwards, into the archaic past, is proceeding along a broader front. I think one may already call it barbarization."

A "clearly czarist" system with an absolute monarch is obviously fully authoritarian. The all-powerful Putin is the supreme leader who determines which policies he will determine (foreign policy, security, and defense, above all) and which he will devolve to his inner circle. He "dictates" in the sense of having the final word on all matters. He stands above the law; he was elected, in 2012 if not before, in violation of the law. But Putin is not just an all-powerful "new tsar," as Myers (2015) calls him. If he were, there would be no grounds for claiming that Russia is anything but fully authoritarian. Two more features of Putin's leadership style need underlining. First, as a variety of scholars have pointed out, it rests on a cult of personality. The cult is not quite as ubiquitous and mandatory as Stalin's, but Putin is a constant presence in Russian media. Second, Putin's leadership style is personalistic and vigorous. That is, Putin's is a peculiar kind of dictatorial rule. Instead of being a gray eminence or a wise personality, he has chosen to construct a cult of vigorous leadership (Cassiday and Johnson, October 2010; Schroeder, 2014: 9), one that, like

Mussolini's, emphasizes his hyper-masculinity and bare-chested prowess (Sperling, 2015). Like Mussolini, Putin favors stylish black clothing that connotes toughness. Like Mussolini, Putin likes being photographed with weapons. And, like the Duce, Putin likes to show off his physical prowess.[14]

## Conclusions

Is, then, Putin's Russia fascist?

All the ten characteristics of fully authoritarian systems listed in Table 1 clearly apply to Putin's Russia at present.[15] As Zimmerman's (2014), Levitsky and Way's (n.d., 2010), and Freedom House's criteria of full authoritarianism lead us to expect, United Russia is the dominant party, elections are rigged, the State Duma and Federation Council (the lower and upper houses of the Russian parliament) are rubber-stamp institutions that eschew debate and take their cues from the president (partly as a result of changes to their structure and procedures, partly as a result of the dominance within them, and the system, of the pro-presidential party of power, United Russia, and mostly because of Putin's dictatorial dominance), and the judiciary retains some autonomy in non-political spheres (Yakovlev, Kazun, and Khodzhayeva, 2015). As I established in the previous section, Putin's rule is a personalistic dictatorship. The official worldview (or what Brian Taylor usefully calls a "code"[16]) is incoherent, while focusing on the exaltation of the Russian state, the Russian nation, and the personalistic, macho leader (Cassiday and Johnson, October 2010; Sperling, 2015).

---

14 The late-2007 election-campaign video showing Putin in a variety of usually bare-chested manly poses—on horseback, with automatic rifles, wading through a river—may have been a watershed in Putin's Duce-like self-representation (www.russia.ru/putin/).
15 Schroeder (2014), and Habdank-Kołaczkowska (2015) provide detailed discussions of most of these points.
16 According to Taylor (2015), Putinism consists of ideas (statism, including great power statism, anti-Westernism and anti-Americanism, conservatism/anti-liberalism), habits (control, order, unity/anti-pluralism, loyalty, hyper-masculinity), and emotions (respect/disrespect and humiliation, resentment, vulnerability/fear). Note the similarity with the fourteen features of fascism listed by Eco (1995).

Putin's popularity has consistently been high—and highest in the last ten years, as he was consolidating fascism in Russia (White and McAllister, 2003; Volkov, 2014). No one would dispute that Russia has a market economy that is dominated by the state, which has formed alliances with key oligarchs or actually owns significant portions of key industries (Dawisha, 2015). The opposition, especially after Boris Nemtsov's killing, is almost completely marginalized. Civil rights are greatly circumscribed and routinely violated (Freedom House, 2015). The *siloviki* constitute a significant portion of the ruling elite (Kryshtanovskaya and White, 2003). The propaganda apparatus—television, print media, radio, and Internet—is huge, actively promoting the official worldview and the cult of the leader,[17] but far short of the ubiquitous machine found in Soviet times (Van Herpen, 2015). Official violence is directed against key critics, with intimidation and coercion being the preferred methods of rule.

The case for Putin's Russia being fascist rests on two reasons. The first reason is empirical. As the above typological exercise demonstrated, the three characteristics that distinguish fascist systems from fully authoritarian ones—personalistic dictator, a leader cult, and mass popular support—apply completely to Putin's Russia. In a word, Putin's Russia is a fascist political system because it shares the defining characteristics of fascism as a subtype of full authoritarianism.

The second reason is logical. Putin's Russia may also be termed fascist because of the syllogism upon which my argument rests. If Putin's Russia is a fully authoritarian system and Putin is a

---

17  According to Anne Applebaum (2015), "In the past decade, for example, the Russian regime has reconstructed a state-run media machine far more sophisticated than anything the USSR ever invented and yet similarly blinkered. Although there are dozens of domestic news outlets, entertainment channels, and magazines, they all toe the same political line, with only a tiny number of exceptions. There is an appearance of variety but a unity of messages. Among them: The United States is a threat; Europe is degenerate; Ukraine is run by Nazis; Russia, unfairly deprived of its role in the world, is finally becoming a superpower again. To anyone who remembers how Communist ideology once sought to express all of history and all of contemporary politics through the lens of one giant conspiracy theory, this is nothing new."

personalistic dictator; and if fascism can be salvaged as a concept and defined as a political system that combines full authoritarianism with a personalistic dictatorship, then it follows that Putin's Russia is indeed fascist.

## References

Allardyce, Gilbert, 1979. What Fascism Is Not: Thoughts on the Deflation of a Concept. *The American Historical Review*, 84 (2), 367-388

Applebaum, Anne, 2015. Russia and the Great Forgetting. *Commentary*, December 1. >https://www.commentarymagazine.com/articles/russia-great-forgetting/<

Applebaum, Anne, Spring 2008. Putinism: Democracy, the Russian Way. *The Berlin Journal*, 16, 43-47.

Billig, Michael, 1995. *Banal Nationalism*. Sage, London.

Bosworth, R.J.B., 2006. *Mussolini's Italy: Life under the Fascist Dictatorship, 1915-1945*. Penguin, New York.

Buchheim, Hans, 1986. *Totalitarian Rule: Its Nature and Characteristics*. Wesleyan University Press, Middletown, CT.

Carafano, James Jay et al., 2015. U.S. Comprehensive Strategy Toward Russia. The Heritage Foundation. Special report no. 173, December 9. >http://www.heritage.org/research/reports/2015/12/us-comprehensive-strategy-toward-russia<

Cassiday, Julie A. and Johnson, Emily D., October 2010. Putin, Putiniana and the Question of a Post-Soviet Cult of Personality. *Slavonic and East European Review*, 681-707.

Connolly, Richard, 2015. Putin Needs to Look Beyond the Rouble. Chatham House, April 20. >https://www.chathamhouse.org/expert/comment/17471?gclid=CPmDhP_l9MkCFQotHwodgXwIdw<

Connolly, William, 1983. *The Terms of Political Discourse*, 2nd ed. Princeton University Press.

Corner, Paul. Italian Fascism: Whatever Happened to Dictatorship? *The Journal of Modern History*, 74 (2) 325-351.

Dawisha, Karen, 2015. *Putin's Kleptocracy: Who Owns Russia?* Simon & Schuster, New York.

Deuber, Gunter und Andreas Schwabe, 2015. Lange Phase der wirtschaftlichen Stagnation wahrscheinlich. *Russland-Analysen*, 299, July 3, 2-8. >http://www.laender-analysen.de/russland/pdf/RusslandAnalysen299.pdf<

Easton, David, 1953. *The Political System*. Knopf, New York.

Eco, Umberto, 1995. Eternal Fascism: Fourteen Ways of Looking at a Blackshirt. *New York Review of Books*, June 22, 12-15. >http://interglacial.com/pub/text/Umberto_Eco_-_Eternal_Fascism.html<

Freedom House, 2015. Russia. Nations in Transit 2015. >https://freedomhouse.org/report/nations-transit/2015/russia<

Gallie, W. B., 1956. Essentially Contested Concepts. Proceedings of the Aristotelian Society, 56, 167–198.

Gel'man, Vladimir, 2015. *Analyzing Post-Soviet Regime Changes*. University of Pittsburgh, Pittsburgh.

Gerasimov, Ilya, 2015. A Forgotten Detour on the Way "Back to the USSR." *Aspen Review Central Europe*, 4 (4) 67-72.

Gerring, John, 1999. What Makes a Concept Good? A Criterial Framework for Understanding Concept Formation in the Social Sciences. *Polity*, 31 (3) 357-393.

Griffin, Roger, 1993, *The Nature of Fascism*, 2nd ed. Routledge, London and New York.

Habdank-Kołaczkowska, Sylvana, 2015. Nations in Transit 2015: Democracy on the Defensive in Europe and Eurasia. Freedom House, Washington, DC. >https://freedomhouse.org/sites/default/files/FH_NIT2015_06.06.15_FINAL.pdf<

Iampolski, Mikhail, 2015. Putin's Russia Is in the Grip of Fascism. *Newsweek*, March 9. >http://www.newsweek.com/putins-russia-grip-fascism-312513<

Ikhlov, Evgenii, 2015. Paradoksal'nost' patriotizma, ili gonki krotov istorii. Kasparov.ru, March 21. >http://www.kasparov.ru/material.php?id=550D90F5A35DC<

Inozemtsev, Vladislav, 2015a. Vstavai, strana ogromnaia: kak fashizm vozvrashchaetsia 70 let spustia. RBK, June 22. >http://daily.rbc.ru/opinions/politics/22/06/2015/5582da729a794713ec1a6b91<

Inozemtsev, Vladislav, 2015b. Obyknovennyi fashizm. Pravda o Vladimire Putine. Novoe vremia, August 5. >http://nv.ua/opinion/Inozemtsev/obyknovennyy-fashizm-pravda-o-vladimire-putine-58980.html<

Kryshtanovskaya, Olga and Stephen White, 2003. Putin's Militocracy. *Post-Soviet Affairs*, 19 (4) 289-306.

Levitsky, Steven and Lucan Way, 2010. *Competitive Authoritarianism: Hybrid Regimes after the Cold War*. Cambridge University Press, New York.

Levitsky, Steven and Lucan Way, n.d. Competitive Authoritarianism: The Origins and Dynamics of Hybrid Regimes in the Post-Cold War Era. >http://iis-db.stanford.edu/evnts/4396/Levitsky-Way-Stanford.pdf<

Linz, Juan J., 1976. Some Notes toward a Comparative Study of Fascism in Sociological Historical Perspective. In: Laqueur, Walter (Ed.), *Fascism: A Reader's Guide*. University of California Press, Berkeley, 3-124.

Lipman, Masha, 2015. Putin's Shaky Tsardom. *The New Yorker*, December 20. >http://www.newyorker.com/news/news-desk/putins-shaky-tsardom<

Lyttleton, Adrian (Ed.), 1973. *Italian Fascisms: From Pareto to Gentile*. Harper & Row, New York.

Mann, Michael, 2004. *Fascists*. Cambridge University Press, Cambridge.

Merriam-Webster Dictionary, 2015. Fascism. >http://www.merriam-webster.com/dictionary/fascism<

Motyl, Alexander, 2010. Russia's Systemic Transformations since Perestroika: From Totalitarianism to Authoritarianism to Democracy — to Fascism? *The Harriman Review*, March, 1-14.

Motyl, Alexander J., 1990. *Sovietology, Rationality, Nationality: Coming to Grips with Nationalism in the USSR*. Columbia University Press, New York.

Mussolini, Benito, 2004. The Doctrine of Fascism. Terence Ball and Richard Dagger (Eds.). *Ideals and Ideologies: A Reader*. Pearson Longman, New York, 304-311.

Myers, Steven Lee, 2015. *The New Tsar: The Rise and Reign of Vladimir Putin*. Knopf, New York.

Oxford Dictionaries, 2015. Fascism. >http://www.oxforddictionaries.com/definition/english/fascism<

Paxton, Robert O., 2004. *The Anatomy of Fascism*. Allen Lane, London.

Paxton, Robert O., 1998. The Five Stages of Fascism. *The Journal of Modern History*, 70 (1) 1-23.

Payne, Stanley G., 1980. *Fascism: Comparison and Definition*. University of Wisconsin Press, Madison.

Payne, Stanley G., 1995. *A History of Fascism, 1914-1945*. University of Wisconsin Press, Madison.

Rawls, John, 2001. *The Law of Peoples*. Harvard University Press, Cambridge, MA.

Riley, Dylan, 2005. Civic Associations and Authoritarian Regimes in Interwar Europe: Italy and Spain in Comparative Perspective. *American Sociological Review*, 70 (2) 288-310.

Roberts, David D., 2000. How Not to Think about Fascism and Ideology: Intellectual Antecedents and Historical Meaning. *Journal of Contemporary History*, 35 (2) 185-211.

Rocco, Alfredo, 2004. The Political Theory of Fascism. Terence Ball and Richard Dagger (Eds.). *Ideals and Ideologies: A Reader*. Pearson Longman, New York, 312-317.

Sartori, Giovanni, 1970. Concept Misformation in Comparative Politics. *American Political Science Review*, 64 (4) 1033-1046.

Schroeder, Hans-Henning, 2014. »Volk« und »Macht«. Die schwache Verankerung des Systems Putin in der Gesellschaft. *Russland-Analysen*, July 18, 6-9. >http://www.laender-analysen.de/russland/pdf/RusslandAnalysen281.pdf<

Scruton, Roger, 1982. *A Dictionary of Political Thought*. Harper & Row, New York.

Shelin, Sergei, 2015. Nash put'—varvarizatsiia. *Rosbalt*, December 12. >http://www.rosbalt.ru/blogs/2015/12/1470681.html<

Shevtsova, Lilia, 2015. Forward to the Past in Russia. *Journal of Democracy*, 26, (2), 22-36. >http://muse.jhu.edu.proxy.libraries.rutgers.edu/journals/journal_of_democracy/v026/26.2.shevtsova.html<

Shiropaev, Aleksei, 2014. Pobedobesie. *Rufabula*, September 8. >http://rufabula.com/articles/2014/09/08/russia-in-the-war-with-ukraine<

Sperling, Valerie, 2015. *Sex, Politics, and Putin*. Oxford University Press.

Taylor, Brian, 2015. The Code of Putinism. PONARS Eurasia Policy Memos, no. 399, November. >http://www.ponarseurasia.org/memo/code-putinism<

Trenin, Dmitri. Russia Needs a Plan C. Carnegie Moscow Center, December 15, 2015. >http://carnegie.ru/commentary/2015/12/15/russia-needs-plan-c/in4j<

Tucker, Jeffrey A., 2015. Is Donald Trump a Fascist? *Newsweek*, July 17. >http://www.newsweek.com/donald-trump-fascist-354690<

Van Herpen, Marcel H., 2015. *Putin's Propaganda Machine: Soft Power and Russian Foreign Policy*. Rowman & Littlefield, Lanham, Maryland.

Volkov, Denis, 2014. Putin's Ratings: Anomaly or Trend? Institute of Modern Russia, December 23. >http://www.worldaffairsjournal.org/content/putin%E2%80%99s-ratings-anomaly-or-trend<

White, Stephen and Ian McAllister, 2003. Putin and His Supporters, *Europe-Asia Studies*, 55 (3) 383-99.

Yakovlev, Andrei, Anton Kazun, and Yekaterina Khodzhayeva, 2015. Wer steht auf Seiten der Verteidigung vor russischen Gerichten? *Russland-Analysen*, 296, May 22, 12-15.

Yampolski, Mikhail, 2015. Putin's Russia is in the grip of fascism. *Newsweek*. March 9. >http://www.newsweek.com/putins-russia-grip-fascism-312513<

Zimmerman, William, 2014. *Ruling Russia: Authoritarianism from the Revolution to Putin*. Princeton University Press, Princeton.

Zubov, Andrei, 2015. Putin stroit bespretsedentnoe gosudarstvo. VOA Golos Ameriki, January 26. >http://www.golos-ameriki.ru/content/russia-zubov/2611952.html<

# SOVIET AND POST-SOVIET POLITICS AND SOCIETY
Edited by Dr. Andreas Umland | ISSN 1614-3515

1 *Андреас Умланд (ред.)* | Воплощение Европейской конвенции по правам человека в России. Философские, юридические и эмпирические исследования | ISBN 3-89821-387-0

2 *Christian Wipperfürth* | Russland – ein vertrauenswürdiger Partner? Grundlagen, Hintergründe und Praxis gegenwärtiger russischer Außenpolitik | Mit einem Vorwort von Heinz Timmermann | ISBN 3-89821-401-X

3 *Manja Hussner* | Die Übernahme internationalen Rechts in die russische und deutsche Rechtsordnung. Eine vergleichende Analyse zur Völkerrechtsfreundlichkeit der Verfassungen der Russländischen Föderation und der Bundesrepublik Deutschland | Mit einem Vorwort von Rainer Arnold | ISBN 3-89821-438-9

4 *Matthew Tejada* | Bulgaria's Democratic Consolidation and the Kozloduy Nuclear Power Plant (KNPP). The Unattainability of Closure | With a foreword by Richard J. Crampton | ISBN 3-89821-439-7

5 *Марк Григорьевич Меерович* | Квадратные метры, определяющие сознание. Государственная жилищная политика в СССР. 1921 – 1941 гг | ISBN 3-89821-474-5

6 *Andrei P. Tsygankov, Pavel A. Tsygankov (Eds.)* | New Directions in Russian International Studies | ISBN 3-89821-422-2

7 *Марк Григорьевич Меерович* | Как власть народ к труду приучала. Жилище в СССР – средство управления людьми. 1917 – 1941 гг. | С предисловием Елены Осокиной | ISBN 3-89821-495-8

8 *David J. Galbreath* | Nation-Building and Minority Politics in Post-Socialist States. Interests, Influence and Identities in Estonia and Latvia | With a foreword by David J. Smith | ISBN 3-89821-467-2

9 *Алексей Юрьевич Безугольный* | Народы Кавказа в Вооруженных силах СССР в годы Великой Отечественной войны 1941-1945 гг. | С предисловием Николая Бугая | ISBN 3-89821-475-3

10 *Вячеслав Лихачев и Владимир Прибыловский (ред.)* | Русское Национальное Единство, 1990-2000. В 2-х томах | ISBN 3-89821-523-7

11 *Николай Бугай (ред.)* | Народы стран Балтии в условиях сталинизма (1940-е – 1950-е годы). Документированная история | ISBN 3-89821-525-3

12 *Ingmar Bredies (Hrsg.)* | Zur Anatomie der Orange Revolution in der Ukraine. Wechsel des Elitenregimes oder Triumph des Parlamentarismus? | ISBN 3-89821-524-5

13 *Anastasia V. Mitrofanova* | The Politicization of Russian Orthodoxy. Actors and Ideas | With a foreword by William C. Gay | ISBN 3-89821-481-8

14 *Nathan D. Larson* | Alexander Solzhenitsyn and the Russo-Jewish Question | ISBN 3-89821-483-4

15 *Guido Houben* | Kulturpolitik und Ethnizität. Staatliche Kunstförderung im Russland der neunziger Jahre | Mit einem Vorwort von Gert Weisskirchen | ISBN 3-89821-542-3

16 *Leonid Luks* | Der russische „Sonderweg"? Aufsätze zur neuesten Geschichte Russlands im europäischen Kontext | ISBN 3-89821-496-6

17 *Евгений Мороз* | История «Мёртвой воды» – от страшной сказки к большой политике. Политическое неоязычество в постсоветской России | ISBN 3-89821-551-2

18 *Александр Верховский и Галина Кожевникова (ред.)* | Этническая и религиозная интолерантность в российских СМИ. Результаты мониторинга 2001-2004 гг. | ISBN 3-89821-569-5

19 *Christian Ganzer* | Sowjetisches Erbe und ukrainische Nation. Das Museum der Geschichte des Zaporoger Kosakentums auf der Insel Chortycja | Mit einem Vorwort von Frank Golczewski | ISBN 3-89821-504-0

20 *Эльза-Баир Гучинова* | Помнить нельзя забыть. Антропология депортационной травмы калмыков | С предисловием Кэролайн Хамфри | ISBN 3-89821-506-7

21 *Юлия Лидерман* | Мотивы «проверки» и «испытания» в постсоветской культуре. Советское прошлое в российском кинематографе 1990-х годов | С предисловием Евгения Марголита | ISBN 3-89821-511-3

22 *Tanya Lokshina, Ray Thomas, Mary Mayer (Eds.)* | The Imposition of a Fake Political Settlement in the Northern Caucasus. The 2003 Chechen Presidential Election | ISBN 3-89821-436-2

23 *Timothy McCajor Hall, Rosie Read (Eds.)* | Changes in the Heart of Europe. Recent Ethnographies of Czechs, Slovaks, Roma, and Sorbs | With an afterword by Zdeněk Salzmann | ISBN 3-89821-606-5

24  *Christian Autengruber* | Die politischen Parteien in Bulgarien und Rumänien. Eine vergleichende Analyse seit Beginn der 90er Jahre | Mit einem Vorwort von Dorothée de Nève | ISBN 3-89821-476-1

25  *Annette Freyberg-Inan with Radu Cristescu* | The Ghosts in Our Classrooms, or: John Dewey Meets Ceauşescu. The Promise and the Failures of Civic Education in Romania | ISBN 3-89821-416-8

26  *John B. Dunlop* | The 2002 Dubrovka and 2004 Beslan Hostage Crises. A Critique of Russian Counter-Terrorism | With a foreword by Donald N. Jensen | ISBN 3-89821-608-X

27  *Peter Koller* | Das touristische Potenzial von Kam"janec'–Podil's'kyj. Eine fremdenverkehrsgeographische Untersuchung der Zukunftsperspektiven und Maßnahmenplanung zur Destinationsentwicklung des „ukrainischen Rothenburg" | Mit einem Vorwort von Kristiane Klemm | ISBN 3-89821-640-3

28  *Françoise Daucé, Elisabeth Sieca-Kozlowski (Eds.)* | Dedovshchina in the Post-Soviet Military. Hazing of Russian Army Conscripts in a Comparative Perspective | With a foreword by Dale Herspring | ISBN 3-89821-616-0

29  *Florian Strasser* | Zivilgesellschaftliche Einflüsse auf die Orange Revolution. Die gewaltlose Massenbewegung und die ukrainische Wahlkrise 2004 | Mit einem Vorwort von Egbert Jahn | ISBN 3-89821-648-9

30  *Rebecca S. Katz* | The Georgian Regime Crisis of 2003-2004. A Case Study in Post-Soviet Media Representation of Politics, Crime and Corruption | ISBN 3-89821-413-3

31  *Vladimir Kantor* | Willkür oder Freiheit. Beiträge zur russischen Geschichtsphilosophie | Ediert von Dagmar Herrmann sowie mit einem Vorwort versehen von Leonid Luks | ISBN 3-89821-589-X

32  *Laura A. Victoir* | The Russian Land Estate Today. A Case Study of Cultural Politics in Post-Soviet Russia | With a foreword by Priscilla Roosevelt | ISBN 3-89821-426-5

33  *Ivan Katchanovski* | Cleft Countries. Regional Political Divisions and Cultures in Post-Soviet Ukraine and Moldova | With a foreword by Francis Fukuyama | ISBN 3-89821-558-X

34  *Florian Mühlfried* | Postsowjetische Feiern. Das Georgische Bankett im Wandel | Mit einem Vorwort von Kevin Tuite | ISBN 3-89821-601-2

35  *Roger Griffin, Werner Loh, Andreas Umland (Eds.)* | Fascism Past and Present, West and East. An International Debate on Concepts and Cases in the Comparative Study of the Extreme Right | With an afterword by Walter Laqueur | ISBN 3-89821-674-8

36  *Sebastian Schlegel* | Der „Weiße Archipel". Sowjetische Atomstädte 1945-1991 | Mit einem Geleitwort von Thomas Bohn | ISBN 3-89821-679-9

37  *Vyacheslav Likhachev* | Political Anti-Semitism in Post-Soviet Russia. Actors and Ideas in 1991-2003 | Edited and translated from Russian by Eugene Veklerov | ISBN 3-89821-529-6

38  *Josette Baer (Ed.)* | Preparing Liberty in Central Europe. Political Texts from the Spring of Nations 1848 to the Spring of Prague 1968 | With a foreword by Zdeněk V. David | ISBN 3-89821-546-6

39  *Михаил Лукьянов* | Российский консерватизм и реформа, 1907-1914 | С предисловием Марка Д. Стейнберга | ISBN 3-89821-503-2

40  *Nicola Melloni* | Market Without Economy. The 1998 Russian Financial Crisis | With a foreword by Eiji Furukawa | ISBN 3-89821-407-9

41  *Dmitrij Chmelnizki* | Die Architektur Stalins | Bd. 1: Studien zu Ideologie und Stil | Bd. 2: Bilddokumentation | Mit einem Vorwort von Bruno Flierl | ISBN 3-89821-515-6

42  *Katja Yafimava* | Post-Soviet Russian-Belarussian Relationships. The Role of Gas Transit Pipelines | With a foreword by Jonathan P. Stern | ISBN 3-89821-655-1

43  *Boris Chavkin* | Verflechtungen der deutschen und russischen Zeitgeschichte. Aufsätze und Archivfunde zu den Beziehungen Deutschlands und der Sowjetunion von 1917 bis 1991 | Ediert von Markus Edlinger sowie mit einem Vorwort versehen von Leonid Luks | ISBN 3-89821-756-5

44  *Anastasija Grynenko in Zusammenarbeit mit Claudia Dathe* | Die Terminologie des Gerichtswesens der Ukraine und Deutschlands im Vergleich. Eine übersetzungswissenschaftliche Analyse juristischer Fachbegriffe im Deutschen, Ukrainischen und Russischen | Mit einem Vorwort von Ulrich Hartmann | ISBN 3-89821-691-8

45  *Anton Burkov* | The Impact of the European Convention on Human Rights on Russian Law. Legislation and Application in 1996-2006 | With a foreword by Françoise Hampson | ISBN 978-3-89821-639-5

46  *Stina Torjesen, Indra Overland (Eds.)* | International Election Observers in Post-Soviet Azerbaijan. Geopolitical Pawns or Agents of Change? | ISBN 978-3-89821-743-9

47  *Taras Kuzio* | Ukraine – Crimea – Russia. Triangle of Conflict | ISBN 978-3-89821-761-3

48  *Claudia Šabić* | „Ich erinnere mich nicht, aber L'viv!" Zur Funktion kultureller Faktoren für die Institutionalisierung und Entwicklung einer ukrainischen Region | Mit einem Vorwort von Melanie Tatur | ISBN 978-3-89821-752-1

49 *Marlies Bilz* | Tatarstan in der Transformation. Nationaler Diskurs und Politische Praxis 1988-1994 | Mit einem Vorwort von Frank Golczewski | ISBN 978-3-89821-722-4

50 *Марлен Ларюэль (ред.)* | Современные интерпретации русского национализма | ISBN 978-3-89821-795-8

51 *Sonja Schüler* | Die ethnische Dimension der Armut. Roma im postsozialistischen Rumänien | Mit einem Vorwort von Anton Sterbling | ISBN 978-3-89821-776-7

52 *Галина Кожевникова* | Радикальный национализм в России и противодействие ему. Сборник докладов Центра «Сова» за 2004-2007 гг. | С предисловием Александра Верховского | ISBN 978-3-89821-721-7

53 *Галина Кожевникова и Владимир Прибыловский* | Российская власть в биографиях I. Высшие должностные лица РФ в 2004 г. | ISBN 978-3-89821-796-5

54 *Галина Кожевникова и Владимир Прибыловский* | Российская власть в биографиях II. Члены Правительства РФ в 2004 г. | ISBN 978-3-89821-797-2

55 *Галина Кожевникова и Владимир Прибыловский* | Российская власть в биографиях III. Руководители федеральных служб и агентств РФ в 2004 г.| ISBN 978-3-89821-798-9

56 *Ileana Petroniu* | Privatisierung in Transformationsökonomien. Determinanten der Restrukturierungs-Bereitschaft am Beispiel Polens, Rumäniens und der Ukraine | Mit einem Vorwort von Rainer W. Schäfer | ISBN 978-3-89821-790-3

57 *Christian Wipperfürth* | Russland und seine GUS-Nachbarn. Hintergründe, aktuelle Entwicklungen und Konflikte in einer ressourcenreichen Region| ISBN 978-3-89821-801-6

58 *Togzhan Kassenova* | From Antagonism to Partnership. The Uneasy Path of the U.S.-Russian Cooperative Threat Reduction | With a foreword by Christoph Bluth | ISBN 978-3-89821-707-1

59 *Alexander Höllwerth* | Das sakrale eurasische Imperium des Aleksandr Dugin. Eine Diskursanalyse zum postsowjetischen russischen Rechtsextremismus | Mit einem Vorwort von Dirk Uffelmann | ISBN 978-3-89821-813-9

60 *Олег Рябов* | «Россия-Матушка». Национализм, гендер и война в России XX века | С предисловием Елены Гощило | ISBN 978-3-89821-487-2

61 *Ivan Maistrenko* | Borot'bism. A Chapter in the History of the Ukrainian Revolution | With a new Introduction by Chris Ford | Translated by George S. N. Luckyj with the assistance of Ivan L. Rudnytsky | Second, Revised and Expanded Edition ISBN 978-3-8382-1107-7

62 *Maryna Romanets* | Anamorphosic Texts and Reconfigured Visions. Improvised Traditions in Contemporary Ukrainian and Irish Literature | ISBN 978-3-89821-576-3

63 *Paul D'Anieri and Taras Kuzio (Eds.)* | Aspects of the Orange Revolution I. Democratization and Elections in Post-Communist Ukraine | ISBN 978-3-89821-698-2

64 *Bohdan Harasymiw in collaboration with Oleh S. Ilnytzkyj (Eds.)* | Aspects of the Orange Revolution II. Information and Manipulation Strategies in the 2004 Ukrainian Presidential Elections | ISBN 978-3-89821-699-9

65 *Ingmar Bredies, Andreas Umland and Valentin Yakushik (Eds.)* | Aspects of the Orange Revolution III. The Context and Dynamics of the 2004 Ukrainian Presidential Elections | ISBN 978-3-89821-803-0

66 *Ingmar Bredies, Andreas Umland and Valentin Yakushik (Eds.)* | Aspects of the Orange Revolution IV. Foreign Assistance and Civic Action in the 2004 Ukrainian Presidential Elections | ISBN 978-3-89821-808-5

67 *Ingmar Bredies, Andreas Umland and Valentin Yakushik (Eds.)* | Aspects of the Orange Revolution V. Institutional Observation Reports on the 2004 Ukrainian Presidential Elections | ISBN 978-3-89821-809-2

68 *Taras Kuzio (Ed.)* | Aspects of the Orange Revolution VI. Post-Communist Democratic Revolutions in Comparative Perspective | ISBN 978-3-89821-820-7

69 *Tim Bohse* | Autoritarismus statt Selbstverwaltung. Die Transformation der kommunalen Politik in der Stadt Kaliningrad 1990-2005 | Mit einem Geleitwort von Stefan Troebst | ISBN 978-3-89821-782-8

70 *David Rupp* | Die Rußländische Föderation und die russischsprachige Minderheit in Lettland. Eine Fallstudie zur Anwaltspolitik Moskaus gegenüber den russophonen Minderheiten im „Nahen Ausland" von 1991 bis 2002 | Mit einem Vorwort von Helmut Wagner | ISBN 978-3-89821-778-1

71 *Taras Kuzio* | Theoretical and Comparative Perspectives on Nationalism. New Directions in Cross-Cultural and Post-Communist Studies | With a foreword by Paul Robert Magocsi | ISBN 978-3-89821-815-3

72 *Christine Teichmann* | Die Hochschultransformation im heutigen Osteuropa. Kontinuität und Wandel bei der Entwicklung des postkommunistischen Universitätswesens | Mit einem Vorwort von Oskar Anweiler | ISBN 978-3-89821-842-9

73 *Julia Kusznir* | Der politische Einfluss von Wirtschaftseliten in russischen Regionen. Eine Analyse am Beispiel der Erdöl- und Erdgasindustrie, 1992-2005 | Mit einem Vorwort von Wolfgang Eichwede | ISBN 978-3-89821-821-4

74  *Alena Vysotskaya* | Russland, Belarus und die EU-Osterweiterung. Zur Minderheitenfrage und zum Problem der Freizügigkeit des Personenverkehrs | Mit einem Vorwort von Katlijn Malfliet | ISBN 978-3-89821-822-1

75  *Heiko Pleines (Hrsg.)* | Corporate Governance in post-sozialistischen Volkswirtschaften | ISBN 978-3-89821-766-8

76  *Stefan Ihrig* | Wer sind die Moldawier? Rumänismus versus Moldowanismus in Historiographie und Schulbüchern der Republik Moldova, 1991-2006 | Mit einem Vorwort von Holm Sundhaussen | ISBN 978-3-89821-466-7

77  *Galina Kozhevnikova in collaboration with Alexander Verkhovsky and Eugene Veklerov* | Ultra-Nationalism and Hate Crimes in Contemporary Russia. The 2004-2006 Annual Reports of Moscow's SOVA Center | With a foreword by Stephen D. Shenfield | ISBN 978-3-89821-868-9

78  *Florian Küchler* | The Role of the European Union in Moldova's Transnistria Conflict | With a foreword by Christopher Hill | ISBN 978-3-89821-850-4

79  *Bernd Rechel* | The Long Way Back to Europe. Minority Protection in Bulgaria | With a foreword by Richard Crampton | ISBN 978-3-89821-863-4

80  *Peter W. Rodgers* | Nation, Region and History in Post-Communist Transitions. Identity Politics in Ukraine, 1991-2006 | With a foreword by Vera Tolz | ISBN 978-3-89821-903-7

81  *Stephanie Solywoda* | The Life and Work of Semen L. Frank. A Study of Russian Religious Philosophy | With a foreword by Philip Walters | ISBN 978-3-89821-457-5

82  *Vera Sokolova* | Cultural Politics of Ethnicity. Discourses on Roma in Communist Czechoslovakia | ISBN 978-3-89821-864-1

83  *Natalya Shevchik Ketenci* | Kazakhstani Enterprises in Transition. The Role of Historical Regional Development in Kazakhstan's Post-Soviet Economic Transformation | ISBN 978-3-89821-831-3

84  *Martin Malek, Anna Schor-Tschudnowskaja (Hgg.)* | Europa im Tschetschenienkrieg. Zwischen politischer Ohnmacht und Gleichgültigkeit | Mit einem Vorwort von Lipchan Basajewa | ISBN 978-3-89821-676-0

85  *Stefan Meister* | Das postsowjetische Universitätswesen zwischen nationalem und internationalem Wandel. Die Entwicklung der regionalen Hochschule in Russland als Gradmesser der Systemtransformation | Mit einem Vorwort von Joan DeBardeleben | ISBN 978-3-89821-891-7

86  *Konstantin Sheiko in collaboration with Stephen Brown* | Nationalist Imaginings of the Russian Past. Anatolii Fomenko and the Rise of Alternative History in Post-Communist Russia | With a foreword by Donald Ostrowski | ISBN 978-3-89821-915-0

87  *Sabine Jenni* | Wie stark ist das „Einige Russland"? Zur Parteibindung der Eliten und zum Wahlerfolg der Machtpartei im Dezember 2007 | Mit einem Vorwort von Klaus Armingeon | ISBN 978-3-89821-961-7

88  *Thomas Borén* | Meeting-Places of Transformation. Urban Identity, Spatial Representations and Local Politics in Post-Soviet St Petersburg | ISBN 978-3-89821-739-2

89  *Aygul Ashirova* | Stalinismus und Stalin-Kult in Zentralasien. Turkmenistan 1924-1953 | Mit einem Vorwort von Leonid Luks | ISBN 978-3-89821-987-7

90  *Leonid Luks* | Freiheit oder imperiale Größe? Essays zu einem russischen Dilemma | ISBN 978-3-8382-0011-8

91  *Christopher Gilley* | The 'Change of Signposts' in the Ukrainian Emigration. A Contribution to the History of Sovietophilism in the 1920s | With a foreword by Frank Golczewski | ISBN 978-3-89821-965-5

92  *Philipp Casula, Jeronim Perovic (Eds.)* | Identities and Politics During the Putin Presidency. The Discursive Foundations of Russia's Stability | With a foreword by Heiko Haumann | ISBN 978-3-8382-0015-6

93  *Marcel Viëtor* | Europa und die Frage nach seinen Grenzen im Osten. Zur Konstruktion ‚europäischer Identität' in Geschichte und Gegenwart | Mit einem Vorwort von Albrecht Lehmann | ISBN 978-3-8382-0045-3

94  *Ben Hellman, Andrei Rogachevskii* | Filming the Unfilmable. Casper Wrede's 'One Day in the Life of Ivan Denisovich' | Second, Revised and Expanded Edition | ISBN 978-3-8382-0044-6

95  *Eva Fuchslocher* | Vaterland, Sprache, Glaube. Orthodoxie und Nationenbildung am Beispiel Georgiens | Mit einem Vorwort von Christina von Braun | ISBN 978-3-89821-884-9

96  *Vladimir Kantor* | Das Westlertum und der Weg Russlands. Zur Entwicklung der russischen Literatur und Philosophie | Ediert von Dagmar Herrmann | Mit einem Beitrag von Nikolaus Lobkowicz | ISBN 978-3-8382-0102-3

97  *Kamran Musayev* | Die postsowjetische Transformation im Baltikum und Südkaukasus. Eine vergleichende Untersuchung der politischen Entwicklung Lettlands und Aserbaidschans 1985-2009 | Mit einem Vorwort von Leonid Luks | Ediert von Sandro Henschel | ISBN 978-3-8382-0103-0

98  *Tatiana Zhurzhenko* | Borderlands into Bordered Lands. Geopolitics of Identity in Post-Soviet Ukraine | With a foreword by Dieter Segert | ISBN 978-3-8382-0042-2

99   *Кирилл Галушко, Лидия Смола (ред.)* | Пределы падения – варианты украинского будущего. Аналитико-прогностические исследования | ISBN 978-3-8382-0148-1

100  *Michael Minkenberg (Ed.)* | Historical Legacies and the Radical Right in Post-Cold War Central and Eastern Europe | With an afterword by Sabrina P. Ramet | ISBN 978-3-8382-0124-5

101  *David-Emil Wickström* | Rocking St. Petersburg. Transcultural Flows and Identity Politics in the St. Petersburg Popular Music Scene | With a foreword by Yngvar B. Steinholt | Second, Revised and Expanded Edition | ISBN 978-3-8382-0100-9

102  *Eva Zabka* | Eine neue „Zeit der Wirren"? Der spät- und postsowjetische Systemwandel 1985-2000 im Spiegel russischer gesellschaftspolitischer Diskurse | Mit einem Vorwort von Margareta Mommsen | ISBN 978-3-8382-0161-0

103  *Ulrike Ziemer* | Ethnic Belonging, Gender and Cultural Practices. Youth Identitites in Contemporary Russia | With a foreword by Anoop Nayak | ISBN 978-3-8382-0152-8

104  *Ksenia Chepikova* | ‚Einiges Russland' - eine zweite KPdSU? Aspekte der Identitätskonstruktion einer postsowjetischen „Partei der Macht" | Mit einem Vorwort von Torsten Oppelland | ISBN 978-3-8382-0311-9

105  *Леонид Люкс* | Западничество или евразийство? Демократия или идеократия? Сборник статей об исторических дилеммах России | С предисловием Владимира Кантора | ISBN 978-3-8382-0211-2

106  *Anna Dost* | Das russische Verfassungsrecht auf dem Weg zum Föderalismus und zurück. Zum Konflikt von Rechtsnormen und -wirklichkeit in der Russländischen Föderation von 1991 bis 2009 | Mit einem Vorwort von Alexander Blankenagel | ISBN 978-3-8382-0292-1

107  *Philipp Herzog* | Sozialistische Völkerfreundschaft, nationaler Widerstand oder harmloser Zeitvertreib? Zur politischen Funktion der Volkskunst im sowjetischen Estland | Mit einem Vorwort von Andreas Kappeler | ISBN 978-3-8382-0216-7

108  *Marlène Laruelle (Ed.)* | Russian Nationalism, Foreign Policy, and Identity Debates in Putin's Russia. New Ideological Patterns after the Orange Revolution | ISBN 978-3-8382-0325-6

109  *Michail Logvinov* | Russlands Kampf gegen den internationalen Terrorismus. Eine kritische Bestandsaufnahme des Bekämpfungsansatzes | Mit einem Geleitwort von Hans-Henning Schröder und einem Vorwort von Eckhard Jesse | ISBN 978-3-8382-0329-4

110  *John B. Dunlop* | The Moscow Bombings of September 1999. Examinations of Russian Terrorist Attacks at the Onset of Vladimir Putin's Rule | Second, Revised and Expanded Edition | ISBN 978-3-8382-0388-1

111  *Андрей А. Ковалёв* | Свидетельство из-за кулис российской политики I. Можно ли делать добро из зла? (Воспоминания и размышления о последних советских и первых послесоветских годах) | With a foreword by Peter Reddaway | ISBN 978-3-8382-0302-7

112  *Андрей А. Ковалёв* | Свидетельство из-за кулис российской политики II. Угроза для себя и окружающих (Наблюдения и предостережения относительно происходящего после 2000 г.) | ISBN 978-3-8382-0303-4

113  *Bernd Kappenberg* | Zeichen setzen für Europa. Der Gebrauch europäischer lateinischer Sonderzeichen in der deutschen Öffentlichkeit | Mit einem Vorwort von Peter Schlobinski | ISBN 978-3-89821-749-1

114  *Ivo Mijnssen* | The Quest for an Ideal Youth in Putin's Russia I. Back to Our Future! History, Modernity, and Patriotism according to Nashi, 2005-2013 | With a foreword by Jeronim Perović | Second, Revised and Expanded Edition | ISBN 978-3-8382-0368-3

115  *Jussi Lassila* | The Quest for an Ideal Youth in Putin's Russia II. The Search for Distinctive Conformism in the Political Communication of Nashi, 2005-2009 | With a foreword by Kirill Postoutenko | Second, Revised and Expanded Edition | ISBN 978-3-8382-0415-4

116  *Valerio Trabandt* | Neue Nachbarn, gute Nachbarschaft? Die EU als internationaler Akteur am Beispiel ihrer Demokratieförderung in Belarus und der Ukraine 2004-2009 | Mit einem Vorwort von Jutta Joachim | ISBN 978-3-8382-0437-6

117  *Fabian Pfeiffer* | Estlands Außen- und Sicherheitspolitik I. Der estnische Atlantizismus nach der wiedererlangten Unabhängigkeit 1991-2004 | Mit einem Vorwort von Helmut Hubel | ISBN 978-3-8382-0127-6

118  *Jana Podßuweit* | Estlands Außen- und Sicherheitspolitik II. Handlungsoptionen eines Kleinstaates im Rahmen seiner EU-Mitgliedschaft (2004-2008) | Mit einem Vorwort von Helmut Hubel | ISBN 978-3-8382-0440-6

119  *Karin Pointner* | Estlands Außen- und Sicherheitspolitik III. Eine gedächtnispolitische Analyse estnischer Entwicklungskooperation 2006-2010 | Mit einem Vorwort von Karin Liebhart | ISBN 978-3-8382-0435-2

120  *Ruslana Vovk* | Die Offenheit der ukrainischen Verfassung für das Völkerrecht und die europäische Integration | Mit einem Vorwort von Alexander Blankenagel | ISBN 978-3-8382-0481-9

121 *Mykhaylo Banakh* | Die Relevanz der Zivilgesellschaft bei den postkommunistischen Transformationsprozessen in mittel- und osteuropäischen Ländern. Das Beispiel der spät- und postsowjetischen Ukraine 1986-2009 | Mit einem Vorwort von Gerhard Simon | ISBN 978-3-8382-0499-4

122 *Michael Moser* | Language Policy and the Discourse on Languages in Ukraine under President Viktor Yanukovych (25 February 2010–28 October 2012) | ISBN 978-3-8382-0497-0 (Paperback edition) | ISBN 978-3-8382-0507-6 (Hardcover edition)

123 *Nicole Krome* | Russischer Netzwerkkapitalismus Restrukturierungsprozesse in der Russischen Föderation am Beispiel des Luftfahrtunternehmens „Aviastar" | Mit einem Vorwort von Petra Stykow | ISBN 978-3-8382-0534-2

124 *David R. Marples* | 'Our Glorious Past'. Lukashenka's Belarus and the Great Patriotic War | ISBN 978-3-8382-0574-8 (Paperback edition) | ISBN 978-3-8382-0675-2 (Hardcover edition)

125 *Ulf Walther* | Russlands „neuer Adel". Die Macht des Geheimdienstes von Gorbatschow bis Putin | Mit einem Vorwort von Hans-Georg Wieck | ISBN 978-3-8382-0584-7

126 *Simon Geissbühler (Hrsg.)* | Kiew – Revolution 3.0. Der Euromaidan 2013/14 und die Zukunftsperspektiven der Ukraine | ISBN 978-3-8382-0581-6 (Paperback edition) | ISBN 978-3-8382-0681-3 (Hardcover edition)

127 *Andrey Makarychev* | Russia and the EU in a Multipolar World. Discourses, Identities, Norms | With a foreword by Klaus Segbers | ISBN 978-3-8382-0629-5

128 *Roland Scharff* | Kasachstan als postsowjetischer Wohlfahrtsstaat. Die Transformation des sozialen Schutzsystems | Mit einem Vorwort von Joachim Ahrens | ISBN 978-3-8382-0622-6

129 *Katja Grupp* | Bild Lücke Deutschland. Kaliningrader Studierende sprechen über Deutschland | Mit einem Vorwort von Martin Schulz | ISBN 978-3-8382-0552-6

130 *Konstantin Sheiko, Stephen Brown* | History as Therapy. Alternative History and Nationalist Imaginings in Russia, 1991-2014 | ISBN 978-3-8382-0665-3

131 *Elisa Kriza* | Alexander Solzhenitsyn: Cold War Icon, Gulag Author, Russian Nationalist? A Study of the Western Reception of his Literary Writings, Historical Interpretations, and Political Ideas | With a foreword by Andrei Rogatchevski | ISBN 978-3-8382-0589-2 (Paperback edition) | ISBN 978-3-8382-0690-5 (Hardcover edition)

132 *Serghei Golunov* | The Elephant in the Room. Corruption and Cheating in Russian Universities | ISBN 978-3-8382-0570-0

133 *Manja Hussner, Rainer Arnold (Hgg.)* | Verfassungsgerichtsbarkeit in Zentralasien I. Sammlung von Verfassungstexten | ISBN 978-3-8382-0595-3

134 *Nikolay Mitrokhin* | Die „Russische Partei". Die Bewegung der russischen Nationalisten in der UdSSR 1953-1985 | Aus dem Russischen übertragen von einem Übersetzerteam unter der Leitung von Larisa Schippel | ISBN 978-3-8382-0024-8

135 *Manja Hussner, Rainer Arnold (Hgg.)* | Verfassungsgerichtsbarkeit in Zentralasien II. Sammlung von Verfassungstexten | ISBN 978-3-8382-0597-7

136 *Manfred Zeller* | Das sowjetische Fieber. Fußballfans im poststalinistischen Vielvölkerreich | Mit einem Vorwort von Nikolaus Katzer | ISBN 978-3-8382-0757-5

137 *Kristin Schreiter* | Stellung und Entwicklungspotential zivilgesellschaftlicher Gruppen in Russland. Menschenrechtsorganisationen im Vergleich | ISBN 978-3-8382-0673-8

138 *David R. Marples, Frederick V. Mills (Eds.)* | Ukraine's Euromaidan. Analyses of a Civil Revolution | ISBN 978-3-8382-0660-8

139 *Bernd Kappenberg* | Setting Signs for Europe. Why Diacritics Matter for European Integration | With a foreword by Peter Schlobinski | ISBN 978-3-8382-0663-9

140 *René Lenz* | Internationalisierung, Kooperation und Transfer. Externe bildungspolitische Akteure in der Russischen Föderation | Mit einem Vorwort von Frank Ettrich | ISBN 978-3-8382-0751-3

141 *Juri Plusnin, Yana Zausaeva, Natalia Zhidkevich, Artemy Pozanenko* | Wandering Workers. Mores, Behavior, Way of Life, and Political Status of Domestic Russian Labor Migrants | Translated by Julia Kazantseva | ISBN 978-3-8382-0653-0

142 *David J. Smith (Eds.)* | Latvia – A Work in Progress? 100 Years of State- and Nation-Building | ISBN 978-3-8382-0648-6

143 *Инна Чувычкина (ред.)* | Экспортные нефте- и газопроводы на постсоветском пространстве. Анализ трубопроводной политики в свете теории международных отношений | ISBN 978-3-8382-0822-0

144 *Johann Zajaczkowski* | Russland – eine pragmatische Großmacht? Eine rollentheoretische Untersuchung russischer Außenpolitik am Beispiel der Zusammenarbeit mit den USA nach 9/11 und des Georgienkrieges von 2008 | Mit einem Vorwort von Siegfried Schieder | ISBN 978-3-8382-0837-4

145 *Boris Popivanov* | Changing Images of the Left in Bulgaria. The Challenge of Post-Communism in the Early 21st Century | ISBN 978-3-8382-0667-7

146 *Lenka Krátká* | A History of the Czechoslovak Ocean Shipping Company 1948-1989. How a Small, Landlocked Country Ran Maritime Business During the Cold War | ISBN 978-3-8382-0666-0

147 *Alexander Sergunin* | Explaining Russian Foreign Policy Behavior. Theory and Practice | ISBN 978-3-8382-0752-0

148 *Darya Malyutina* | Migrant Friendships in a Super-Diverse City. Russian-Speakers and their Social Relationships in London in the 21st Century | With a foreword by Claire Dwyer | ISBN 978-3-8382-0652-3

149 *Alexander Sergunin, Valery Konyshev* | Russia in the Arctic. Hard or Soft Power? | ISBN 978-3-8382-0753-7

150 *John J. Maresca* | Helsinki Revisited. A Key U.S. Negotiator's Memoirs on the Development of the CSCE into the OSCE | With a foreword by Hafiz Pashayev | ISBN 978-3-8382-0852-7

151 *Jardar Østbø* | The New Third Rome. Readings of a Russian Nationalist Myth | With a foreword by Pål Kolstø | ISBN 978-3-8382-0870-1

152 *Simon Kordonsky* | Socio-Economic Foundations of the Russian Post-Soviet Regime. The Resource-Based Economy and Estate-Based Social Structure of Contemporary Russia | With a foreword by Svetlana Barsukova | ISBN 978-3-8382-0775-9

153 *Duncan Leitch* | Assisting Reform in Post-Communist Ukraine 2000–2012. The Illusions of Donors and the Disillusion of Beneficiaries | With a foreword by Kataryna Wolczuk | ISBN 978-3-8382-0844-2

154 *Abel Polese* | Limits of a Post-Soviet State. How Informality Replaces, Renegotiates, and Reshapes Governance in Contemporary Ukraine | With a foreword by Colin Williams | ISBN 978-3-8382-0845-9

155 *Mikhail Suslov (Ed.)* | Digital Orthodoxy in the Post-Soviet World. The Russian Orthodox Church and Web 2.0 | With a foreword by Father Cyril Hovorun | ISBN 978-3-8382-0871-8

156 *Leonid Luks* | Zwei „Sonderwege"? Russisch-deutsche Parallelen und Kontraste (1917-2014). Vergleichende Essays | ISBN 978-3-8382-0823-7

157 *Vladimir V. Karacharovskiy, Ovsey I. Shkaratan, Gordey A. Yastrebov* | Towards a New Russian Work Culture. Can Western Companies and Expatriates Change Russian Society? | With a foreword by Elena N. Danilova | Translated by Julia Kazantseva | ISBN 978-3-8382-0902-9

158 *Edmund Griffiths* | Aleksandr Prokhanov and Post-Soviet Esotericism | ISBN 978-3-8382-0903-6

159 *Timm Beichelt, Susann Worschech (Eds.)* | Transnational Ukraine? Networks and Ties that Influence(d) Contemporary Ukraine | ISBN 978-3-8382-0944-9

160 *Mieste Hotopp-Riecke* | Die Tataren der Krim zwischen Assimilation und Selbstbehauptung. Der Aufbau des krimtatarischen Bildungswesens nach Deportation und Heimkehr (1990-2005) | Mit einem Vorwort von Swetlana Czerwonnaja | ISBN 978-3-89821-940-2

161 *Olga Bertelsen (Ed.)* | Revolution and War in Contemporary Ukraine. The Challenge of Change | ISBN 978-3-8382-1016-2

162 *Natalya Ryabinska* | Ukraine's Post-Communist Mass Media. Between Capture and Commercialization | With a foreword by Marta Dyczok | ISBN 978-3-8382-1011-7

163 *Alexandra Cotofana, James M. Nyce (Eds.)* | Religion and Magic in Socialist and Post-Socialist Contexts. Historic and Ethnographic Case Studies of Orthodoxy, Heterodoxy, and Alternative Spirituality | With a foreword by Patrick L. Michelson | ISBN 978-3-8382-0989-0

164 *Nozima Akhrarkhodjaeva* | The Instrumentalisation of Mass Media in Electoral Authoritarian Regimes. Evidence from Russia's Presidential Election Campaigns of 2000 and 2008 | ISBN 978-3-8382-1013-1

165 *Yulia Krasheninnikova* | Informal Healthcare in Contemporary Russia. Sociographic Essays on the Post-Soviet Infrastructure for Alternative Healing Practices | ISBN 978-3-8382-0970-8

166 *Peter Kaiser* | Das Schachbrett der Macht. Die Handlungsspielräume eines sowjetischen Funktionärs unter Stalin am Beispiel des Generalsekretärs des Komsomol Aleksandr Kosarev (1929-1938) | Mit einem Vorwort von Dietmar Neutatz | ISBN 978-3-8382-1052-0

167 *Oksana Kim* | The Effects and Implications of Kazakhstan's Adoption of International Financial Reporting Standards. A Resource Dependence Perspective | With a foreword by Svetlana Vlady | ISBN 978-3-8382-0987-6

168 *Anna Sanina* | Patriotic Education in Contemporary Russia. Sociological Studies in the Making of the Post-Soviet Citizen | With a foreword by Anna Oldfield | ISBN 978-3-8382-0993-7

169 *Rudolf Wolters* | Spezialist in Sibirien Faksimile der 1933 erschienenen ersten Ausgabe | Mit einem Vorwort von Dmitrij Chmelnizki | ISBN 978-3-8382-0515-1

170 *Michal Vít, Magdalena M. Baran (Eds.)* | Transregional versus National Perspectives on Contemporary Central European History. Studies on the Building of Nation-States and Their Cooperation in the 20th and 21st Century | With a foreword by Petr Vágner | ISBN 978-3-8382-1015-5

171 *Philip Gamaghelyan* | Conflict Resolution Beyond the International Relations Paradigm. Evolving Designs as a Transformative Practice in Nagorno-Karabakh and Syria | With a foreword by Susan Allen | ISBN 978-3-8382-1057-5

172 *Maria Shagina* | Joining a Prestigious Club. Cooperation with Europarties and Its Impact on Party Development in Georgia, Moldova, and Ukraine 2004–2015 | With a foreword by Kataryna Wolczuk | ISBN 978-3-8382-1084-1

173 *Alexandra Cotofana, James M. Nyce (Eds.)* | Religion and Magic in Socialist and Post-Socialist Contexts II. Baltic, Eastern European, and Post-USSR Case Studies | With a foreword by Anita Stasulane | ISBN 978-3-8382-0990-6

174 *Barbara Kunz* | Kind Words, Cruise Missiles, and Everything in Between. The Use of Power Resources in U.S. Policies towards Poland, Ukraine, and Belarus 1989–2008 | With a foreword by William Hill | ISBN 978-3-8382-1065-0

175 *Eduard Klein* | Bildungskorruption in Russland und der Ukraine. Eine komparative Analyse der Performanz staatlicher Antikorruptionsmaßnahmen im Hochschulsektor am Beispiel universitärer Aufnahmeprüfungen | Mit einem Vorwort von Heiko Pleines | ISBN 978-3-8382-0995-1

176 *Markus Soldner* | Politischer Kapitalismus im postsowjetischen Russland. Die politische, wirtschaftliche und mediale Transformation in den 1990er Jahren | Mit einem Vorwort von Wolfgang Ismayr | ISBN 978-3-8382-1222-7

177 *Anton Oleinik* | Building Ukraine from Within. A Sociological, Institutional, and Economic Analysis of a Nation-State in the Making | ISBN 978-3-8382-1150-3

178 *Peter Rollberg, Marlene Laruelle (Eds.)* | Mass Media in the Post-Soviet World. Market Forces, State Actors, and Political Manipulation in the Informational Environment after Communism | ISBN 978-3-8382-1116-9

179 *Mikhail Minakov* | Development and Dystopia. Studies in Post-Soviet Ukraine and Eastern Europe | With a foreword by Alexander Etkind | ISBN 978-3-8382-1112-1

180 *Aijan Sharshenova* | The European Union's Democracy Promotion in Central Asia. A Study of Political Interests, Influence, and Development in Kazakhstan and Kyrgyzstan in 2007–2013 | With a foreword by Gordon Crawford | ISBN 978-3-8382-1151-0

181 *Andrey Makarychev, Alexandra Yatsyk (Eds.)* | Boris Nemtsov and Russian Politics. Power and Resistance | With a foreword by Zhanna Nemtsova | ISBN 978-3-8382-1122-0

182 *Sophie Falsini* | The Euromaidan's Effect on Civil Society. Why and How Ukrainian Social Capital Increased after the Revolution of Dignity | With a foreword by Susann Worschech | ISBN 978-3-8382-1131-2

183 *Valentyna Romanova, Andreas Umland (Eds.)* | Ukraine's Decentralization. Challenges and Implications of the Local Governance Reform after the Euromaidan Revolution | ISBN 978-3-8382-1162-6

184 *Leonid Luks* | A Fateful Triangle. Essays on Contemporary Russian, German and Polish History | ISBN 978-3-8382-1143-5

185 *John B. Dunlop* | The February 2015 Assassination of Boris Nemtsov and the Flawed Trial of his Alleged Killers. An Exploration of Russia's "Crime of the 21st Century" | ISBN 978-3-8382-1188-6

186 *Vasile Rotaru* | Russia, the EU, and the Eastern Partnership. Building Bridges or Digging Trenches? | ISBN 978-3-8382-1134-3

187 *Marina Lebedeva* | Russian Studies of International Relations. From the Soviet Past to the Post-Cold-War Present | With a foreword by Andrei P. Tsygankov | ISBN 978-3-8382-0851-0

188 *Tomasz Stępniewski, George Soroka (Eds.)* | Ukraine after Maidan. Revisiting Domestic and Regional Security | ISBN 978-3-8382-1075-9

189 *Petar Cholakov* | Ethnic Entrepreneurs Unmasked. Political Institutions and Ethnic Conflicts in Contemporary Bulgaria | ISBN 978-3-8382-1189-3

190 *A. Salem, G. Hazeldine, D. Morgan (Eds.)* | Higher Education in Post-Communist States. Comparative and Sociological Perspectives | ISBN 978-3-8382-1183-1

191 *Igor Torbakov* | After Empire. Nationalist Imagination and Symbolic Politics in Russia and Eurasia in the Twentieth and Twenty-First Century | With a foreword by Serhii Plokhy | ISBN 978-3-8382-1217-3

192 *Aleksandr Burakovskiy* | Jewish-Ukrainian Relations in Late and Post-Soviet Ukraine. Articles, Lectures and Essays from 1986 to 2016 | ISBN 978-3-8382-1210-4

193 *Natalia Shapovalova, Olga Burlyuk (Eds.)* | Civil Society in Post-Euromaidan Ukraine. From Revolution to Consolidation | With a foreword by Richard Youngs | ISBN 978-3-8382-1216-6

194 *Franz Preissler* | Positionsverteidigung, Imperialismus oder Irredentismus? Russland und die „Russischsprachigen", 1991–2015 | ISBN 978-3-8382-1262-3

195 *Marian Madeła* | Der Reformprozess in der Ukraine 2014-2017. Eine Fallstudie zur Reform der öffentlichen Verwaltung | Mit einem Vorwort von Martin Malek | ISBN 978-3-8382-1266-1

196 *Anke Giesen* | „Wie kann denn der Sieger ein Verbrecher sein?" Eine diskursanalytische Untersuchung der russlandweiten Debatte über Konzept und Verstaatlichungsprozess der Lagergedenkstätte „Perm'-36" im Ural | ISBN 978-3-8382-1284-5

197 *Alla Leukavets* | The Integration Policies of Belarus and Ukraine vis-à-vis the EU and Russia. A Comparative Case Study Through the Prism of a Two-Level Game Approach | ISBN 978-3-8382-1247-0

198 *Oksana Kim* | The Development and Challenges of Russian Corporate Governance I. The Roles and Functions of Boards of Directors | With a foreword by Sheila M. Puffer | ISBN 978-3-8382-1287-6

199 *Thomas D. Grant* | International Law and the Post-Soviet Space I. Essays on Chechnya and the Baltic States | With a foreword by Stephen M. Schwebel | ISBN 978-3-8382-1279-1

200 *Thomas D. Grant* | International Law and the Post-Soviet Space II. Essays on Ukraine, Intervention, and Non-Proliferation | ISBN 978-3-8382-1280-7

201 *Slavomír Michálek, Michal Štefansky* | The Age of Fear. The Cold War and Its Influence on Czechoslovakia 1945–1968 | ISBN 978-3-8382-1285-2

202 *Iulia-Sabina Joja* | Romania's Strategic Culture 1990–2014. Continuity and Change in a Post-Communist Country's Evolution of National Interests and Security Policies | With a foreword by Heiko Biehl | ISBN 978-3-8382-1286-9

203 *Andrei Rogatchevski, Yngvar B. Steinholt, Arve Hansen, David-Emil Wickström* | War of Songs. Popular Music and Recent Russia-Ukraine Relations | With a foreword by Artemy Troitsky | ISBN 978-3-8382-1173-2

204 *Maria Lipman (Ed.)* | Russian Voices on Post-Crimea Russia. An Almanac of Counterpoint Essays from 2015–2018 | ISBN 978-3-8382-1251-7

205 *Ksenia Maksimovtsova* | Language Conflicts in Contemporary Estonia, Latvia, and Ukraine. A Comparative Exploration of Discourses in Post-Soviet Russian-Language Digital Media | With a foreword by Ammon Cheskin | ISBN 978-3-8382-1282-1

206 *Michal Vít* | The EU's Impact on Identity Formation in East-Central Europe between 2004 and 2013. Perceptions of the Nation and Europe in Political Parties of the Czech Republic, Poland, and Slovakia | With a foreword by Andrea Pető | ISBN 978-3-8382-1275-3

207 *Per A. Rudling* | Tarnished Heroes. The Organization of Ukrainian Nationalists in the Memory Politics of Post-Soviet Ukraine | ISBN 978-3-8382-0999-9

208 *Kaja Gadowska, Peter Solomon (Eds.)* | Legal Change in Post-Communist States. Progress, Reversions, Explanations | ISBN 978-3-8382-1312-5

209 *Pawel Kowal, Georges Mink, Iwona Reichardt (Eds.)* | Three Revolutions: Mobilization and Change in Contemporary Ukraine I. Theoretical Aspects and Analyses on Religion, Memory, and Identity | ISBN 978-3-8382-1321-7

210 *Pawel Kowal, Georges Mink, Adam Reichardt, Iwona Reichardt (Eds.)* | Three Revolutions: Mobilization and Change in Contemporary Ukraine II. An Oral History of the Revolution on Granite, Orange Revolution, and Revolution of Dignity | ISBN 978-3-8382-1323-1

211 *Li Bennich-Björkman, Sergiy Kurbatov (Eds.)* | When the Future Came. The Collapse of the USSR and the Emergence of National Memory in Post-Soviet History Textbooks | ISBN 978-3-8382-1335-4

212 *Olga R. Gulina* | Migration as a (Geo-)Political Challenge in the Post-Soviet Space. Border Regimes, Policy Choices, Visa Agendas | With a foreword by Nils Muižnieks | ISBN 978-3-8382-1338-5

213 *Sanna Turoma, Kaarina Aitamurto, Slobodanka Vladiv-Glover (Eds.)* | Religion, Expression, and Patriotism in Russia. Essays on Post-Soviet Society and the State. ISBN 978-3-8382-1346-0

214 *Vasif Huseynov* | Geopolitical Rivalries in the "Common Neighborhood". Russia's Conflict with the West, Soft Power, and Neoclassical Realism | With a foreword by Nicholas Ross Smith | ISBN 978-3-8382-1277-7

215 *Mikhail Suslov* | Geopolitical Imagination. Ideology and Utopia in Post-Soviet Russia | With a foreword by Mark Bassin | ISBN 978-3-8382-1361-2

216 *Alexander Etkind, Mikhail Minakov (Eds.)* | Ideology after Union. Political Doctrines, Discourses, and Debates in Post-Soviet Societies | ISBN 978-3-8382-1388-0

217 *Jakob Mischke, Oleksandr Zabirko (Hgg.)* | Protestbewegungen im langen Schatten des Kreml. Aufbruch und Resignation in Russland und der Ukraine | ISBN 978-3-8382-0926-5

218 *Oksana Huss* | How Corruption and Anti-Corruption Policies Sustain Hybrid Regimes. Strategies of Political Domination under Ukraine's Presidents in 1994-2014 | With a foreword by Tobias Debiel and Andrea Gawrich | ISBN 978-3-8382-1430-6

219 *Dmitry Travin, Vladimir Gel'man, Otar Marganiya* | The Russian Path. Ideas, Interests, Institutions, Illusions | With a foreword by Vladimir Ryzhkov | ISBN 978-3-8382-1421-4

220 *Gergana Dimova* | Political Uncertainty. A Comparative Exploration | With a foreword by Todor Yalamov and Rumena Filipova | ISBN 978-3-8382-1385-9

221 *Torben Waschke* | Russland in Transition. Geopolitik zwischen Raum, Identität und Machtinteressen | Mit einem Vorwort von Andreas Dittmann | ISBN 978-3-8382-1480-1

222 *Steven Jobbitt, Zsolt Bottlik, Marton Berki (Eds.)* | Power and Identity in the Post-Soviet Realm. Geographies of Ethnicity and Nationality after 1991 | ISBN 978-3-8382-1399-6

223 *Daria Buteiko* | Erinnerungsort. Ort des Gedenkens, der Erholung oder der Einkehr? Kommunismus-Erinnerung am Beispiel der Gedenkstätte Berliner Mauer sowie des Soloveckij-Klosters und -Museumsparks | ISBN 978-3-8382-1367-5

224 *Olga Bertelsen (Ed.)* | Russian Active Measures. Yesterday, Today, Tomorrow | With a foreword by Jan Goldman | ISBN 978-3-8382-1529-7

225 *David Mandel* | "Optimizing" Higher Education in Russia. University Teachers and their Union "Universitetskaya solidarnost'" | ISBN 978-3-8382-1519-8

226 *Mikhail Minakov, Gwendolyn Sasse, Daria Isachenko (Eds.)* | Post-Soviet Secessionism. Nation-Building and State-Failure after Communism | ISBN 978-3-8382-1538-9

227 *Jakob Hauter (Ed.)* | Civil War? Interstate War? Hybrid War? Dimensions and Interpretations of the Donbas Conflict in 2014–2020 | With a foreword by Andrew Wilson | ISBN 978-3-8382-1383-5

228 *Tima T. Moldogaziev, Gene A. Brewer, J. Edward Kellough (Eds.)* | Public Policy and Politics in Georgia. Lessons from Post-Soviet Transition | With a foreword by Dan Durning | ISBN 978-3-8382-1535-8

229 *Oxana Schmies (Ed.)* | NATO's Enlargement and Russia. A Strategic Challenge in the Past and Future | With a foreword by Vladimir Kara-Murza | ISBN 978-3-8382-1478-8

230 *Christopher Ford* | Ukapisme – Une Gauche perdue. Le marxisme anti-colonial dans la révolution ukrainienne 1917-1925 | Avec une préface de Vincent Présumey | ISBN 978-3-8382-0899-2

231 *Anna Kutkina* | Between Lenin and Bandera. Decommunization and Multivocality in Post-Euromaidan Ukraine | With a foreword by Juri Mykkänen | ISBN 978-3-8382-1506-8

232 *Lincoln E. Flake* | Defending the Faith. The Russian Orthodox Church and the Demise of Religious Pluralism | With a foreword by Peter Martland | ISBN 978-3-8382-1378-1

233 *Nikoloz Samkharadze* | Russia's Recognition of the Independence of Abkhazia and South Ossetia. Analysis of a Deviant Case in Moscow's Foreign Policy | With a foreword by Neil MacFarlane | ISBN 978-3-8382-1414-6

234 *Arve Hansen* | Urban Protest. A Spatial Perspective on Kyiv, Minsk, and Moscow | With a foreword by Julie Wilhelmsen | ISBN 978-3-8382-1495-5

235 *Eleonora Narvselius, Julie Fedor (Eds.)* | Diversity in the East-Central European Borderlands. Memories, Cityscapes, People | ISBN 978-3-8382-1523-5

236 *Regina Elsner* | The Russian Orthodox Church and Modernity. A Historical and Theological Investigation into Eastern Christianity between Unity and Plurality | With a foreword by Mikhail Suslov | ISBN 978-3-8382-1568-6

237 *Bo Petersson* | The Putin Predicament. Problems of Legitimacy and Succession in Russia | With a foreword by J. Paul Goode | ISBN 978-3-8382-1050-6

238 *Jonathan Otto Pohl* | The Years of Great Silence. The Deportation, Special Settlement, and Mobilization into the Labor Army of Ethnic Germans in the USSR, 1941–1955 | ISBN 978-3-8382-1630-0

239 *Mikhail Minakov (Ed.)* | Inventing Majorities. Ideological Creativity in Post-Soviet Societies | ISBN 978-3-8382-1641-6

240 *Robert M. Cutler* | Soviet and Post-Soviet Foreign Policies I. East-South Relations and the Political Economy of the Communist Bloc, 1971–1991 | With a foreword by Roger E. Kanet | ISBN 978-3-8382-1654-6

241 *Izabella Agardi* | On the Verge of History. Life Stories of Rural Women from Serbia, Romania, and Hungary, 1920–2020 | With a foreword by Andrea Pető | ISBN 978-3-8382-1602-7

242 *Sebastian Schäffer (Ed.)* | Ukraine in Central and Eastern Europe. Kyiv's Foreign Affairs and the International Relations of the Post-Communist Region | With a foreword by Pavlo Klimkin | ISBN 978-3-8382-1615-7

243 *Volodymyr Dubrovskyi, Kalman Mizsei, Mychailo Wynnyckyj (Eds.)* | Eight Years after the Revolution of Dignity. What Has Changed in Ukraine during 2013–2021? | With a foreword by Yaroslav Hrytsak | ISBN 978-3-8382-1560-0

244 *Rumena Filipova* | Constructing the Limits of Europe Identity and Foreign Policy in Poland, Bulgaria, and Russia since 1989 | With forewords by Harald Wydra and Gergana Yankova-Dimova | ISBN 978-3-8382-1649-2

245 *Oleksandra Keudel* | How Patronal Networks Shape Opportunities for Local Citizen Participation in a Hybrid Regime A Comparative Analysis of Five Cities in Ukraine | With a foreword by Sabine Kropp | ISBN 978-3-8382-1671-3

246 *Jan Claas Behrends, Thomas Lindenberger, Pavel Kolar (Eds.)* | Violence after Stalin Institutions, Practices, and Everyday Life in the Soviet Bloc 1953–1989 | ISBN 978-3-8382-1637-9

247 *Leonid Luks* | Macht und Ohnmacht der Utopien Essays zur Geschichte Russlands im 20. und 21. Jahrhundert | ISBN 978-3-8382-1677-5

248 *Iuliia Barshadska* | Brüssel zwischen Kyjiw und Moskau Das auswärtige Handeln der Europäischen Union im ukrainisch-russischen Konflikt 2014-2019 | Mit einem Vorwort von Olaf Leiße | ISBN 978-3-8382-1667-6

249 *Valentyna Romanova* | Decentralisation and Multilevel Elections in Ukraine Reform Dynamics and Party Politics in 2010–2021 | With a foreword by Kimitaka Matsuzato | ISBN 978-3-8382-1700-0

250 *Alexander Motyl* | National Questions. Theoretical Reflections on Nations and Nationalism in Eastern Europe | ISBN 978-3-8382-1675-1

251 *Marc Dietrich* | A Cosmopolitan Model for Peacebuilding. The Ukrainian Cases of Crimea and the Donbas | ISBN 978-3-8382-1687-4

252 *Eduard Baidaus* | An Unsettled Nation. State-Building, Identity, and Separatism in Post-Soviet Moldova | With forewords by John-Paul Himka and David R. Marples | ISBN 978-3-8382-1582-2

253 *Igor Okunev, Petr Oskolkov (Eds.)* | Transforming the Administrative Matryoshka. The Reform of Autonomous Okrugs in the Russian Federation, 2003–2008 | With a foreword by Vladimir Zorin | ISBN 978-3-8382-1721-5

254 *Winfried Schneider-Deters* | Ukraine's Fateful Years 2013–2019. Vol. I: The Popular Uprising in Winter 2013/2014 | ISBN 978-3-8382-1725-3

255 *Winfried Schneider-Deters* | Ukraine's Fateful Years 2013–2019. Vol. II: The Annexation of Crimea and the War in Donbas | ISBN 978-3-8382-1726-0

256 *Robert M. Cutler* | Soviet and Post-Soviet Russian Foreign Policies II. East-West Relations in Europe and the Political Economy of the Communist Bloc, 1971–1991 | With a foreword by Roger E. Kanet | ISBN 978-3-8382-1727-7

257 *Robert M. Cutler* | Soviet and Post-Soviet Russian Foreign Policies III. East-West Relations in Europe and Eurasia in the Post-Cold War Transition, 1991–2001 | With a foreword by Roger E. Kanet | ISBN 978-3-8382-1728-4

258 *Paweł Kowal, Iwona Reichardt, Kateryna Pryshchepa (Eds.)* | Three Revolutions: Mobilization and Change in Contemporary Ukraine III. Archival Records and Historical Sources on the 1990 Revolution on Granite | ISBN 978-3-8382-1376-7

259 *Mikhail Minakov (Ed.)* | Philosophy Unchained. Development of Philosophy after the Fall of the Soviet Union. | ISBN 978-3-8382-1768-0

*ibidem*.eu